Economics Imperialism and Interdisciplinarity

Critical Reconstructions of Political Economy, Volume 2

Studies in Critical Social Sciences Book Series

Haymarket Books is proud to be working with Brill Academic Publishers (www.brill.nl) to republish the *Studies in Critical Social Sciences* book series in paperback editions. This peer-reviewed book series offers insights into our current reality by exploring the content and consequences of power relationships under capitalism, and by considering the spaces of opposition and resistance to these changes that have been defining our new age. Our full catalog of *SCSS* volumes can be viewed at https://www.haymarketbooks.org/series_collections/4-studies-in-critical-social-sciences.

Series Editor
David Fasenfest (York University, Canada)

Editorial Board
Eduardo Bonilla-Silva (Duke University)
Chris Chase-Dunn (University of California–Riverside)
William Carroll (University of Victoria)
Raewyn Connell (University of Sydney)
Kimberlé W. Crenshaw (University of California–LA and Columbia University)
Heidi Gottfried (Wayne State University)
Alfredo Saad-Filho (King's College London)
Chizuko Ueno (University of Tokyo)
Sylvia Walby (Lancaster University)
Raju Das (York University)

Economics Imperialism and Interdisciplinarity

The Watershed and After

CRITICAL RECONSTRUCTIONS OF POLITICAL ECONOMY, VOLUME 2

BEN FINE

Haymarket Books
Chicago, IL

First published in 2023 by Brill Academic Publishers, The Netherlands
© 2023 Koninklijke Brill NV, Leiden, The Netherlands

Published in paperback in 2024 by
Haymarket Books
P.O. Box 180165
Chicago, IL 60618
773-583-7884
www.haymarketbooks.org

ISBN: 979-8-88890-334-6

Distributed to the trade in the US through Consortium Book Sales and Distribution (www.cbsd.com) and internationally through Ingram Publisher Services International (www.ingramcontent.com).

This book was published with the generous support of Lannan Foundation, Wallace Action Fund, and the Marguerite Casey Foundation.

Special discounts are available for bulk purchases by organizations and institutions. Please call 773-583-7884 or email info@haymarketbooks.org for more information.

Cover design by Jamie Kerry and Ragina Johnson.

Printed in the United States.

Library of Congress Cataloging-in-Publication data is available.

Contents

Preface VII

1 **The Emperors of Economics Imperialism Have No Clothes** 1
   1 Picking Up the Threads 1
   2 Twin Peaks 5

2 **Economics Imperialism: A History of a Revolution in Economics That Never Was (Acknowledged)** 12
   1 Introduction 12
   2 The Forward March of "Economics Imperialism" Halted 13
   3 The (In)Visibility of Economics Imperialism 14
   4 Balance against the Unbalanced/Imbalanced? 21
   5 Economics Imperialism Is as Variegated as Economics Imperialism Does 33
   6 Strategic Considerations by Way of Conclusion 41

3 **'Economic Imperialism': A View from the Periphery** 49
   Postscript as Personal Preamble 49
   1 Introduction 50
   2 The Historical Anomaly 52
   3 The Anomaly of Scope 55
   4 The Anomaly of Resistance 59
   5 The Prospects for Radical Political Economy 61

4 **"Household Appliances and the Use of Time: The United States and Britain since the 1920s" – A Comment** 70
   Postscript as Personal Preamble 70
   1 Introduction 74
   2 A False Economy of Time? 74
   3 From Time to Demand 76
   4 The Appliance of Economic Science? 80
   5 Towards a Durable Alternative 81

5 **The Economics of Identity and the Identity of Economics?** 87
   Postscript as Personal Preamble 87
   1 Introduction 93
   2 Identity as Individual Choice 95

	3	Identity as Social Choice 100
	4	Identity and the Social 101
	5	The Economics of Identity as Economics Imperialism 108
	6	Concluding Remarks 113
6	*Collective Choice and Social Welfare*: Economics Imperialism in Action and Inaction 120	
		Postscript as Personal Preamble 120
	1	Disciplinary and Personal Beginnings 123
	2	Bringing Back in (BBI) as Analytical Context 125
	3	Economics and Social Choice: Marriage and Divorce 129
	4	Interpreting the History of Social Choice Theory in Reverse? 130
7	From Freakonomics to Political Economy 134	
		Postscript as Personal Preamble 134
	1	Introduction 138
	2	Economic Crisis and Economic Theory 140
	3	The (General) Criticisms 141
	4	Clearing the Ground 144
	5	Methodological Issues 145
	6	Questions of the History of Economic Thought 150
	7	Economics Imperialism and the Role of Finance 154
	8	The Road Ahead 158
8	Freakonomics as Thickening End of the Symbolic Wedge 164	
		Postscript as Personal Preamble 164
	1	Response to Jack Vromen 168
9	Vicissitudes of Economics Imperialism 179	
		Postscript as Personal Preamble 179
	1	Speaker's Corner 179
10	Economics and Interdisciplinarity: One Step Forward, N Steps Back? 186	
		Postscript as Personal Preamble 186
	1	Economics Is as Economics Does 187
	2	Economics Imperialism 188
	3	Acknowledging the Strengths, Exposing and Exploiting the Weaknesses 196

Index   205

Preface

This is the second volume in a series of edited pieces (co-)authored by myself. This and the first volume, with the next to be on economic history, are concerned with economics imperialism, the trajectory of the colonisation of other disciplines and subject matter by mainstream economics far beyond its traditional boundaries from the 1950s onwards and, currently, gathering ever greater momentum. The motivation for these volumes, and the others to follow – on development, mainstream economics, heterodox economics, Marxist political economy, neoliberalism, South Africa, and policy, each of which touches upon economics imperialism to a greater or lesser extent without its being the main business – is covered in the Preface to the first volume and will not be reproduced here. Suffice it to say that the exercise of revisiting my published work, and placing it in the context not only of scholarship but also more general engagements, has been extremely rewarding for me personally and, hopefully, will prove so for the reader, especially if interested in both the contemporary scene and its history, not least as a means by which to engage critically with what has been, is, and will be.

Significantly, for this volume at least, my endeavours were a cause of surprise and disappointment. Whilst I amply confirmed the forward march of economics imperialism was still proceeding apace, its doing so had not been increasingly acknowledged by each of its proponents and its critics. My warnings from twenty-five years ago seemed to have gone unheeded. As a heterodox critic of mainstream economics, that I had not turned around the juggernaut of economics imperialism even with decades of effort did not surprise me. After all, I had suffered a similar experience with social capital (Fine 2001, 2010 and, most recently, 2023). But, whilst social capital has continued to expand in scale and scope, it is done so openly by those that use it, with a continuing guerrilla movement of opposition which can, on occasion, be acknowledged to suit by "social capitalists". As far as economics imperialism is concerned, by comparison it would be is as if globalisation, neoliberalism, and even the environment and climate change had disappeared from the scholarly lexicon. Much of this volume is devoted to explaining how it is that economics imperialism has got away with it, without being explicitly called to account, despite my efforts to bring it under critical scrutiny.

One part of the previous preface, I am pleased and obliged to reproduce. For, last, and by no means least, I cannot begin to thank enough those who have supported me throughout my career, particularly co-authors and collaborators but ranging beyond this to family and friends. Appreciation must also go to David Fasenfest and Brill for making the venture possible, and for encouraging and supporting its coming to fruition.

References

Damodaran, S., S. Gupta, S. Mitra and D. Sinha (eds) (2023) *Development, Transformations and the Human Condition: Volume in Honour of Professor Jayati Ghosh*, New Delhi: Routledge, forthcoming.

Fine, B. (2001) *Social Capital versus Social Theory: Political Economy and Social Science at the Turn of the Millennium*, London: Routledge.

Fine, B. (2010) *Theories of Social Capital: Researchers Behaving Badly*, London: Pluto.

Fine, B. (2023) "Social Capital: the Indian Connection", in Damodaran et al (eds) (2023), forthcoming.

CHAPTER 1

The Emperors of Economics Imperialism Have No Clothes

1   Picking Up the Threads

The purpose of this chapter is, understandably, to give an overview of the main thrust of the chapters that follow, some (uneven) indication of their content and a context in which to situate them.[1] I am mindful that this volume is preceded by another where much of the groundwork in understanding the nature and trajectory of economics imperialism, and the challenges posed for heterodox economists, have already been covered in some detail, especially for the period leading up to what I call a watershed in economics imperialism, dating from about a decade ago at the time of writing. I intend that this chapter should make sense to the reader unfamiliar with the first volume but reference to it will render richer the reading of this second volume.

The first volume closed with a debate within heterodox economics over whether economics imperialism constituting a revolution in economics was, or was liable to become, valid. In a sense, the next twenty years and, hopefully, this second volume on economics imperialism, and its continuing if not accelerating momentum, amply confirm the hypothesis. However, despite this initial debate and much that was soon to follow, the hypothesis of economics imperialism has suffered, not so much from lack of acceptance as such let alone refutation. Rather, the situation has been far worse since the incidence and impact of economics imperialism has simply and primarily been overlooked. In short, whilst the thrust of this volume is that the forward momentum of economics imperialism has been sustained and even accelerated by a third phase based on core economic principles plus whatever analytical factors take the fancy through plunder from other social sciences, critical commentary upon economics imperialism peaked after the first decade of the twentieth century. That peak marks what I have dubbed a watershed, not least as signified in the subtitles of the first two of the volumes on economics imperialism, the third being on its relationship to economics history. There is something Cassandra-like about economics imperialism – the more the incidence and warning, the

---

1   This chapter is newly drafted for this volume.

less it is noticed let alone explicitly acted upon. At least everybody knows about climate change, and denialists have become a minority, even if remedial action remains sorely deficient.

The next chapter is primarily concerned with a robust explanation of why economics imperialism should be so strong and yet so little remarked. It does so by offering a select, if long, overview of the literature on economics imperialism followed by evidence for its neglect by reference to the limited discussion that there has been. Close consideration is given to one of the literature's major themes, the nature of balance (and unification) between economics and other disciplines. Together with a discussion of the variegated nature of economics imperialism, a multifaceted explanation for the neglect of economics imperialism is formulated drawing out broader implications for pluralism and the promotion of alternatives to mainstream economics, themes also taken up in Chapters 2, 9 and 10.

One of the reasons for the neglect of economics imperialism is that it is not seen, for it has dropped out of intellectual consciousness, and so cannot be commented upon. Chapter 3 indirectly suggests one reason why this should have been so. At one level, the chapter should have appeared in the previous volume, as it is concerned with what has been termed the first phase of economics imperialism, its Becker-like, as if a perfect market treatment of the social/non-economic as opposed to the later, second phase of economics imperialism based on (responses to) market imperfections as a template for the social/non-economic. As is highlighted, Lazear (2000), to which I offer a response in the chapter, is wedded to the first phase of economics imperialism, lauding Becker in particular, even though I have already detected in Fine (1997) that the first phase has been superseded by the second. Indeed, Lazear is gung ho, more or less anticipating that economics imperialism will become the only social science as it subordinates other disciplines because of its superior rigour. Such an argument is shown to be fundamentally flawed, not least because, if economics (imperialism) were so great, why had it not prevailed so much earlier and longer in the history of the social sciences. And, if there were obstacles to this, why should they be overcome now. If God could create the world in a week, surely economics could overcome the other social sciences in less than a century or more? In other words, not only the substance of economics imperialism but also its rhythm over time needs to be contextualised and explained.

Now, what the piece by Lazear, and my response to it, neatly illustrates is that the first phase of economics imperialism lives on beyond its natural life, even after it has become new and improved by the second, market-imperfections phase. This allows that second phase to be seen by its proponents, and, perversely by many of its critics as not imperialistic at all. Indeed, the second phase is seen as critical rather than part of economics imperialism as if economics imperialism is confined to its Becker-style, first phase alone. This is so whether the new phase is welcome or not (for being more rounded in its interdisciplinarity as is claimed by some heterodoxy, see Chapter 8). But the result is to confine mainstream criticism of economics imperialism as its first phase erodes and overlaps with, but gives way to, its second phase. And potential heterodox criticism is muted because, unlike the first phase, the second phase does not promote itself as imperialistic and can even present itself and be seen as engaging with interdisciplinarity at the expense of its mainstream principles and practices. As it were, economics imperialism only has a short life because it is perceived to be confined to its first, crude phase alone rather than progressing through what will be identified here, and in the previous volume, to be two further phases, each of which purports to be critical of economics as imperialistic whilst being more successful at it in scope and depth.

As mentioned, the piece by Lazear raises questions of the evolution of economics imperialism in rhythm and range, placing us in the history of economic thought and interdisciplinarity. For the first time, I explicitly point to the logic of economics imperialism – that the scope of application of its technical apparatus is not, in principle, confined to the market/economy. So, once established, it can range more or less without limit subject to the nature of its core concepts. There is also implicit reference to the historical nature of economics imperialism, although the term is not used as such, with emphasis upon the initial confinement of the technical apparatus to market supply and demand. As would be explicitly established later, the evolution of economics imperialism can be framed in terms of its *historical* logic – that mainstream economics is established through its technical apparatus of production and utility functions, but confined at its birth to the market, only for that technical apparatus to be increasingly used according to the *logic* of its general applicability. Crucially, this is a logic with outcomes in practice – the scale and scope of economics imperialism –contingent upon developments within and between disciplines and the factors that influence these.

By the same token, there are parallel logics informing the prospects for criticism of, and alternatives to, economics imperialism as also addressed in the next chapter, with some degree of balance and even optimism being sought with the economics imperialism beastie as it moves from its old to its new (putatively non-imperialistic) phase. On the positive side, the retreat from postmodernism across the social sciences and the focus upon explaining major material developments, such as globalisation and neoliberalisation, opened up the potential for the enhanced role for political economy within the social sciences other than economics. In addition, whilst economics imperialism does itself take advantage of this opportunity on the basis of what it perceives to be its core strengths, doing so exposes its extreme weaknesses from the perspectives of its intended 'colonies' and their own traditional methodologies, methods, theories and conceptualisations.

This is especially so of the failure of mainstream economics to question the asocial and ahistorical nature of its approach, even in its second market-imperfections phase, something that is unacceptable to most social science, especially in the postmodernist period and its aftermath. Whilst all of this means that heterodox alternatives to the mainstream are able to contest the 'economic', and even prosper across the other social sciences, their presence within the discipline itself is eroded even further by both its extreme intolerance to alternatives and its putative claims to having become more rounded in light of its incorporation of the social, the institutional, etc, in the second phase of economics imperialism and beyond.

The critique of Lazear is followed by another critique, this time in the context of the new economic history and, more specifically, the new household or family economics associated with Becker and its application to consumer durables, Chapter 4. As with Lazear, for the reasons already given, the commentary on papers by Bowden and Offer could easily have appeared in the first volume on economics imperialism or, indeed, in the next volume given it is an application to economic history. But it too offers a chance to understand how economics imperialism tends to be overlooked, especially if cloaked in history, as there is an apparently more rounded approach in looking at things over a longer time and with the benefit of adding ad hoc variables like culture, demography, etc.

Many of the issues raised by these oddly placed examples of economics imperialism are intensified by the emergence of the third phase of economics imperialism, which is still not so much absent from consideration in these earlier chapters to this volume as unimagined if not unimaginable. Indeed, I do recall believing that the mainstream had nowhere to go beyond the second phase of market-imperfections economics, on top of perfect-market economics, other than more of the same on an ever-widening terrain. I even wrote of economics as being "undead", reflecting a past life but stumbling in search of satisfaction for a voracious appetite for new material whilst offering none of its own (Fine 2009b and 2010, and 2017 later on). But I was wrong, as will be seen below, for which I confess only to a degree of naivety and even some degree of belief in the intellectual integrity of the mainstream. For, although aware of its glaring inconsistencies on its own terms of 'rigour', these would be taken to extremes with the third phase of economics imperialism, see Chapter 10.

2 Twin Peaks

In this light, Fine (2009a), in critique of Akerlof and Kranton, A&K, and their putative economics of identity, occupies something of an interregnum in the evolution of economics imperialism, between second and third phases. A&K remain deeply rooted in market imperfection economics – indeed, they basically treat identity as if it were a market imperfection, a special type of externality, as covered in Chapter 5. But A&K also meander into incorporating other motivations for behaviour, whether underpinned by individual optimisation or not. What is clear is that pure reliance on Becker-style economics imperialism had been superseded.

But there is also one other major factor at work during the interregnum, accelerating the presence of economics imperialism as well as the transition to its third phase. It is the astonishing, meteoric rise of freakonomics, marked by the publication and success of Levitt and Dubner (2005), although this was primarily made up of previously published articles by Levitt. As Wikipedia reports, https://en.wikipedia.org/wiki/Freakonomics:[2]

> By late 2009, the book had sold over 4 million copies worldwide. Based on the success of the original book, Levitt and Dubner have grown the *Freakonomics* brand into a multi-media franchise, with a sequel book, a feature film, a regular radio segment on National Public Radio, and a weekly blog.

Essentially, freakonomics offered the prospect of economists deploying whatever variables they liked on whatever subject matter – specifically dealing, for example, with cheating in Suomi wrestling, the relationship between legalised abortion and crime, and drug dealers cohabiting with their mothers. It was third phase economics imperialism par excellence, with its own idiosyncrasies (more concerned with statistical analyses than economics as such), both ahead of and pushing forward the third phase.

These developments were very much in mind when the critique of A&K was drafted. There is reference to Fine and Milonakis (2009), cited as 2007 and forthcoming in early drafts, and with the title *From Economics Imperialism to Freakonomics: The Shifting Boundaries between Economics and Other Social Sciences*, explicitly acknowledging the impact of freakonomics on economics

---

2 The resonances with the subsequent rise to prominence of Piketty are striking albeit with less of the razzamatazz for the latter.

imperialism although motivated in part to jump critically on the freakonomics bandwagon.

In this and other respects, Fine and Milonakis (2009), together with its companion volume (Milonakis and Fine 2009),[3] marks a key point in the evolving exposure of economics imperialism in our work for a number of reasons. First, as already indicated, the shift from second to third phase of economics imperialism was recognised in all but name. All of the elements were in place: the continuing reliance upon the mainstream's technical apparatus and technical architecture, dubbed TA^2 in the previous volume; the shift to a vision based on imperfectly as opposed to (as if) perfectly working markets; the expanding scope of application; the complementing of market imperfections with other aspects drawn from across the social sciences; and the cumulating inconsistencies and conceptual incoherences as a result of the bringing back in, so common as to warrant an acronym (BBI), of those factors that had to be excluded to allow the TA^2 to be established. For the latter, for example, we assume preferences are given in order to explain how they change. Or we posit a production function on the basis of fixed technologies in order to explain how technologies change (and we might even have the equivalent of a production function for production functions).

Second, then, as already indicated, the key term that I mobilised to signify the third phase of economics imperialism, 'suspension', was already in draft contributions in 2010, almost immediately after the publication of Milonakis and Fine (2009) and Fine and Milonakis (2009), and see Chapter 8, first drafted in April, 2010, but unpublished at the time. The term is explained for the first time in print as follows (Fine 2011, pp. 208–9), as involving:[4]

> adoption of topics for analysis by economists on the basis of the methods developed, with whatever legitimacy, for entirely different purposes. This is well-illustrated by the rise of neuroeconomics in particular and freakonomics more generally (Levitt and Dubner 2005)) and the presumption there can be an economic theory of (almost) everything. These, together, to use a crude dialectics, illustrate a remarkable process of 'suspension'.

---

3 The co-production of these two volumes explains the delay between drafting and publication as we sought to finish each and publish them together. Initially, a single volume was intended, but it became too large.

4 'Suspension' also appears in 2010 in a draft for the Deutscher Prize lecture but did not make it into the published version (Fine and Milonakis 2011). See the forthcoming volume on the mainstream for the longer version. Note Stillwell (2023, p. 191) can be seen as interpreting suspension in terms of the "gravitational force" of the mainstream's core.

Precisely, because it has become a set of techniques and statistical methods of universal applicability, economics is capable of both floating free of its origins and core material whilst remaining irrevocably attached to them. It can go anywhere but it never departs.

Subsequently, over the next decade, 'suspension' is deployed across a number of applications. For example, the new industrial policy of Justin Lin, the World Bank's Chief Economist, is found to depend upon so-called "dynamic" comparative advantage, with the goal of matching economic and social infrastructure to economies of scale as development proceeds. But comparative advantage can only be defined in the absence of economies of scale (and scope) (Fine and Van Waeyenberge 2013). Suspension is also used in 2013 in the preface to the Turkish edition of Fine and Milonakis (2009), signalling its previous absence. Its role is crucial in contesting Tony Lawson's dismissal of mainstream economics being neoclassical on grounds of mathematical determinism serving as its leading characteristic as opposed to TA^2.[5] Suspension explains the latter's leading role even in its absence (just as divorce is evidence for, not against, a system of marriage) (Fine 2015). The World Bank's take on nudging in its World Development Report of 2015 is the target for suspension in Fine et al (2016). Suspension as the enhanced living death of the mainstream's TA^2 is taken up in Fine (2017) and as a lever for teaching in and against orthodoxy in Fine (2018b). Ultimately, in Fine (2019), the final chapter in this volume, in a retrospective account of economics imperialism and corresponding interdisciplinarity, breaking with suspension through its use as critical point of departure is seen as vital in moving forward against the mainstream.[6]

A third key aspect of the two books co-authored with Dimitris Milonakis was their location of economics imperialism in the history of economic thought, itself involving two broad aspects alongside much detail. One aspect has been the intra-disciplinary developments of economics itself, with classical political economy giving way to neoclassical economics through the marginalist revolution of the 1870s (although its completion and predominance only came in the period after the second world war). On the other hand, the trajectory of economics imperialism, in interdisciplinary terms, could be located in terms of its historical logic. Historically, TA^2 was derived by what had already been designated as an implosion – a focus upon market supply and demand, and the disregard for any obstacle in the way of establishing the framework, whether

---

5 For a recent (re)statement of his case, see Lawson (2021).
6 The paper is based on the plenary address to the founding conference of the Portuguese Association of Political Economy, held at Lisbon, ISCTE-IUL, 25–27, January 2018.

it be unacceptable assumptions, such as given preferences, goods and technologies, perfect competition, or the absence of the non-economic.[7] Logically, though, the TA² so derived is universal in its application, in the sense of not being confined to the market, not least in its use of ahistorical and asocial categories such as utility, production, equilibrium and efficiency. The corresponding historical logic of economics imperialism set the scene for the implosion associated with the establishing of its core apparatus and overall architecture, to be followed by an explosion of application across the social sciences, not least through the three phases of economics imperialism identified.

Fourth, partly because of its relationship with the history of economic thought, economic history figured extremely strongly in our specification of economics imperialism. It served as a leading illustration, as cliometrics, alongside human and social capital, as well as public choice. But, in addition, Douglass North straddled many of these developments, not least as a founding father of cliometrics, a leading figure in the new institutional economics, and as a scholar who, albeit with idiosyncrasies, exemplified the trajectory of economics imperialism through its three phases. Indeed, the relationship between economics and economic history became so prominent, and voluminous, in our work that we decided to hive it off for separate volumes.[8]

Last, the two books marked a key personal highlight, if not watershed, in work on economics imperialism, with each being awarded a prize, with corresponding prominence to whatever degree. More specifically, this gave rise to organised commentary from more or less sympathetic scholars, for which our response to one symposium, Fine and Milonakis (2012) is reproduced in its longer version as Chapter 7, and another response to the tacit rejection of

---

7   Interestingly, if as a bi-product, taking Veblen to have defined neoclassical economics as supply and demand plus – most notably in the inconsistent stances of the older (J. N.) Keynes and Marshall and as reiterated by Lawson (2021) most recently – offers strong evidence for the implosion hypothesis, as this is equivalent to the dropping of the plus. This does not imply, however, that discarding the plus through the implosion leaves neoclassical economics without a coherent specification by TA² even if complemented by the subsequent restoration of the plus, especially in the third phase of economics imperialism). See also Pratten (2023), below in passing, Chapter 1 of the first volume on economics imperialism, and each of the forthcoming volumes on heterodoxy and the mainstream for more on the complex relationships between the ontological critique of mainstream economics, critical realism in economics, and the definition of neoclassical economics and whether it exists.

8   The treatment of the relationship between economics and economic history was projected to be covered in one, then two, separate volumes although this never materialised, but see the forthcoming volume on (economics imperialism and) economic history. The intention was to publish one book covering the evolving historical content of economics and the other to address the evolving economics content of economic history.

economics imperialism as Chapter 8.[9] Subsequently, our work on economics imperialism did continue, as already indicated, for example in the above select account of use of 'suspension' across various contributions. But it was to become more fragmented in its presence or, more exactly, figuring as one factor amongst many across disparate topics. An example is provided by Chapter 6, Fine (2018a), tracing the trajectory of Amartya Sen's work through its origins in social choice theory and how his own concerns and methods became increasingly incompatible with economics, even in the third phase of its imperialistic versions.[10] This is followed by Chapter 7, drafted but unpublished at the time, that criticises Vromen (2009) for casually dismissing the hypothesis of economics imperialism and treating freakonomics as a bit of fun. The final chapter in this volume offers an overall assessment of economics imperialism by bringing together a synthesis of earlier work, with an emphasis upon interdisciplinarity. Our work on economics imperialism continued but it had peaked and so,[11] as suggested and will be seen in Chapter 2 in detail, had its prominence within the literature.

References

Birch, K. and V. Mykhnenko (eds) (2010) *The Rise and Fall of Neoliberalism: the Collapse of an Economic Order?* London: Zed Books.

Decker, S., W. Elsner and S. Flechtner (eds) (2018) *Advancing Pluralism in Teaching Economics*, London: Routledge.

Fine, B. (1997) "The New Revolution in Economics", *Capital and Class*, no 61, Spring, pp. 143–48.

---

9   Yet another response, Fine and Milonakis (2012), in debate with Geoff Hodgson (2011 and 2012), is included in a forthcoming volume, on heterodoxy rather than economics imperialism since, of symbolic significance, it is more focused on orthodoxy and heterodoxy and their role rather than on economics imperialism as such.

10 As a result, my own continuing contributions on economics imperialism are scattered across other forthcoming volumes, on heterodoxy, orthodoxy and development. Dimitris Milonakis, in part with his PhD students, has tended to focus upon specific topics, such as paradigm shifts, and Coase, property rights, transactions costs and institutional economics. See Meramveliotakis and Milonakis (2010 and 2018), Milonakis and Meramveliotakis (2012) and Tzotzes and Milonakis (2021 and 2022).

11 My contributions before and after the "peak", as listed in the Auto-Bibliography Appendix in the first volume on economics imperialism, roughly lie in the ratio of two-to-one, respectively.

Fine, B. (2009a) "The Economics of Identity and the Identity of Economics?", *Cambridge Journal of Economics*, vol 33, no 2, pp. 175–91. See also Chapter 5.

Fine, B. (2009b) "Development as Zombieconomics in the Age of Neo-Liberalism", *Third World Quarterly*, vol 30, no 5, pp. 885–904.

Fine, B. (2010) "Zombieconomics: the Living Death of the Dismal Science", in Birch and Mykhnenko (eds) (2010), pp. 53–70.

Fine, B. (2011) "Prospecting for Political Economy", *International Journal of Management Concepts and Philosophy*, vol 5, no 3, pp. 204–17.

Fine, B. (2015) "Neoclassical Economics: an Elephant Is Not a Chimera But Is a Chimera Real?", in Morgan (ed.) (2015), pp. 180–99.

Fine, B. (2017) "The Undead World of Mainstream Economics", SOAS Department of Economics Working Paper, no 206, translated as "Die Untote Welt der Mainstream-Ökonomik", *Zeitschrift für Kulturwissenschaften*, 2017, vol 11, no 2, pp. 85–102.

Fine, B. (2018a) "*Collective Choice and Social Welfare*: Economics Imperialism in Action and Inaction", *Ethics and Social Welfare*, vol 12, no 4, pp. 393–399. See also Chapter 6.

Fine, B. (2018b) "In and Against Orthodoxy: Teaching Economics in the Neoliberal Era", in Decker et al (eds) (2018), pp. 78–94.

Fine, B. (2019) "Economics and Interdisciplinarity: One Step Forward, N Steps Back?" *Revista Crítica de Ciências Sociais*, no 119, pp. 131–48. See also Chapter 10.

Fine, B., D. Johnson, A. Santos and E. Van Waeyenberge (2016) "Nudging or Fudging: the World Development Report 2015", *Development and Change*, vol 47, no 4, pp. 640–63.

Fine, B. and D. Milonakis (2009) *From Economics Imperialism to Freakonomics: The Shifting Boundaries between Economics and Other Social Sciences*, London: Routledge.

Fine, B. and D. Milonakis (2011) "'Useless but True': Economic Crisis and the Peculiarities of Economic Science", *Historical Materialism*, vol 19, no 2, pp. 3–31.

Fine, B. and D. Milonakis (2012) "From Freakonomics to Political Economy", *Historical Materialism*, vol 20, no 3, pp. 81–96. See also Chapter 7.

Fine, B. and E. Van Waeyenberge (2013) "A Paradigm Shift that Never Was: Justin Lin's New Structural Economics", *Competition and Change*, vol 17, no 4, pp. 355–71; for longer version, "A Paradigm Shift that Never Will Be?: Justin Lin's New Structural Economics", with E. Van Waeyenberge, SOAS Department of Economics Working Paper Series, no 179, 2013, http://www.soas.ac.uk/economics/research/workingpapers/file81928.pdf.

Hodgson, G. (2011) "Sickonomics: Diagnoses and Remedies", *Review of Social Economy*, vol 69, no 3, pp. 357–76.

Hodgson, G. (2012) "From Social Theory to Explaining Sickonomics: a Response to Dimitris Milonakis and Ben Fine", *Review of Social Economy*, vol 70, no 4, pp, 492–507.

Lawson, T. (2021) "Whatever Happened to Neoclassical Economics?", *Revue de Philosophie Economique*, vol 22, no 1, pp. 39–84, cited from https://www.researchgate.net/publication/356832620_Whatever_happened_to_neoclassical_economics/link/61b07b361a5f480388c187e4/download.

Lazear, E. (2000) "Economic Imperialism", *Quarterly Journal of Economics*, vol 115, no 1, pp. 99–146, previously National Bureau of Economic Research, Working Paper no 7300, 1999.

Levitt, S. and S. Dubner (2005) *Freakonomics: a Rogue Economist Explores the Hidden Side of Everything*, New York: Harper Collins.

Meramveliotakis, G. and D. Milonakis (2010) "Surveying the Transaction Cost Foundations of New Institutional Economics: a Critical Inquiry", *Journal of Economic Issues*, vol 44, no 4, pp. 1045–1071.

Meramveliotakis, G. and D. Milonakis (2018) "Coasean Theory of Property Rights and Law Revisited: a Critical Inquiry", *Science and Society*, vol 82, no 1, pp. 39–67.

Milonakis, D. and B. Fine (2009) *From Political Economy to Economics: Method, the Social and the Historical in the Evolution of Economic Theory*, London: Routledge.

Milonakis, D. and G. Meramveliotakis (2012) "Homo Economicus and the Economics of Property Rights: History in Reverse Order", *Review of Radical Political Economics*, vol 45, no 1, pp. 5–23.

Morgan, J. (ed.) (2015) *What Is This 'School' Called Neoclassical Economics?: Debating the Origins, Meaning and Significance*, London: Routledge.

Pratten, S. (2023) "Veblen, Marshall and Neoclassical Economics", *Journal of Classical Sociology*, vol 23, no 1, pp. 63–88.

Tzotzes, S. and D. Milonakis (2021) "Paradigm Change or Assimilation? The Case of Behavioral Economics", *Review of Radical Political Economics*, vol 53, no 1, pp. 173–92.

Tzotzes, S. and D. Milonakis (2022) "Scientific Communities, Recent Crisis and Change in Economics: a Kuhnian Perspective", *Journal of Economic Methodology*, 10.1080/1350178X.2022.2147980, forthcoming.

Vromen, J. (2009) "The Booming Economics-Made-Fun Genre: More than Having Fun, but Less than Economics Imperialism" *Erasmus Journal for Philosophy and Economics*, vol 2, no 1, pp. 70–99.

CHAPTER 2

Economics Imperialism: A History of a Revolution in Economics That Never Was (Acknowledged)

1   Introduction[1]

This chapter faces two formidable tasks. The first, which I hope to have met, is to argue that critical commentary on economics imperialism has been subject to a watershed, having declined significantly over the past decade. I am less upbeat over the second task, and suspect that I will fail miserably. It is to persuade heterodox economists and those engaged across the other social sciences, with or without inclusion of political economy, to engage critically with economics imperialism. This is not only to defend and promote continuing analyses, traditions and disciplines against the incursions of economics imperialism but also for these to rebound back upon mainstream economics and reinforce efforts for it to be more pluralistic and to allow for overwhelming reform within the academic and scholarly discipline of (mainstream) economics. The reason for my pessimism is that the scholarly neglect of economics imperialism has, perversely, gone hand in hand with its ever-expanding presence in scope and range. The more there is, the less it is observed and brought to account.

In the next Section, I set the scene in the context of my own work and how it relates to a watershed in critical commentary on economics imperialism. Apart from the closing section which draws out some strategic considerations, the rest of the chapter is concerned to establish the presence of that watershed and to seek explanations for it through a review of literature, especially the relatively recent (which, is relatively sparse).

Section 3 offers some evidence of the limited attention to economics imperialism leading to a focus in Section 4 upon how interdisciplinarity with economics has been discussed in terms of balance between disciplines and how to achieve it. This is questioned as a goal precisely because of the nature of mainstream economics and how it engages with other disciplines and the non-economic.

---

[1]   This chapter is newly drafted for this volume.

Section 5 draws upon the preceding analyses to argue that economics imperialism is variegated within and across disciplines and subject matter. Precisely because it is differentiated, even fragmented, in how it colonises, critical response to economics imperialism, of which there is much and much that is invaluable, tends to overlook how it is part and parcel of a common phenomenon which, consequently, remains more or less invisible.

2 The Forward March of "Economics Imperialism" Halted

It was always my intention, at least as starting point, for the volumes on economics imperialism (and the other volumes on other themes) to introduce the contributions included, more or less chronologically as they were published, and then to offer an overall update in light of subsequent contributions across the literature. I changed my mind, at least in part, for this volume upon reviewing the literature because I did not find what I had expected. As a result, I decided not to continue the narrative of the forward march of economics imperialism as laid out in the previous volume, and its critical exposure within heterodox economics and across the social sciences, but to shift instead to look back upon the trajectory of economics imperialism in the opposite direction – not on how was it evolving from the past forward, but on how is it now and how does this shed qualified if not new light on economic imperialism's past.

My starting point is that economics imperialism is alive, well and expanding extensively (to pastures new) and intensively (within economics whether for the first time or in renewal through the three phases of economics imperialism). I have had no reason to revise my assessment, laid out in the previous volume, and see Chapter 10 in this, and especially that economics imperialism has gone through three phases: the old (as if perfect market); followed by the new (as if – response to – market imperfections); and currently the newer ("suspension" or whatever mainstream economics has to offer plus anything else it chooses to append).

Further, whilst the genus of no-go areas for economics imperialism is bordering on an endangered species, the depth of penetration and the forms it takes is highly variegated across disciplines and subject matter. The word variegated is used advisedly, especially as it has been increasingly popular in attachment as a qualifier to each of neoliberalism and financialisation (Fine 2022a). In my mind, it reflects common determinants that lead to complex and contextually contingent outcomes according to subject matter, material and policy imperatives (pandemics, wars, climate change, austerity, etc, make a difference) and disciplinary traditions and dynamics within evolving conditions of teaching and research. Such systemic factors do not all point in the same direction and outcomes in all cases. In short, there are no templates for outcomes for case studies of economics imperialism.

None of this was unexpected, it was even anticipated from the outset, not least in light of my first contribution on economics imperialism in Fine (1997), designating it as a revolution in economics once this assessment was prompted by the second phase of economics imperialism based on market imperfections and their non-economic and inter-disciplinary implications. Initial critical exposure of economics imperialism, especially jointly with Dimitris Milonakis, peaked around the end of the first decade of the new millennium, after which our concerted concentration upon it waned. Occasional forays continued into the evolving character and incidence of economics imperialism. Two areas in particular, social capital and development economics/studies, offered striking, contrasting and evolving examples of economics imperialism.

What did come as a retrospective surprise in surveying the economics imperialism literature in 2022 is that the 2010-watershed in our own engagement was complemented by a corresponding limited weight of the critical literature over the last decade despite the burgeoning of economics imperialism in practice. The correlation may have been accidental, although a flurry of (critical) discussion did arise out of the publication of our two 2009 books, as well as the reaction to *Freakonomics* by Levitt and Dubner (2005) if on a monumentally grander scale. In addition, following the self-designating triumphalism of the first phase of economics imperialism, the literature in the subsequent phases understandably saw itself as engaging with, and drawing upon, the other social sciences with the result that it certainly did not describe itself in imperialistic terms – even the opposite as a (market imperfections plus) reaction against the first phase of economics imperialism. Indeed, the later phases have presented themselves as rejecting the first phase even if building upon it by adding market imperfections and, ultimately, whatever other factors according to fancy.

3 The (In)Visibility of Economics Imperialism

In short, the single most important feature of the economics imperialism literature is just how little there is that explicitly refers to it – both its proponents and its critics seem to have eschewed the term. This is massively paradoxical given just how much economics imperialism there has been – no one now seems to deny this whether it is judged positively or critically – and just how much heterodox economics has prospered whether around the margins of the mainstream or within social science as political economy (especially in the wake of the Global Financial Crisis, GFC, and attention to globalisation, neoliberalism and financialisation). Whilst I have not gone out of my way to undertake a comprehensive survey of literature that incorporates 'economic(s) imperialism', running a search on Web of Science in titles, abstracts and keywords yields far less than a hundred items in total after necessary pruning of those dealing with (Leninist) economic imperialism de facto. Whatever social scientists have been doing, they do not themselves, nor their critics, see it primarily in terms of economics imperialism.

Thus, whilst economics imperialism has prospered, 'economics imperialism' has been in the doldrums. This raises two important questions. Why should this be so and what are the implications? Before addressing these questions, it is helpful to take a look at the literature that there has been coming out of my modest literature search. I begin with what might be termed case studies before looking successively at the 'balance' sought around economics imperialism and its variegated nature.

Although my literature research was thin, it did yield some insight into critical (lack of) contributions on individual topics. There are, for example, just three on education (and human capital) – Allais (2012), Gilead (2015) and Jabbar and Menashy (2022). The latter undertook what was clearly a more extensive search than my own for economics imperialism in the field. They report, pp. 279/80:

> Through a systematic literature review that yielded 62 published academic works from 1961 through 2020, covering all disciplinary areas, we examine how economic imperialism has been conceptualized and applied across fields, including education. We identify promising directions for applying the concept of economic imperialism more widely in [criticism of] education research.

Of those 62 contributions, only eight are within education studies itself, suggesting in both relative and absolute terms how limited has been the discipline's resistance to economics imperialism. Not unreasonably, they conclude, "Despite these robust contributions to the education literature, we view this body of scholarship as minimal", p. 283, drawing upon Romer's (2020) critique of the undue power of economists in social policy and public affairs,[2] proposing that, p. 284:

---

2   Without any sense of his own mea culpa as Nobel prizewinner for new growth theory and as Chief Economist at the World Bank, see Fine (2019).

> Researchers can use economic imperialism to critique existing policies that exacerbate inequities and advance more just education policies, rather than offering solutions that are embedded within the framework of economics ... Most of the research on economic imperialism has been theoretical, but we argue for more empirical testing of the concept. Through empirical studies, education researchers can trace the influence of economists and economic ideas, track how this influence happens, and by whom. The discipline's influence has likely led to an outsized influence of economists in education policy spaces, as advisors, providers of expert testimony, and dominant presences in news media, which in turn perpetuates economic imperialism.

How telling that such a recommendation should be made in 2022 – what a commentary on the weakness of the counter, even guerilla, movement against human capital over more than half a century.

For economic sociology, the overt presence of economics imperialism is equally limited. For Davern and Eitzen (1995), unsurprisingly given its vintage, the field is perceived as a duality of dualities, depending upon whether it is approached from the side of sociology (and the social as well as the more rounded individual)[3] or from the side of economics (and a confined rational choice) which is more or less positive depending upon whether it is based on imperialism or hubris, p. 80/81:

> Economic imperialism, which has been well documented, occurs when economists use their own theory, namely neo-classical theory based on the three assumptions of (1) constant preferences (2) maximizing behavior, and (3) market coordination of social participants ... to explain social phenomena ... Economic hubris, which has not been well documented, is when economists fail to recognize the important contributions by sociologists concerning topics of interest to both sociologists and economists. Economic imperialism is a good thing for social science in general, and sociology in particular, because it allows for a new approach to, and debate about, traditional sociological problems. Economic hubris, on the other hand, is not beneficiary to the social sciences. Economic hubris comes about when economists feel that the 'elegant' and 'clean models' of economics are superior to the 'dirty hands' verstehen approach of sociology. This feeling among economists tends to produce one-sided

---

3 See also Kuorikoski and Lehtinen (2010) and Convert and Heilbron (2007).

research that could benefit from more sociological input and would produce stronger theory and better policy recommendations.

Indeed, they conclude, p. 85, "Sociologists have taken the economists advances into sociology seriously, but mainstream economists, as demonstrated, fail to take the writings of sociologists on economic topics seriously".

Velthuis (1999) looks at the same dualities, noting how sociology in the passage from Parsons to Granovetter has resisted the unsubtle methods, theories and conceptualisations of the economic by economics. Zafirowski (2000) argues that rational choice sociology has a more rounded notion of rationality than economics, and wonders how this will be resolved in going forward. In short, there were and remain fuzzy boundaries around economic sociology, even for common subject matter, contingent upon degree of rational choice or not, and what sort of rational choice.

In case of personnel economics, the brainchild of Becker-style economics imperialist, Edward Lazear,[4] Spencer (2011, p. 129) comments:[5]

> At root, personnel economics is an exercise in 'economics imperialism': it draws on and promotes a discourse and ideology that asserts that economics is the superior social science and rejects a genuine marriage of different perspectives and approaches in the realm of work studies.

However, it should be observed that personnel economics is a (small) part and parcel of labour economics, in which longstanding macro/social traditions around institutionalism (and John Dunlop) have given way to micro market imperfections approaches, leading to the dilution of industrial relations as a discipline and field, if not its incorporation into business and management studies and human resource management for institutionalised reasons whether for teaching, research or commercial promotion through consultancy.

Not least with a telling title, Medema (1997) asks, "The Trial of Homo Economicus: What Law and Economics Tells Us About the Development of Economic Imperialism". His answer, tied to its time, is more of the same but with its own peculiar features. For, in the assault on law by economics imperialism in its first phase, p. 140:

---

4 See Chapter 3.
5 See also p. 125, and Bailly (2022).

> The field arose as a unidirectional phenomenon, applying economics to law and not the other way around, and as the economic analysis of law, rather than as part of a general social-scientific approach to legal thinking. In both of these senses, post-1960 law and economics arose as an imperialistic movement, purporting, in the hands of some at least, to provide the key to legal reasoning.

As a result:

> Law and economics rocketed to prominence because, in the hands of its most able exponents, the field seemed to offer substantial insights into the legal arena at a time when legal thinking was in search of moorings and economists were armed with rather new, sophisticated weaponry for analyzing individual choices. And, following the Beckerian dictum, this weaponry was "relentlessly and unflinchingly" applied.

Nonetheless, Medema reports a reaction against this dictum, prompted in part by developments within economics itself (especially around behavioural economics). He is ambiguous over prospects, pp. 140/141, for:

> it would be wrong to think that law and economics is coming full circle, back to its early-twentieth-century form. Indeed, it would be unfortunate if it did so, since post-1960 law and economics has done a great deal to enrich our understanding of legal-economic processes. Great insights often come from pushing an idea (even an incorrect one) to the limit to see what happens; then, when the dust settles, you see what you've got and proceed accordingly. In the process of doing this, the field of law and economics seems to be moving back toward its roots in its incorporation of the insights of other social sciences, a movement that holds the promise of a richer law and economics.

In short, surprisingly, hopes seemed to be pinned on richer models of the individual and the reaction against pure rational choice, as opposed to the pursuit of the social, the structural, the relational quite apart from how the law is interpreted, its meaning, and how its processes reflect powers and hierarchies.[6]

---

6 A telling, if superficial, index of the contemporary absence of critique of "economics imperialism" in the interdisciplinary interaction between economics and law is to be found by examining the articles in the newly-founded, *Journal of Law and Political Economy*, which is commendably concerned with the exercise of power, etc. Nonetheless, across all of the

Other contributions include: ecology for which are "highlighted three aspects of [economics] imperialism: the failure to achieve unification (or integration), the failure to observe epistemological pluralism (when pluralism is appropriate), and the failure to account adequately for the appropriate values",[7] Thorén and Stålhammar (2018); Andersson (2021) who seeks Hayekian analysis of social, not just market, spontaneous order as a weapon against economics imperialism; Marchionatti and Cedrini (2016) and Cedrini and Marchionatti (2017) who deploy the gift as a weapon against economics imperialism (and how primitive societies are conceived) from Adam Smith onwards, see below; and Hadjimichalis (2006, p. 699/700) for whom:[8]

> The introduction of non-economic factors into economic geography and regional development studies was a welcome contribution and could lead to a much-needed renewal of the radical critique of the contemporary space-economy of capitalist societies. But, in practice, it often seems instead to be trapped in many questionable aspects, particularly in ignoring first, the power asymmetries and exploitative relations inherent in reciprocity, trust, routines and habits; second, in ignoring macroeconomic processes, inter-regional relations, the scalar organization of space and the role of the state; and third, in ignoring those places that remain stuck in the doldrums of persistent decline, underdevelopment or socio-economic weakness, and how this relates to combined and uneven development.

Only with Michie et al (2002) is there any concerted attempt to observe the relationship between economics imperialism and economic realities (it's neoliberalism, and it's economics, stupid) with important observations on

---

pieces published in its first seven issues, sixteen do include the word "imperial*", but just one, in a reference, makes reference to economics imperialism (and then more concerned with the property rights attached to markets than assessing interdisciplinary capture). Yet its aims and scope state that, "*JLPE* welcomes contributions ... on any theme at the intersection between law and political economy", https://escholarship.org/uc/lawandpoliticaleconomy/aimscope.

7 See also Pinto (2016).
8 Hadjimichalis offers a neat quotation from Myrdal, p. 692: "Economic theory has disregarded ... non-economic factors and kept them outside the analysis. As they are among the main vehicles for the circular causation in the cumulative processes of economic change, this represents one of the principal shortcomings of economic theory (Myrdal, 1957: 30)". However, in reductionist form, such is the thrust of the new economic geography (and international trade) inspired by Krugman, on which see Fine (2010).

the implications of economics imperialism for studying economics itself, as opposed to its spread to the non-economic, touching upon macroeconomics, finance, labour markets, production and competition.

The theme of an enriched mainstream economics has now become important although it is not usually posed by reference to economics imperialism as such; rather it is in terms of whether economics is changing to the better through the positive influences garnered from the other social sciences and a more rounded view of individuals and, to such an extent that weak heterodox alternatives should be abandoned in favour of encouraging the disintegration of the erstwhile mainstream and its reconstruction. These issues are taken up below, and elsewhere[9] – especially questioning the characterisation of both the mainstream and heterodoxy and the strategic relations between them. The related, even bigger, issue is how to relate developments within economics to developments within the economy and society more generally. Most of my (and other) contributions remain confined to a history of thought, at the expense of social influences. However, clearly Keynesianism has something to do with a response to the Great Depression, just as the monetarist counterrevolution, and its even more extreme progeny, New Classical Economics (Fine and Dimakou 2016), had something to do with neoliberalism. And there are clear affinities between the first phase of economics imperialism and the shift between Keynesianism and monetarism, and between subsequent shifts within neoliberalism and shifts in economics imperialism through its two later phases, especially in the context of development policy (Fine 2020).[10]

More generally, Kellecioglu (2017, p. 4) expresses the issue well and leans towards the priority of external influences:

> there are both intra-scientific (internal) and extra-scientific (external) structures and mechanisms in shaping and transforming economics and

---

9   See forthcoming volumes on heterodoxy and orthodoxy and, most recently, Fine (2022b).
10 Interestingly, Fleury (2010) rejects Robbins' definition of economics in the 1930s as the reason for the rise of economics imperialism in the 1960s since it would be necessary to explain a thirty-year delay. Instead, he puts the economists' ventures into interdisciplinarity down to the post-war social policies associated with extensive state intervention and the wish to be engaged in policymaking. What is sauce, however, for the goose is sauce for the gander, not least as interwar economics was already heavily interdisciplinary (not least with the old or classic institutional economics, predominant in the USA), and equally heavily policy-oriented (from anti-trust to New Deal). What has to be explained is both the delay **and** acceptance/acceptability of neoclassical forms of interdisciplinarity and policymaking, with the latter contingent on both external factors **and** those within economics itself.

the conduct of economists, but that the latter is much more important than the former.

But I remain to be convinced that this relative emphasis is correct other than, at most, in broad thrust. Economics as a discipline is heavily driven by the evolution of its own internal logic, especially how it relates to it technical apparatus and technical architecture, TA^2, production and utility functions, equilibrium, etc. The issues considered and, to some degree, how, are heavily influenced by the external environment. But the details of intellectual developments are extremely open and subject to contestation, and much more important is the extent to which alternatives are driven out by internal, institutionalised intolerance – something that is crucial not only for the inner development of economics as a discipline but also for the terms and conditions on which it relates to other disciplines and topics that are not within its traditional terrain. It should also be borne in mind that there is a tension between arguing that mainstream economics is both lacking realism and capable of fundamentally serving particular interests and/or policymaking as is often offered as an explanation for the theoretical and ideological positions adopted by mainstream economics. In short, the relationships across economics, economic conditions, policymaking and ideology are far from simple nor necessarily conforming with one another. Nor is there a simple relationship between academic hegemony and policy hegemony, otherwise scientists would have long since been seen to have addressed climate change in practice, and every country in the world would have long been on the way to adopting the social policy gold standard of a Scandinavian-style welfare state.

4   Balance against the Unbalanced/Imbalanced?

From its origins, the literature on economics imperialism has long exhibited a strong, dominant current in search of balance in economics' relations with other social sciences, initially in reaction against the imbalanced designs of the first phase of economics imperialism. The question of balance is worthy of discussion at some length as it spans the entire history of economics imperialism and is vital in how it is understood and addressed. A useful starting point, across various contributions, is Bögenhold (2017, 2018 and 2020) who seeks the reincorporation of institutions as well as history, history of economic thought, sociology and psychology, concluding Bögenhold (2018, p. 1126):

sociology's public reputation may have declined, while simultaneously economics is shifting its attention to the social dimension of economic behavior and moving toward the other social sciences ... those developments can also be seen as chances to upgrade the social sciences "around" economics.

This begs the question of why this should not be an upgrading of economics around the social sciences. But, significantly, he is also able to cite the much earlier Solow (1985, p. 328/9) to the same effect (Bögenhold 2018, p. 1131):

> All narrowly economic activity is embedded in a web of social institutions, customs, beliefs, and attitudes. ... Few things should be more interesting to a civilized economic theorist than the opportunity to observe the interplay between social institutions and economic behavior over time and place.

But even earlier still is Stillman (1955, p. 83) on the relations between economics and anthropology:

> Until better mathematical devices are discovered to handle human whims, and those impulses which for want of a better name we call tensions, or needs, I can see nothing that economics can contribute in suggesting why people want one object more than another, apples rather than oranges, mink coats rather than true love, and so on. I am excluding economics from the area of the psychodynamic; ... That economists have invaded this sphere, I think is explicable only in terms of imperialistic thinking. It is attributable to the use by economists of their thought-ways to explain more of the world about them than is justified by the nature of the intellectual tools with which they work. This limitation in no way cuts out the usefulness of economic theory; it requires, only, that economists work with given assumptions regarding preferences and refrain from going behind those preferences to explain the reason for the array.
>
> A second conclusion, which grows out of the first, is that economics is applicable to those areas of human activity in which people are rational. That is, economics applies in instances in which people really do wish to find the most efficient way of securing from a pile of resources the best possible satisfaction of a range of wants, given their ability and knowledge.

And, moving forward fifty years if still thirty years ago, for public choice theory, PCT, and economics applied to politics, we have Frey (1993, p. 101/2) for whom:[11]

> Public choice, and economic imperialism more generally, has been a great success within the social sciences. While progress can certainly be made by further applying the economic approach to politics (and other areas), diminishing returns have set in. Public choice has joined the ranks of normal science, originality and innovation play an increasingly smaller role.
>
> It is time now to embark on a new course and to switch from an exporter to an importer of ideas. The social and literary sciences contain many ideas which can enrich future public choice without giving up its sound foundations. The areas of behavioural anomalies and human motivation are two fields where political economy can benefit from insights from psychology; and discourse and personal embeddedness are aspects which public choice can learn from philosophy and sociology. Many other concepts and ideas can fruitfully be borrowed from other social sciences. If political economists are ready to take this challenge, public choice will prosper in the coming 25 years.

Move forward a further decade or more, and Chuah (2006) observes a boundary line for economics imperialism in terms of culture wars, a theme taken up by Krijnen (2016) after a further decade, with the added nuance that preferences are reflexive and multidimensional and, ironically, inapplicable to the purveyors of economics imperialism itself given their other-oriented intellectual goals and ambitions as opposed to pursuit of self-interest.

On a different tack, Lehtinen and Kuorikoski (2007, p. 134) are more concerned with realism of assumptions:

> the most effective (theoretical) way of criticizing an imperialistic model would be to demonstrate that unrealistic psychological or institutional assumptions actually matter in terms of the conclusions, although we agree that the burden of proof should in principle lie on those using the unrealistic assumptions in the first place. Explicit robustness analysis would thus be a valuable theoretical means of assessing the merits of economic models applied outside the traditional field of economics.

---

11   See also pp. 95 and 97.

A more scathing approach is taken by McRorie (2016, p. 218):

> Economic analyses of trust, reciprocity, "the warm glow," and "sophistication effects" have proliferated in recent decades, each adding their own ad hoc amendment to the framework of rational choice in an attempt to approximate moral decision making with mathematical precision. Such piecemeal and ineffectual efforts to quantify the complexities of moral agency are not likely to find much appreciation from scholars of religious ethics, who may suspect that fascination with the apparently scientific patina of such terms will render facile conversations about human nature by displacing richer, multifaceted and more complex debates over moral anthropology and psychology. Behavioral economic research is just as susceptible as other science of morality scholarship to be used to promote reductionistic accounts of causality, agency, habit, and identity, and to bolster the hope that science can itself become the lingua franca of a time of fractious pluralism – that perhaps one day sciences such as cognitive psychology and neurobiology can replace philosophy in explaining our lives to us. Given the immense cultural draw of this kind of scientism, surely one of the duties of a responsible engagement with this literature is avoiding the temptation to unadvisedly appropriate behavioral economic research for our own understanding of human nature.

Noting that economics imperialism comes in pure and plus forms, lack of balance in specifying the nature of individuals is deployed by Rothschild (2008, p. 724) to point to the presumed superiority of economics in interdisciplinarity endeavours, with other disciplines and their insights to be used as supplements rather than to be treated as an equal partner:[12]

> Nobody will object to holding on to neoclassical theory when it can be shown to work in practice, but why should that not also hold for behavioural economics and its refinement?

And he closes, p. 733:

> success stories do not support the EI ideology with its claims for universality and superiority. They rather support the view that in the complex

---

12   See also pp. 728 and 729. Rothschild puts such imbalance within economics down to the influence of Walras and physics envy as applied to, and generalised from, markets.

world in which we live we need several theories and methods as a box of tools from which one has to choose according to the nature of the object and the questions asked. Analogies and heuristic elements can and do play a role in this process. But there is no reason to assume that one method (which is particularly suited for a certain branch!) is a superior ideal to be adopted in all cases. What is required is a give-and-take relationship and this is also true for economics which benefits from the research results of other social sciences obtained by different methods.

Usefully and most recently, and unusually, in seeking interdisciplinarity between engineering and economics, Mariotti (2022, p. 19/20) offers a balanced view of (lack of proper) balance and how it has come about and can be strengthened:[13]

> associated with economics imperialism, a position of social superiority of economists has emerged, which has bred self-confidence, allowed the discipline to maintain its epistemological insularity over time and fueled an inclination toward a sense of entitlement. Fourcade et al. (2015), for example, cited a survey conducted in the United States in 2006 which showed that mainstream economists were the only social scientists who opposed interdisciplinarity to a great extent: 57.3% of American economics professors disagreed with the statement that "in general, interdisciplinary knowledge is better than knowledge obtained by a single discipline" while, on average, 20.8% of other social scientists did so (professors in finance, history, political science, psychology, sociology).
>
> In contrast, and quite ironically, in more recent times, we have witnessed an increasing assimilation by economics of other social sciences, with the incorporation of knowledge from psychology, sociology, neuroscience, biology, anthropology, etc. … as well as from engineering … The most relevant case is perhaps that of behavioral economics, which has begun to question the mainstream … More generally, after economics had exported its view of rationality to other social sciences, new approaches have emerged within economics that import insights from other sciences, thus giving rise to a process that has been called "reverse imperialism".

---

13 For a very different take on interdisciplinarity with engineering, see the results of the iBUILD project on UK infrastructure in which my own system of provision approach played a role, as well as in the Lili project for more sustainable consumption, https://research.ncl.ac.uk/ibuild/ and https://lili.leeds.ac.uk/ See also Bayliss and Fine (2021).

Significantly, Mariotti's balance includes reference to what has been an occasional theme in the literature, namely 'reverse imperialism', to put it bluntly the idea that we are witnessing sociological or other interdisciplinary imperialisms against or within economics. In doing so, his emphasis is upon more complex, mixed and balanced models of individual behaviour, ones in which there is evolving interaction with the social, structures and the like, with complexity economics, experimental economics, RCT and neuroeconomics as the more prominently favoured descendants of behavioural economics. As it were, and unsurprisingly, these can be traced from Simon's bounded rationality and from game theory to their currently elevated status within the realm of the third phase of economics imperialism and be seen as not only reverse imperialism but also a reaction against, and rejection of, earlier/earliest phases of economics imperialism with their lack of balance.

Note, though, that Mariotti immediately continues from the quotation above, p. 20:

> Imperialism and reverse imperialism are criticized for envisioning an epistemological domain that would constrain and stifle the development of the interpretative and creative capacities of the disciplines. However, both reflect the aspiration of sciences toward unification. Mäki (2009, p. 357) noted: "[w]hatever the formulation, unification is widely celebrated as a major goal and achievement of the best of science. … There is little doubt that large segments of the economics profession share the view that unification is a major virtue of theorizing".

Strangely, "the aspiration of sciences toward unification" is contradicted for economists earlier in the passage cited above from Mariotti in citing Fourcade et al. In addition, Mariotti presents an unduly balanced view as being taken by Mäki in the following, p. 20:

> As Mäki [2009, p.377] argued, there is good and bad in economics expansionism. The 'good thing' is that it "manifests a respectable philosophy of science" when searching for knowledge unification. The 'bad thing' is that "economics imperialism suffers from unjustified radicalism and dogmatism that should deny it any support".

However, Mäki distinguishes two types of economics imperialism, on pastures previously unoccupied by other disciplines and on those being incorporated from other disciplines, the latter being denoted by the addition of a * which has been omitted by Mariotti himself in the quotation. This means that Mäki does not, as is implied, suggest economics imperialism is a "bad thing" unworthy of support, especially where it seeks unification across disciplines.

More generally, Mäki has made a number of contributions on economics imperialism, the thrust of which is to seek balance although I would argue that the implications of his, and others', inputs are to achieve the opposite of balance in practice.[14] One way to approach this is to view Mäki as having taken economics imperialism as an issue and to have imported it into the philosophy and methodology of economics, just as others have done the same with the history of economic thought, bearing in mind this is not a matter of intra-economics discourse as both of these fields had abandoned economics (or, more exactly, been forced out as irrelevant) to seek greener pastures within the philosophy and history of science. In this vein, Mäki asks what do we mean by economics imperialism, what are its various aspects, and what makes for good as opposed to bad economics imperialism.

These all seem, and can be, reasonable, balanced questions, and a first, necessary step towards unpicking economics imperialism in practice, especially in avoiding what is viewed as heated and emotive debate. But these questions are extraordinarily lacking in sufficient mindfulness of the substance and context of economics imperialism – not least in allowing for balance. Indeed, so balanced is Mäki (2009, p. 354) that he describes his stance as follows:[15]

> It is important to understand what this paper does not seek to do. It does not offer any historical account of economics imperialism, but is

---

14 I remember being somewhere between disappointed and irritated by the contributions of Mäki and others for reasons that will become clear, although presented in more temperate form here with the benefit of age, wisdom and the passage of time, but see also Chapter 8. To Mäki's credit, he did in the most flattering terms invite me to participate at a conference where economics imperialism was to be discussed but I was unable to attend for personal reasons (special needs childcare). Fortunately, I have a copy of my response to him which, in part, reads: "What I find most interesting is the extent to which the *limits* on EI are stressed by economists and non-economists until most recently, even by the imperialists themselves. Today, though, economists do not even seem to be aware of the problem". As a footnote in the history of emailing, I only have this draft, from as early as 25th May, 2004, but not the original to which it is a response, because internet access was limited at the time to internet-connected desktops. For many emails, for convenience, I would draft to be able to send them in batches (transporting on a floppy disk). Otherwise, there were no records of "sent" and so none for those drafted online unless copied – and limitations on server storage space did not allow for retention of emails received.

15 Note the much earlier contribution, Mäki (2002, p. 255) for which: "My question was whether economics imperialism is a justified project of explanatory unification in being able to meet certain ontological and pragmatic constraints".

supposed to be compatible with a number of different historical accounts concerned with its origins, actual trajectories, and stages of development. Neither does the paper attempt to explain the phenomenon of economics imperialism, it rather seeks to develop tools that could be employed in its evaluation.

Indeed, "The proposed account is intended as neutral with regard to any particular ideas concerning the contents of any particular economics that behaves imperialistically", p. 354.

By contrast, I would argue that such neutrality is not an option. To adopt it is to side with economics imperialism. In the abstract, and in total generality, this cannot be argued convincingly. But, put in some context and some other examples, and you will see what I have in mind. Consider something similar for racism or sexism for example – no need for their origins, histories, trajectories or stages of development, just a neutral scheme by which to evaluate them. It would also make sense to throw global warming into the neutrality pot – an exclusive concern with the methods and criteria for evaluating whether it is happening or not, surely would provide succour to climate change denialists.

The imperative of balance recurs throughout Mäki's contributions, bending over backwards to give economics a fair crack, if not hold, of the whip. Thus, Mäki and Marchionni (2011, p. 662):

> Our general conclusion is that one should not rush to pass judgement on whether a given academic phenomenon is an instance of economics imperialism, nor on whether to welcome or resist it. One should first examine the complex phenomenon using refined concepts that highlight its multiple aspects and variations.

And, Mäki (2013, p. 328):

> many critics of economics imperialism (controversially) argue that economics seeks to imperialistically impose ideas that are bad also in their original domain ... This sequence should not be ruled out by definition.

In other words, bad economics might make good social science. Just to rub home the lofty lesson, p. 328:

> It may be that evolutionary psychology and Gary Becker's economics of the family ... are bad science. But it is not at all clear that they are bad simply because they are examples of interdisciplinary trespassing.

Rather, they would be bad for the same reasons as disciplinary science may be bad: they do not meet the standards of good science (whatever these are).

But, to put it bluntly, Becker's economics of the family *is* bad science, as is all economics imperialism in general because its foundations are bad, and none of it meets the standards of good science, so why are we dwelling on this point?

More substantively, Mäki draws upon a whole series of criteria by which to assess economics imperialism: scope, standing and style; the ontological, pragmatic, and epistemological; consilience and unification; and pluralism, tolerance and fallibilism. Other aspects could be added more or less indefinitely, according to what we study and how, across methodology, methods, theories, substance, conceptualisation and values,[16] see Kellecioglu (2017) for example. These criteria might not apply to economics imperialism in the same way in the round, not least as it is both variegated and evolving. There is not one economics imperialism but many across three different phases, and across multitudes of disciplines and topics. Even in the first step of disaggregating, Mäki gets it wrong, drawing an apparently valid distinction between economics imperialisms that do or do not seek to occupy the domain of other disciplines. But this is too fuzzy a boundary upon close examination, not least as divisions *within* economics have themselves shifted, especially as more applied fields, more aligned to the other social sciences or its methods, have been internally colonised. The example of segmented labour market theory is telling – initially dismissed by the orthodoxy as sociological and atheoretical, it has become incorporated through the theory of imperfectly working labour markets (Fine 1987 and 1998).

In short, economics imperialism cannot be satisfactorily assessed without taking a position on the nature of mainstream economics and its history and context – something, to be fair, that Mäki (2009, p. 373) seems to accept himself in concluding:

> The upshot … can be expressed by saying, first, that economics expansionism, whether imperialistic or not [NOTE THE RESERVATION], manifests

---

16 See Rolin (2015, p. 427) for whom: "By crossing the boundaries between disciplines, economics imperialists come to have epistemic responsibilities towards those scientists whose domain they enter. That economics imperialists have epistemic responsibilities beyond the boundaries of economics, is a normative basis for the moral evaluation of economics imperialism".

a respectable philosophy of science, ceteris paribus; and secondly, that the ceteris paribus condition often may not hold.

As all critics of mainstream economics know, all the action is in the ceteris paribus. And, in this light, Mäki's project of creating a framework for evaluating economics imperialism can be considered to have failed on a number of grounds. First, there has been limited reference to, and even less application of his approach. It has primarily remained at the level of abstract posturing rather than detailed application.[17] His own application to economic geography (Mäki and Marchionni 2011) does not begin to get to grips with the issues involved, on which see Fine (2010).

Second, this project has not engaged economics imperialists themselves. They are simply uninterested in, even ignorant of, the issues involved. Whilst Mäki (2009) offers some support for his positions on qualifying, or drawing boundaries around, economics imperialism from Coase, Williamson and even Becker himself, this seems to overlook how inconsistent they are (as Mäki observes of Coase), whether they take their methodology into practice, and, most important of all, what they intend themselves even if followed through in practice (in the breach) is of lesser relevance than how they are interpreted and used – with Coase a treasure trove of misinterpretation around his theorem that is presumed to abolish externalities through property rights and open the way for economics imperialism to appropriate law (Medema 2020).

Third, quite apart from seeking balance in framing economics imperialism, Mäki seeks balance in engaging with it, as opposed to dismissing it out of hand through fear or arrogance – with the implicit presumption that this has been driving responses to economics imperialism, something which entirely misrepresents the heterodox economics community by pigeonholing them into either constructive engagers or fearful or arrogant ostrich heads in the sand. Equally, his proposal is wrapped up in the warm collegiality of open debate and pluralism, with Mäki and Marchionni (2011, p. 662) closing:

---

17 More generally, if by reference to one past economist in particular, Yay (2021, p. 96) observes: "the ongoing debate between economists and economic methodologists on the interactions between economics and other disciplines (with the titles like 'interdisciplinarity-multidisciplinarity', 'economics imperialism-reverse imperialism' or 'insulation-social scienciation') … is the main subject matter that was on Schumpeter's agenda throughout his academic life. What is surprising is that no reference is made to Schumpeter's works in the relevant studies".

Intellectual imperialism is potentially progressive, but it may also generate scientific loss and regress. Because passing judgement on these matters is highly fallible, it should take place in circumstances that support criticism and self-criticism, tolerance and pluralism, mutual respect and understanding. Disciplinary boundaries are not carved in stone. Neither are theories and methods, nor the standards for measuring their quality. We join those commentators who see that the best strategy to resist the dangers of economics imperialism and to exploit its potential for scientific progress lies in open communication and cross-fertilization rather than arrogant neglect and fearful rejection.

But this is entirely to overlook the nature of economics (imperialism) and its conscious or unconscious practitioners not only, as previously observed, in their lack of engagement with criticism and alternatives, alongside their institutionalised power to proceed regardless. It is as if the case for economics imperialism is to be made in its strongest possible form, far over and beyond the capabilities and knowledge of its own practitioners, only for this enhanced economics imperialism to be balanced with a bit more roundedness across criteria and substance of which those engaging in the real world of economics imperialism have neither knowledge nor interest.

To conclude this lengthy digression into economics imperialism as balance, only rarely does the literature move fully beyond potential for balance, through lack of appropriate balance to the conclusion of the impossibility or denial of the desirability of balance – the scope of applicability and use of rational choice is not generally perceived to be an empty set – we are all homo economicus to some degree and this needs to be balanced with homo sociologicus and any other disciplinary homos you care to include. However, for Michie et al (2002, p. 364) on the new political economy but with more general relevance:

> The new political economy has sought to apply the methods of neoclassical economics in analysing issues that had previously been regarded as falling within the remit of other disciplines. The realism of behavioural assumptions continues to be regarded as being of no analytical consequence, with only the accuracy of a theory's predictions being of any significance. Far from enriching economic analysis, new political economy simply imposes the assumptions and methods of neoclassical economics. This new economic imperialism needs to be replaced with a genuinely multidisciplinary and interdisciplinary approach to analysing economic issues.

There are two important messages here, more than ready for filling out and bringing up to date. One, the most obvious, is that it is economics itself, the dedicated study of the economy, that is in the greatest need of reform and that it is economics imperialism that exposes that need without criticism to be confined to that terrain alone. If only economics were different, so would be economics imperialism or, if itself turned back, the nature of interdisciplinarity with economics and the economic. In short, the critical target has to be mainstream economics irrespective of its range of application, not only for its substantive content but also for its institutionalised monopoly and intolerance as has been closely observed by its heterodox critics.[18]

The second message, requiring heavy reading between the lines, is for those who peddle the particular balances attached to the imperative of pluralism. The dogmatic and dogma aside, within the context of reforming economics and, on a lesser scale, in opposition to economics imperialism in the search for balance, pluralism has become an almost unquestionable virtue. And those who might oppose it are perceived to have some sort of dogma of their own that they wish to impose in place of the mainstream (and, to be blunt, such accusations have been regularly levelled against me as a purveyor of Marxist political economy even though casual knowledge of my research and teaching reveals not just my tolerance of, but dependence upon, appropriately cast pluralism, including from the mainstream).

So pluralism as such is not the issue. But what cannot be set aside is the extremes of power and influence exercised by the mainstream and its intolerance of alternatives bordering on the obsessive, let alone its unwillingness to engage in any, let alone critically constructive, debate. The demand for pluralism, and strategies to achieve it, cannot ignore such imbalances over what is taught, who is appointed and what is published and funded in research and teaching, within academia and with corresponding, if not necessarily simple, consequences for representation of the economic and economics in the media and in policymaking.[19] In short, the demand for pluralism can only be undertaken effectively by an assault upon the mainstream, paradoxical though this may appear in terms of the ethos of pluralism itself, as the mainstream is the main barrier to pluralism in sharp contrast to most other approaches, their practitioners and their ethos.

---

18 See forthcoming volumes on mainstream economics and heterodox economics but, for now, especially Javdani and Chang (2019) and Aigner (2021).

19 For overviews, bringing out the dominance of a concentrated elite within the USA, with global reach increasingly subordinating, if not displacing the presence of, alternatives within other countries, see Javdani and Chang (2019) and Aigner (2021).

Debates about taking a balanced view over economics imperialism, and seeking to categorise and judge it, especially in individual instances (this bit ok, this bit not), by various criteria is to miss the wood for the trees. Economics imperialism is what (mainstream) economics is whatever forms it takes across topics, disciplines and even internally and in its contestation, however much engaged with alternatives whether from heterodox economics or other social sciences. This is not to say that all of economics imperialism is the same, only that it shares some underlying, if shifting, aspects.

5   Economics Imperialism Is as Variegated as Economics Imperialism Does

As already emphasised, then, the search for balance with and from economics imperialism is complex as it straddles different disciplines, topics and criteria; it is not and cannot be a little bit more or less of this and that. In part that is why it is so elusive even if there were both potential and willingness on the part of all of those involved to be balanced/pluralistic, which there is not. But the complexities of the (im)balance issue is to return to the variegated nature of economics imperialism as this does itself reflect where the imbalances are drawn in practice and in the round, and sheds light on a number of distinct but overlapping aspects in economics imperialism's evolution. Some of these may not have been sufficiently acknowledged in my previous contributions but have become unavoidable in a retrospective reading. First, despite a long gestation into its first Becker phase,[20] waiting upon the contested passage from

---

20   Note that Marchionatti and Cedrini (2016) – see also Cedrini and Marchionatti (2017) and, if more muted, Cedrini and Dagnes (2022) – locate economics imperialism as deriving from the "original sin" of Adam Smith and his understanding of primitive societies, p. 2: "Still, in a reconstruction of the story of the uneasy relationships between economics and social sciences expressly centred upon the problem of economics imperialism, Ben Fine and Dimitris Milonakis (2009) consider the marginalist revolution as the key passage. Marginalism, they argue, allowed economists to shift the boundaries separating their own discipline from other social sciences, and to colonize the subject matter of sociology, anthropology and political science. Fine and Milonakis (2009: 1) regard the 'desocialization and dehistoricization' of economics occurred with the passing from the political economy of the fathers of economics to the marginalist revolution as the conditions that made economics imperialism possible. To the contrary, we advance the thesis that an imperialist orientation characterizes economics since the dawn of the discipline with Adam Smith. We thus devote a substantial part of this book to showing how economists' early analyses of primitive societies – a fundamental issue in the foundation of political economy – can be taken as shining illustration of the pugilistic attitude of

the marginalist revolution of the 1870s to the formalist revolution of the 1950s, subsequently the pace of evolution of economics imperialism has been astonishing. It has gone through two further phases in little more than two decades, with prodigious developments within each of these later phases in critically departing from, or adding to, their predecessors.

Second, the (accelerating) pace of evolution of economics imperialism has exceeded the capacity of those commenting upon it to keep up. In terms of its practitioners, this has meant that the boundaries between the three phases are not hard and fast chronologically, adding to the variegation in its application. Thus, Lazear (2000), for example, is lavishing praise on Becker's "economic approach" long after it has been superseded or enhanced by the market imperfections approach as Akerlof and Kranton (2000) had already been engaging in the economics of identity, see Chapter 5. On the other hand, critics of economics imperialism equally tend to lag behind the curve, working against a model of it that has already been supplemented if not abandoned. This is especially true of critics from disciplines other than economics, for whom the dismal science tends to be seen as remaining embedded in some ante-diluvian, unapologetic scholarly support for neoliberal ideology (as if market imperfections economics, in its new forms, had not emerged).

Third, over and above playing economics imperialism catch up, both its proponents and its critics have also anticipated what was to come even if not entirely fully. For, in the first phase of economics imperialism, some emphasis was placed upon the borders between disciplines and their corresponding methods. Only those at the extremes inside and outside economics saw TA^2, if usually specified as rational choice, as applicable across all social science. Instead, there were both boundaries for the scope of application of rational choice and the need to supplement it with the contributions from other social sciences. If in a different way, without the intermediate step of market imperfections economics that renders it more palatable, this is to engage in the third phase of economics imperialism. Variegated outcomes arise out of where the

---

economics towards other social sciences". This commentary clearly conflates "desocialization and dehistoricization", of which Smith is innocent, with economics imperialism which is its reverse albeit on reduced terms. That Smith projected his understanding of primitive societies from his understanding of capitalism (the commercial stage) is not disputed but is positively emphasised by Milonakis and Fine (2009) both in methodology and substance (value theory, division of labour versus extent of market, and propensity to truck, barter and exchange derived from speech). Further, their alternative to Smith of opposing gift to commodity suffers from its own dualistic reductionism, paralleling if not identical to, Smith's calculus of self-interest alongside desire for social regard. For rejection of the gift/commodity dualism, see Fine (2002, Chapter 3).

boundaries of the application of economics lie and how those boundaries are or are not transgressed.

Indeed, rationality plays a curious and evolving role within economics in this respect. At its core, as with TA^2, it is confined to utility maximisation. Of necessity, this defines an 'other' world of irrationality. The first phase of economics imperialism considers (social) science should be reduced to the application of the core understanding of rationality and everything else is irrational. As neatly put by Lecouteux (2022, p. 4):

> The recurrent use of terms such as 'myopic', 'naïve', 'impulsive', or even 'idiotic' to characterize individual behaviours, and the systematic references to expressions such as 'deviation' or 'mistake', implying that individuals 'suffer' from their 'biases' clearly tend to pathologise the individual, by comparison to his 'far-sighted' and 'sophisticated' neoclassical alter ego.

With the second phase of economics imperialism, this approach to rationality remains the same but is situated in the context of market imperfections with the result that apparently irrational behaviours can be construed as rational, and/or the effects of rationality in the presence of market imperfections require correction by such rational/irrational behaviour or rationally-constructed external intervention whether through custom, norms, trust, institutions and the state and public policy.

Where these give rise to, or are accompanied by, persistent irrational behaviour and dysfunctional outcomes, interventions can be used to deploy the irrational to attain what would be rational behaviour in their absence, with nudge and behavioural economics being the leading thrust in explaining and deploying the irrational to capture the rational. Again, Lecouteux (2022, p. 2) specifies this extremely well:

> emphasising the cognitive limitations of 'real' individuals compared to their neoclassical alter ego, and which lies at the core of nudging policies – offers a distorted view of behavioural public policies by shifting the focus from social institutions and markets ... to consumers' cognition.

Lecouteux offers the telling metaphor of Homer economicus versus Spock economicus – no, not Iliad versus babies but the humanly-flawed Simpson versus the inhumanly-flawed character from Star Trek. One version of nudge, at least, is seeking to shift the former to the latter. But, in the third phase of economics imperialism, the boundaries between the rational and the irrational are shifted (as was always the case for anyone other than head-banging economists) and rationality is both suspended and supplemented by whatever factors are fancied. In other words, narrow rationality can be core for analytical and policy purposes but, equally, range across other forms of rationality and objectives to suit. In general, in the third phase of economics imperialism, practitioners vary willy-nilly and unwittingly across what is rational and what is irrational, and whether outcomes are better for realising or rejecting rationality. All that matters is the model.

The tensions across the rational/irrational border are complemented by those concerning how economics can be more realistic. This is brought out by Grayot's (2020, p. 105) discussion of the dualism imminent in behavioural economics and neuroeconomics, if without any reference to economics imperialism:

> the case can be made that the popularity of dual process theory in economics has less to do with the empirical success of dualistic decision models, and more to do with the convenience that the dual process narrative provides economists looking to explain away decision anomalies. This leaves behavioral economists and neuroeconomists with something of a dilemma: either they stick to their purported ambitions to give a realistic description of human decision-making and give up the narrative, or they revise and restate their scientific ambitions.

Fourth, then, more generally than for (ir)rationality and (ir)realism, where and how the balance of interdisciplinary content is struck is a source of variegation across the incidence and impact of economics imperialism, although the issue of balance is most readily seen, inappropriately, as one-dimensional and linear rather than multidimensional and contradictory. In short, to be balanced, economics is lectured on the need to know its limits and learn from other disciplines, rather than to invade and impose a narrow version of rational choice upon them. This means the third phase of economics imperialism, of economics plus, has always been at least latent if only fully taking root once relying upon market imperfections plus.

If the role of balance reflects variegation across economics imperialism, so does the fifth aspect, the presumption that economics has become more specialised and fragmented. Thus, Marchionatti and Cedrini (2017, p. 5) refer to:[21]

---

21 See also Cedrini and Fontana (2018).

Unprecedented specialization in a more and more fragmented discipline ... For sure, mainstream economics is changing face ... Collaboration with other disciplines is a crucial but critical factor of this transformation ... Thereby, it is argued, economics will be able to help solve the "scandalous" ... problem of today's "social sciences pluralism" ... by contributing to developing a common model of human behaviour.

And Ambrosino et al (2021, p. 632) assess "recent proposals for unifying the social sciences [i.e. economics imperialism] that have originated within the economics profession at a time of pervasive specialisation and increasing fragmentation". This posture, however, is also another example of missing the woods for the trees. Surely, economics imperialism does lead to the spread of the discipline across an increasing number of specialised topics, with corresponding fragmentation in application. And this has all been intensified by the third phase of economics imperialism. But this is to overlook what such specialisation and fragmentation retains in common, TA^2 with or without suspension/plus. Otherwise, economics is essentially no longer economics.

Significantly, there would appear to be a common position across a group of scholars, as indicated by co-authorships, and including Mäki, Davis, Cedrini, Marchionatti, Vromen[22] and Ambrosino, with the notion of balance that we have imputed to Mäki being framed as trade between (disciplinary) nations, rather than imperialism, by Ambrosino et al (2021) and Davis (2016).[23] What is crucial in this posture, however, is that, irrespective of the origins of economics imperialism in its first phase, it is now perceived to be becoming more balanced (Ambrosino et al 2021, p. 634):

> The advent, since the 1980s, of a series of different research programs (the most important being evolutionary game theory, experimental economics, behavioral economics, evolutionary economics, neuroeconomics, complexity theory), all of them significantly deviating from

---

22 See Chapter 8.
23 See also Falgueras-Sorauren (2018) who questions the extent to which Robbins' (in)famous definition of economics as the allocation of scarce resources between competing ends (in the midst of the world's worst ever economic depression) is a true reflection of his beliefs. It should, however, be borne in mind that Robbins was more than capable of changing his mind and contradicting himself (as is obvious over his opposition to Keynesian policies in the thirties) and, in any case, how he is perceived and used is more important than his own qualifications. In passing, it is much easier in retrospect to exaggerate Robbins as the source of the original sins of mainstream economics than it is to establish his influence in practice. The same cannot be said of Chicago.

the neoclassical core of mainstream economics, signals the transition "from neoclassical dominance to mainstream pluralism" (Davis 2006). Mainstream economics is changing face (see Colander, Holt, and Rosser 2004) and exploring new research paths. The rise and success of complexity economics and evolutionary game theory promote a new conception of social interaction, one that involves heterogeneous agents endowed with bounded rationality, helps focus on institutional structures, and draws attention to unpredictable, emerging properties of social systems shaped by interactions themselves.

Not least through reference to Colander et al., this involves a presumption that economics is disintegrating from its boundaries inwards with corresponding implications for the gathering weight of reverse imperialism and how to strategise in response. We discuss the latter after first returning to the issue of why there should have been so little literature on economics imperialism although, to be fair to Davis, he is much less upbeat than might be imagined around the prospects for economics, presuming mainstream economics' reaction against reverse imperialism is to blame (Davis 2016, p. 17):

> it seems entirely justified to recommend that science environments be open and pluralistic. Needless to say, the details of securing this goal are many and demanding in economics, because neoclassicism since the early reverse imperialism incursions from the 1980s has arguably become an increasingly defensive and yet aggressive approach. No support for pluralism seems likely to be found among the ranks of neoclassical economists. The risk is just too high to core principles. Thus, as has only been too long clear, the defense of pluralism falls to heterodoxy.

Why then has the literature critical of economics imperialism been so weak? As with so many other things, as will be adopted here, it is easy and commonplace to divide explanatory factors into two, the internal and the external, as well as acknowledging that there are overlaps and interactions between the two factors. Criticism from within economics is almost inevitably going to be from heterodoxy, other than in the first phase of economics imperialism, but the mainstream within other social sciences is also a potential source of antipathy.

First and foremost, for the external factors (from a heterodox perspective), is the nature and role of the mainstream. As emphasised in our discussion of balance around economics imperialism, alongside and following its first phase, the mainstream has always heavily and openly opposed economics imperialism as the application of rational choice to everything with those, such as Becker who claim otherwise, being seen as extreme. With the passage out of the first phase, economics imperialism proceeded apace but with muted presence and successes. Accordingly, the mainstream was wont to see itself not as imperialistic but as interdisciplinary and positively incorporating the insights of other disciplines. In other words, economics imperialism prevailed in everything other than name except when claiming reverse imperialism. In short, the exaggerated claims for economics (as the only rigorous) social science of the first phase of economics imperialism allowed the discipline to present itself as reacting against such extremes without addressing the concerns of heterodoxy around the social, the historical, etc, content of economic theorising.

Second, then, alongside its apparent abandonment of the first phase of economics imperialism, the mainstream was hardly likely to look favourably upon heterodox contributions, if and when they did arise, with any more favour than upon heterodoxy more generally. Absolute intolerance in teaching, appointments and research would inevitably extend to claims and claimants of economics imperialism.

Third, by the same token, whether by strategy to survive and prosper within the mainstream or by deliberate strategy to engage with it in the belief that its (reverse) economics imperialism signified a process of mainstream transformation that could be deepened and accelerated, heterodox criticism of economics imperialism has itself been muted and even rejected as a way forward.

Fourth, and closely related, the variegated nature of economics imperialism – its different depth and forms across disciplines and topics – certainly allowed for it to be acknowledged and criticised but on its own terms case by base, but without reference to the much more general and common processes of economics imperialism. In other words, I am claiming that there is much magnificent criticism of the mainstream for its economics imperialism but without this being acknowledged as such. If the mainstream itself is specified as fragmented and specialised (and disintegrating), it is less readily able to be seen as imperialistic.

Fifth, the hypothesis of economics imperialism (and its evolving nature) does itself depend upon a number of issues, each of which is controversial between heterodox economists and beyond. They include the history of economic thought, the evolving nature of both the mainstream and heterodoxy, and questions of methodology and strategy in relation to the mainstream. Disagreement and/or focus on one or more of these is more than enough to set economics imperialism aside as a common critical rallying call and understanding of the nature of the mainstream, quite apart from obscuring the main issue by side-tracking into those with which it is associated.[24]

Sixth, given the vulnerability of heterodoxy to the intolerance of the mainstream, it is understandable that those who do survive, and even prosper, should see their own interests, fields and engagements as strategic in criticising the mainstream and promoting alternatives as imperative, thereby constraining attention to economics imperialism as such. In different ways, this is true of Lawson's emphasis upon social ontology, of Hodgson on institutions, of complexity and behavioural economics, and of the migration of history, philosophy and methodology of economic thought from within (heterodox) economics to other fields/disciplines.

This is not to denigrate these contributions – except to the extent that they misread the mainstream as positively transforming to which heterodoxy should engage and contribute, and do themselves denigrate heterodoxy for not being dedicated to their own favoured theme. Rather it is merely to locate their role in contributing to the invisibility of economics imperialism. To some degree, this is paradoxical, as those promoting a one-strand heterodoxy are guilty of the most blatant rejection of pluralism even if generally insisting upon it in practice as the means to promote a well-grounded interdisciplinarity.[25] Significantly, the most prominent heterodox economist, although he himself rejects the term, is Ha-Joon Chang whose success in popular promotion of alternatives to the mainstream has been accompanied by a determined dedication not only to unremittingly critical exposure of the mainstream, but also to pluralism, history of thought, the social and cultural, attention to policy, and the seamless shift from one topic to another, most recently Chang (2022) following Chang (2010 and 2014).

Seventh, in terms of the other social sciences, there have been mixed (variegated) results in response and in outcomes to economics imperialism in practice but, unsurprisingly given the muted response from perpetrators and their critics within economics, these too have been limited, reflecting the specialisations and fragmentations of their origins, with human capital and the

---

24 See Chapter 7 in which this syndrome is observed of a symposium to assess the two books (Fine and Milonakis 2009; Milonakis and Fine 2009), which lay out economics imperialism in full and historical detail. In addition, on a more personal note, the misunderstanding and/or misperception of the significance of economics imperialism derives from false interpretations of my (and Dimitri Milonakis') own work as in Vromen (2009) and Nik-Khah and Van Horn (2012). See Chapters 7 and 8.

25 For disputes with Hodgson around these issues, see Fine and Milonakis (2012) and Fine (2022b), for Lawson, for methodology, Fine (2015).

economics of education as the leading example of the incursions that dare not speak their name. I cannot but recall my frustrated appeal to other social scientists to use their energies to waste social capital – the response was often, no one serious takes it seriously in our discipline. Possibly, much the same is true of much social science in response to economics imperialism, at least until there has been some damage done that has become irreversible.

Eighth, this in part also reflects the intellectual and material environment within which the social sciences have been situated since the displacement of the first phase of economics imperialism. For globalisation and neoliberalism (and social capital) have been the first ports of call for the social sciences as they have retreated from the extremes of postmodernism. In addition, in the wake of the Global Financial Crisis, the most significant emerging concept and issue across the social sciences over the last decade, leaving aside the environment and the pandemic, has been financialisation. It has enjoyed the almost total absence of contributions from mainstream economics. In addition, on its own terms, the heterodox economics literature has focused upon the dysfunctions deriving from financialisation which can be readily incorporated and supplemented by the broader social science literature by reference to the corresponding dysfunctions of social and environmental reproduction (and the impacts upon everyday life). By contrast, had the various mainstream theories of finance sought to displace "financialisation" within other social sciences, the chances are that they would have been firmly rejected and even been perceived as a leading instance of economics imperialism with broader implications for other case studies. Indeed, financialisation offers a wonderful illustration of economics imperialism in terms of the dog that did not bark.

6 Strategic Considerations by Way of Conclusion

Against this account of the reasons for the invisibility of economics imperialism and, mindful of my own failure to have placed it other than minimally on the agenda of heterodox economists and other social scientists,[26] what

---

26 To be fair to myself, apart from initiating the setting up of the International Initiative for Promoting Political Economy, iippe.org, I found in searching through electronic files that I had forgotten that I had created a website for works on economics imperialism, long since deceased, and also taught an MSc optional course on economics imperialism at SOAS, available to the 200 or so students of both economics and development studies. It also died, due to lack of student demand and yet, especially through the leading initiatives taken by the World Bank, economics imperialism is arguably at its most virulent in development economics/studies if both criticised and not acknowledged as such.

strategic implications can be drawn other than disabling pessimism in light of the mainstream's parasitism, intolerance, ignorance and stranglehold over the discipline of economics whilst its scale and scope of application presses forward remorselessly. First is to recognise how much political economy has strengthened across the social sciences as a result of the GFC, and the continuing dysfunctions in economic performances and failings in offering explanations for them.

Second is to harness the increasing dissatisfaction with mono-economics and the inability of the mainstream to respond to this in a meaningful way and make anything more than a paper commitment to engage in pluralism. However, as emphasised, the rallying call around pluralism must be set in the context of a pluralism amongst unequals in terms of the mainstream's domination of the discipline and what will be attempts to determine the nature of the plural where it cannot be resisted.

Last, and by no means least, the motivation behind signposting economics imperialism is twofold – to bring about the reconstruction of economics as political economy and to guard against the appropriation of other topics and disciplines by economics imperialism.

Priority in principle must be assigned to the reform of mainstream economics, without which imperialistic designs will be sustained, with strategic implications for seeking alternatives by reintroducing methodology, conceptualisation, the historical and social, and the history of economic thought in ways in which the contributions of other disciplines can be incorporated into and against the mainstream. This is the route through which genuine pluralism can be embraced rather than one conventional and dominant view conceding that others may be allowed on the margins alongside on sufferance. In this way, as I have argued, economics has a chance of becoming interdisciplinary by instinct as opposed to being an add on (Fine 2022b).

But, equally, as also argued, the conditions under which progress can be achieved are highly mixed. Within economics, with heterodox departments few and far between and heavily besieged (Aigner 2021) and the need to contribute to core teaching around TA^2 and econometrics, and the fragmentation and specialisations associated within economics and through economics imperialism,

---

See forthcoming volume on development. My piece in *Review of Social Economy* (Fine 2008, Chapter 9) exhorted the struggle against economics imperialism. Note also that the Appendix to the previous volume on economics imperialism lists as many as eighty (joint) contributions by myself critical of economics imperialism – I may have been ineffective but I was not idle in my endeavours. Clearly, more or different is needed to become a Freakeconomist, a Piketty, or a Ha-Joon Chang.

those seeking to teach and research within economics departments will need to adopt varieties of compromising strategies to survive let alone prosper – needing to finesse the dividing lines between principle, pragmatism and succumbing to, and being incorporated by, the unsubtle charms of the dismal science. Perversely, more latitude and opportunity will be found in addressing economic issues as heterodox economics or political economy in departments other than economics.

I am acutely aware from my own experience of benefitting from what was at the time the comparative advantage of a degree in mathematics that allowed me to establish a career as an academic economist as the basis on which to take on the alternative path of political economy both constructively and in critical command of the mainstream (whilst occasionally revisiting mathematical economics for my own indulgent pleasure and, possibly deceiving myself that it would allow for more leverage in criticism of the mainstream). That route no longer seems open as the requirements for (particular types of) mathematics have been ramped up within the discipline and have become commonplace. Other routes must and can be found. For, otherwise, there will be at best a flight of political economy and political economists to other disciplines, leaving economics without criticism delivered from a position commanding knowledge of its shifting content, including its imperialistic designs.

References

Aigner, E. (2021) "Global Dynamics and Country-Level Development in Academic Economics: an Explorative Cognitive-Bibliometric Study", Department of Socio-Economics, Institute for Multi-Level Governance & Development, Vienna University of Economics and Business, Social-Ecological Discussion Paper in Economics, no 7, https://www-sre.wu.ac.at/sre-disc/sre-disc-2021_07.pdf.

Akerlof, G. and R. Kranton (2000) "Economics and Identity", *Quarterly Journal of Economics*, vol 115, no 3, pp. 715–53.

Allais, S. (2012) "'Economics Imperialism', Education Policy and Educational Theory", *Journal of Education Policy*, vol 27, no 2, pp. 253–74.

Ambrosino, A., M. Cedrini and J. Davis (2021) "The Unity of Science and the Disunity of Economics", *Cambridge Journal of Economics*, vol 45, no 4, pp. 631–54.

Andersson, D. (2021) "Spontaneous Order and the Hayekian Challenge to Interdisciplinary Social Scientists", *Atlantic Economic Journal*, vol 49, no 4, pp. 363–375.

Bailly F. (2022) "When Mainstream Economics Does Human Resource Management: a Critique of Personnel Economics' Prescriptive Ambition", *PSL Quarterly Review*, vol 75, no 301, pp. 103–17.

Bayliss, K. and B. Fine (2021) *A Guide to the Systems of Provision Approach: Who Gets What, How and Why*, Basingstoke: Palgrave MacMillan.

Bögenhold, D. (2017) "The Order of Social Sciences: Sociology in Dialogue with Neighbouring Disciplines", *Journal of Philosophical Economics: Reflections on Economic and Social Issues*, vol XI, no 1, pp. 27–52.

Bögenhold, D. (2018) "Economics between Insulation and Social-Sciencication: Observations by a Sociology of Economics", *Journal of Economic Issues*, vol 52, no 4, pp. 1125–42.

Bögenhold, D. (2020) "History of Economic Thought as an Analytic Tool: Why Past Intellectual Ideas Must Be Acknowledged as Lighthouses for the Future", *International Advances in Economic Research*, vol 26, pp. 73–87.

Cedrini, M. and J. Dagnes (2022) "Economics Imperialism and a Transdisciplinary Perspective", in Stilwell et al (eds) (2022), pp. 428–442.

Cedrini, M. and M. Fontana (2018) "Just Another Niche in the Wall? How Specialization Is Changing the Face of Mainstream Economics", *Cambridge Journal of Economics*, vol 42, no 2, pp. 427–51.

Cedrini, M. and R. Marchionatti (2017) "On the Theoretical and Practical Relevance of the Concept of Gift to the Development of a Non-Imperialist Economics", *Review of Radical Political Economics*, vol 49, no 4, pp. 633–49.

Chang, H.-J. (2010) *23 Things They Don't Tell You About Capitalism*, London: Penguin.

Chang, H.-J. (2014) *Economics: the User's Guide: a Pelican Introduction*, London: Pelican Books. .

Chang, H.-J. (2022) *Edible Economics: a Hungry Economist Explains the World*, London: Penguin.

Chester, L. and T.-H. Jo (eds) (2022) *Heterodox Economics: Legacy and Prospects*, Bristol: World Economics Association Books.

Chuah, S. (2006) "Anthropology and Economic Imperialism: the Battlefield of Culture", NUBS Industrial Economics Division Working Paper, Nottingham University Business School, https://papers.ssrn.com/Sol3/papers.cfm?abstract_id=722401.

Colander, D., R. Holt and B. Rosser (2004) "The Changing Face of Mainstream Economics", *Review of Political Economy*, vol 16, no 4, pp. 485–99.

Convert, B. and J. Heilbron (2007) "Where Did the New Economic Sociology Come from?", *Theory and Society*, vol 36, no 1, pp. 31–54.

Davern, M. and D. Eitzen (1995) "Economic Sociology: an Examination of Intellectual Exchange", *Journal of Economics and Sociology*, vol 54, no 1, pp. 79–88.

Davis, J. (2006) "The Turn in Economics: Neoclassical Dominance to Mainstream Pluralism?", *Journal of Institutional Economics*, vol 2, no 1, pp. 1–20.

Davis, J. (2016) "Economics Imperialism versus Multidisciplinarity", *History of Economic Ideas*, vol 24, no 3 , pp. 77–94, downloaded and quoted from https://epublications.marquette.edu/cgi/viewcontent.cgi?article=1573&context=econ_fac.

Falgueras-Sorauren, I. (2018) "The Convoluted Influence of Robbins's Thinking on the Emergence of Economics Imperialism", *Cambridge Journal of Economics*, 42, no 5, pp. 1473–94.

Fasenfest, D. (ed.) (2022) *Marx Matters*, Leiden: Brill.

Fine, B. (1987) "Segmented Labour Market Theory: a Critical Assessment", *Birkbeck Discussion Papers in Economics*, no 87/12.

Fine, B. (1997) "The New Revolution in Economics", *Capital and Class*, no 61, Spring, pp. 143–48.

Fine, B. (1998) *Labour Market Theory: a Constructive Reassessment*, London: Routledge.

Fine, B. (2002) *The World of Consumption: the Material and Cultural Revisited*, London: Routledge.

Fine, B. (2008) "Vicissitudes of Economics Imperialism", *Review of Social Economy*, vol 66, no 2, pp. 235–40. See Chapter 9.

Fine, B. (2010) "Flattening Economic Geography: Locating the World Development Report for 2009", *Journal of Economic Analysis*, vol 1, no 1, pp. 15–33, http://users.ntua.gr/jea/JEA%20Vol.%20I,%20No%20I,%202010/jea_volume1_issue1_pp15_33.pdf.

Fine, B. (2015) "Neoclassical Economics: an Elephant is Not a Chimera But Is a Chimera Real?", in Morgan (ed.) (2015), pp. 180–99.

Fine, B. (2019) "Post-Truth: an Alumni Economist's Perspective", *International Review of Applied Economics*, vol 33, no 4, pp. 542–67, shortened version of, SOAS Department of Economics Working Paper No. 219, 2019, https://www.soas.ac.uk/economics/research/workingpapers/file139489.pdf.

Fine, B. (2020) "Situating PPPs", in Gideon and Unterhalter (eds) (2020), pp. 26–38.

Fine, B. (2022a) "From Marxist Political Economy to Financialisation or Is It the Other Way About?", in Fasenfest (ed.), pp. 43–66.

Fine, B. (2022b) "Towards Interdisciplinarity as Instinctive", in Chester and Jo (eds) (2022), pp. 290–325.

Fine, B. and O. Dimakou (2016) *Macroeconomics: a Critical Companion*, London: Pluto.

Fine, B. and D. Milonakis (2009) *From Economics Imperialism to Freakonomics: the Shifting Boundaries between Economics and Other Social Sciences*, London: Routledge.

Fine, B. and D. Milonakis (2012) "Interrogating Sickonomics, From Diagnosis to Cure: a Response to Hodgson", *Review of Social Economy*, vol 70, no 4, pp. 477–91.

Fleury, J.-B. (2010) "Drawing New Lines: Economists and Other Social Scientists on Society in the 1960s", *History of Political Economy,* vol 42, Supplement 1, pp. 315–42.

Fourcade, M., E. Ollion and Y. Algan (2015) "The Superiority of Economists", *Journal of Economic Perspectives*, vol 29, no 1, pp. 89–114.

Frey, B. (1993) "From Economic Imperialism to Social Science Inspiration", *Public Choice*, vol 77, no 4, pp. 95–105.

Gideon, J. and E. Unterhalter (eds) (2020) *Critical Reflections on Public Private Partnerships*, London: Routledge.

Gilead, T. (2015) "Economics Imperialism and the Role of Educational Philosophy", *Educational Philosophy and Theory*, vol 47, no 7, pp. 715–733.

Grayot, D. (2020) "Dual Process Theories in Behavioral Economics and Neuroeconomics: a Critical Review", *Review of Philosophy and Psychology*, vol 11, no 1, pp. 105–36.

Hadjimichalis, C. (2006) "Non-Economic Factors in Economic Geography and in 'New Regionalism': a Sympathetic Critique", *International Journal of Urban and Regional Research*, vol 30, no 3, pp. 690–704.

Jabbar, H. and F. Menashy "Economic Imperialism in Education Research: a Conceptual Review", *Educational Researcher*, vol 51, no 4, pp. 279–88.

Javdani, M. and H.-J. Chang (2019) "Who Said or What Said?: Estimating Ideological Bias in Views among Economists", Institute of Labor Economics, IZA, Bonn, Discussion Paper, no 12738, https://www.iza.org/publications/dp/12738/who-said-or-what-said-estimating-ideological-bias-in-views-among-economists, published in *Cambridge Journal of Economics*, 2023, beaco71, https://doi.org/10.1093/cje/beaco71.

Kellecioglu, D. (2017) "How to Transform Economics? A Philosophical Appraisal", *Journal of Philosophical Economics: Reflections on Economic and Social Issues*, vol XI, no 1, pp. 1–26.

Krijnen, C. (2016) "Values – Limits of Economic Rationality and Imperialism of Culture", *Economic and Political Studies*, vol 4, no 2, pp. 101–21.

Kuorikoski, J. and A. Lehtinen (2010) "Economics Imperialism and Solution Concepts in Political Science", *Philosophy of the Social Sciences*, vol 40, no 3, pp. 347–74.

Lazear, E. (2000) "Economic Imperialism", *Quarterly Journal of Economics*, vol 115, no 1, pp. 99–146, previously National Bureau of Economic Research, Working Paper no 7300, 1999.

Lecouteux, G. (2022) "The Homer Economicus Narrative: from Cognitive Psychology to Individual Public Policies", hal-03791951.

Lehtinen, A. and J. Kuorikos (2007) "Unrealistic Assumptions in Rational Choice Theory", *Philosophy of the Social Sciences*, vol 37, no 2, pp. 115–38.

Levitt, S. and S. Dubner (2005) *Freakonomics: a Rogue Economist Explores the Hidden Side of Everything*, New York: Harper Collins.

Mäki, U. (2002) "Symposium on Explanations and Social Ontology 2: Explanatory Ecumenism and Economics Imperialism", *Economics and Philosophy*, vol 18, no 2, pp. 235–57.

Mäki, U. (2009) "Economics Imperialism Concept and Constraints", *Philosophy of the Social Sciences*, vol 39, no 3, pp. 351–80.

Mäki, U. (2013) "Scientific Imperialism: Difficulties in Definition, Identification, and Assessment", *International Studies in the Philosophy of Science*, vol 27, no 3, pp. 325–39.

Mäki, U. and C. Marchionni (2011) "Is Geographical Economics Imperializing Economic Geography?" *Journal of Economic Geography*, vol 11, no 4, pp. 645–65.

Marchionatti, R. and M. Cedrini (2016) *Economics as Social Science: Economics Imperialism and the Challenge of Interdisciplinarity*, London: Routledge.

Mariotti, S. (2022) "The Economics–Engineering Nexus: Response to the Commentaries", *Journal of Industrial and Business Economics*, vol 49, pp. 1–29. https://link.springer.com/article/10.1007/s40812-021-00203-z#citeas.

McRorie, C. (2016) "Rethinking Moral Agency in Markets: a Book Discussion on Behavioral Economics", *Journal of Religious Ethics*, vol 44, no 1, pp. 195–226.

Medema, S. (1997) "The Trial of *Homo Economicus*: What Law and Economics Tells Us About the Development of Economic Imperialism", *History of Political Economy*, vol 29, Supplement 1, pp. 122–42.

Medema, S. (2020) "The Coase Theorem at Sixty", *Journal of Economic Literature*, vol 58, no 4, pp. 1045–128.

Michie, J., C. Oughton and F. Wilkinson (2002) "Against the New Economic Imperialism: Some Reflections", *American Journal of Economics and Sociology*, vol 61, no 1, pp. 351–65.

Milonakis, D. and B. Fine (2009) *From Political Economy to Economics: Method, the Social and the Historical in the Evolution of Economic Theory*, London: Routledge.

Morgan, J. (ed.) (2015) *What Is This 'School' Called Neoclassical Economics?: Debating the Origins, Meaning and Significance*, London: Routledge.

Myrdal, G. (1957) *Economic Theory and Underdeveloped Regions*, London: Duckworth.

Nik-Khah, E. and R. Van Horn (2012) "Inland Empire: Economics Imperialism as an Imperative of Chicago Neoliberalism", *Journal of Economic Methodology*, 19, no 3, pp.

Parker, W. (ed.) (1986) *Economic History and the Modern Economist*, Oxford: Basil Blackwell.

Pinto, F. (2016) "Economics Imperialism in Social Epistemology: a Critical Assessment", *Philosophy of the Social Sciences*, vol 46, no 5, pp. 443–72.

Rolin, K. (2015) "Economics Imperialism and Epistemic Cosmopolitanism", *International Studies in the Philosophy of Science*, vol 29, no 4, pp. 413–29.

Romer, P. (2020) "The Dismal Kingdom: Do Economists Have Too Much Power?", *Foreign Affairs*, March/April, https://www.foreignaffairs.com/reviews/dismal-kingdom.

Rothschild, K. (2008) "Economic Imperialism", *Analyse and Kritik*, vol 30, no 2, p. 723–733.

Solow, R. (1985) "Economic History and Economics", *American Economic Review*, vol 75, no 2, pp. 328-31, reproduced in Parker (ed.) (1986), pp. 21-29.

Spencer, D. (2011) "Getting Personnel: Contesting and Transcending the 'New Labour Economics'", *Work, Employment and Society*, vol 25, no 1, pp. 118–31.

Stillman, C. (1955) "Academic Imperialism and Its Resolution – The Case of Economics and Anthropology", American Scientist, vol 43, no 1, pp. 77–88.

Stilwell, F., D. Primrose and T. Thornton (eds) (2022) *Handbook of Alternative Theories of Political Economy*, Cheltenham: Edward Elgar.

Thorén, H. and S. Stålhammar (2018) "Ecosystem Services between Integration and Economics Imperialism", *Ecology and Society*, vol 23, no 4, article 44, https://www.ecologyandsociety.org/vol23/iss4/art44/.

Velthuis, O. (1999) "The Changing Relationship between Economic Sociology and Institutional Economics: from Talcott Parsons to Mark Granovetter", *American Journal of Economics and Sociology*, vol 58, no 4, pp. 629–49.

Vromen, J. (2009) "The Booming Economics-Made-Fun Genre: More than Having Fun, but Less than Economics Imperialism", *Erasmus Journal for Philosophy and Economics*, vol 2, no 1, pp. 70–99.

Yay, T. (2021) "Method and Scope in Joseph A. Schumpeter's Economics: a Pluralist Perspective", *Journal of Philosophical Economics*, vol XIV, no 1–2, pp. 63–107.

Zafirovski, M. (2000) "The Rational Choice Generalization of Neoclassical Economics Reconsidered: Any Theoretical Legitimation for Economic Imperialism?", *Sociological Theory*, vol 18, no 3, pp. 448–71.

CHAPTER 3

'Economic Imperialism': A View from the Periphery

Postscript as Personal Preamble

This article was originally submitted to the *Quarterly Journal of Economics* as a comment but was returned, without review, at editorial discretion on the grounds of being inappropriate for "mainly focusing on the history of ideas", with Lazear's (2000a) original piece, on which it commented, only having been published as "part of a special symposium on the state of economics at the turn of the millennium". Apart from a few minor changes, and the propositions at the end directed at radical political economists, the piece remains as before. As a courtesy, I sent the piece to Lazear and, equally courteous, he thanked me and promised to respond. I never heard from him again.

Possibly this was because he was preparing himself for bigger and better things. He served as Chief Economic Advisor to President George W. Bush from 2006 to 2009, straddling the Global Financial Crisis. He was on the staff of the neoliberal Hoover Institute, and closely associated with Mont Pèlerin, having presented lectures at its meetings including one on free health markets.[1] His own retrospective on the crisis is unremarkable and borders on the pragmatic as opposed to the analytical, for example laying the blame on the inflow of foreign finance, reducing anticipated returns on financial markets, see also Hennessey and Lazear (2013). He is even credited with "playing a leading role in the establishment of the Troubled Asset Relief Program (TARP), for which Congress initially authorized $700 billion to stabilize the banking, auto, insurance, housing and other industries. The program was deeply unpopular but, according to Dr. Lazear and many other administration officials, urgently necessary", to save workers from losing their jobs.[2] None of this seems to derive from a Becker-style commitment to economics imperialism.

In this respect at least, he seems to have exceeded his use-by-date because, and by way of contrast, he had been preceded as Chief Economic Advisor (to President Clinton) by none other than Joe Stiglitz, from 1995 to 1997. Stiglitz's then, and subsequent, prominence could not have been more marked by comparison with Lazear both in promoting the new phase of

---

1 In 2013, if not in 2010, https://www.desmog.com/mont-pelerin-society/.
2 https://www.washingtonpost.com/local/obituaries/edward-p-lazear-dead/2020/12/01/50415 2ac-3359-11eb-b59c-adb7153d10c2_story.html.

economics imperialism and in seeing it applied to finance, alongside pretty much everything else. Significantly, then, whilst Lazear seems to have been on the ball in acknowledging the imperialistic designs of economics, in doing so he was already a decade or more out of date in relying upon its old as opposed to its new phase and, not least, as acutely revealed as such by the financial crisis for which his prominence in personnel economics and use of individual incentives as explanandum proved sorely wanting if not absented.

1   Introduction[3]

Radical political economists must experience a mixture of gratification and bemusement if finding themselves in agreement with Edward Lazear's (2000a) assessment that economics has been colonising the other social sciences over the past four decades. It is now occupying territory that has previously been the more or less exclusive preserve of other disciplines.[4] Lazear demonstrates a feel for what is going on in, and around, economics that is notably absent from other economists' thinking. The latter is true both of the other millennium contributions to the special issue of the *Quarterly Journal of Economics* and of, for example, the colloquium contributions to the *Journal of Economic Perspectives*, vol 14, no 1, 2000, an imagined retrospect on economics from fifty years hence. Possibly Lazear's broader perspective is a consequence of his having moved within the University of Chicago from the economics to the business department. He has also made pioneering contributions to "personnel economics", the internal management of firms from the perspective of neoclassical

---

3   Originally appearing as Fine (2002). This paper was written whilst in receipt of a Research Fellowship from the UK Economic and Social Research Council, ESRC, under award number R000271046 to study The New Revolution in Economics and Its Impact upon Social Sciences. Thanks to colleagues and referees for comments on earlier versions. Note that the inappropriate term, economic (rather than economics) imperialism is used throughout, since it was used by Lazear and commonly by, insensitive, mainstream economists.

4   See also Olson and Kähkönen (2000) who reject the idea of economics as imperialism relative to the other social sciences, since there is no use of armed force or denial of free choice. They prefer the equally revealing metaphor of economics as the metropolis, extending its influence to the social science suburbs. For my first publication positing the current significance of economic imperialism, see Fine (1997a). See also Fine (1997b, 1998a and b, 1999a and d, 2000a-f, and 2001a and b, and 2004) and Fine and Milonakis (2000) – and Fine (1999c) in debate with Bowden and Offer (1994, 1996 and 1999) and Fine (1999b) with Thompson (1997 and 1999), and Fine and Lapavitsas (2000) with Zelizer (2000) – for the general argument as well as for specific case studies. In the absence of precise quantification of economic imperialism, these contributions offer some evidence of its breadth and depth.

economics in place of psychology and sociology (Lazear 1995, 1998, 1999a and 2000b).[5] Last, but not least, Lazear freely and fulsomely acknowledges his debt to Gary Becker who is explicit about his imperialistic designs upon the other social sciences.[6]

Nor is Lazear's account of economic imperialism the eccentric meandering of an isolated academic. For the imperialist hypothesis garners support from the *Economist*. In a Christmas issue, it repeats an exercise of ten years earlier by speculating about who are to become the rising stars within academic economics. Deploying the metaphor of astronomy's big bang, it claims that the previous predictions had been borne out as "the effects of new analytical tools developed in the 1970s spread out from the profession's core like a shockwave". This is a reference to the new micro-foundations of economics, those drawing upon market, especially informational, imperfections. Further, with explicit reference to "economic imperialism", it suggests that, "unlike the stars of the 1980s, today's impressive young academics are using the tools of economics in fields on or beyond the traditional borders of their discipline" (Economist 1998, p. 143). In particular, "these economists take seriously what every layman knows: that people don't always behave in selfish or even rational ways". *The Economist* had identified two important and closely related developments within economics. On the one hand, it has been colonising the other social sciences. On the other hand, it appears to be addressing the social in the form of customary as opposed to individualistic behaviour.

Despite this apparent confluence of opinion on what is happening, not surprisingly, Lazear's response is not the only one possible. For his account is (little short of) triumphant,[7] as the only truly scientific and rigorous social science is perceived to be sweeping the board by virtue of its intellectual superiority. Tellingly, for him, other social sciences are more rounded in the problems they pose, but economics is superior in the solutions it offers. The perspective from radical political economy is less sanguine. Dissatisfaction with economics' contribution to the understanding of the economy is hardly conducive to

---

5 The first of these is his published Wicksteed Lectures and contains material on economics as scientific and rigorous that is reproduced in the "Economic Imperialism" article. The last but one of the contributions is as founding President of the Society of Labor Economists for which he was founding editor of the *Journal of Labor Economics*. For a critique of personnel economics in general, and of Lazear in particular, with passing reference to economics imperialism, see Bailly (2022).

6 As Becker (1990, p. 39) puts it himself, "'Economic imperialism' is probably a good description of what I do".

7 The parenthesis has been added in deference to a referee who has pointed out that Lazear (2000a) claims superiority for the rigour of economics on no less than twelve occasions!

welcoming its extension to other social sciences. The purpose of this response to Lazear, however, is not to rehearse directly what is wrong with mainstream economics, but to address certain anomalies or absences in Lazear's account of economic imperialism itself and to use these to reveal opportunities for radical political economy.

2   The Historical Anomaly

The first of these is his acknowledgement that the currently evolving overlap between economics and the other social sciences is not new. Previously, with classical political economy and earlier, there was no separate economics as such. This raises a number of issues.[8] If economics was previously integrated with other social sciences, how and why did it become separate? Further, why once it had become separate, has it successfully sought to become integrated again? And what explains the timing of these developments?

Lazear does not confront these issues, concerned with the history of economic thought and the sociology of knowledge more generally. The possible exception is an implicit, if limited, explanation for the current phase of imperialism. It rests on the purported superiority of economics as a science, with emphasis being placed upon its positing empirically refutable hypotheses, leading to three features in particular – its focus upon individual optimisation, equilibrium and efficiency. However, whatever the merits of this account of contemporary mainstream economics, it cannot apply to classical political economy. For it is notably based on classes, rather than individuals, and on the prospects for accumulation, rather than equilibrium or efficiency as such. Presumably, until the marginalist revolution of the 1870s, economics was caught in a low-level equilibrium that allowed for it to be integrated with other social sciences but not to be a science. Indeed, it is appropriate to understand the marginalist revolution as having established much of economics as we know it today by breaking with classical political economy. It did so not merely by becoming scientific in Lazear's terms but also by creating a science of the economy by separating the economy from society. Economics became exclusively concerned with market relations, as in supply and demand, with only limited reference, until recently, to the broader social relations within which the economy is embedded.

---

8   These issues are addressed at length in Milonakis and Fine (2009) and Fine and Milonakis (2009).

In short, the marginalist revolution was responsible for taking the social (or the political) out of the economy. It did so in part because of the simultaneous emergent consolidation of other social science disciplines but also because of perceived limitations in the scope of application of marginalist principles. Significantly, Talcott Parsons, well-trained in economics, hardly a radical, and to become the leading figure in sociology, was adamantly opposed to the integration of the two disciplines. This was because he saw them as dealing in different methods, not subject matters, with the social and the individual being targeted for sociology and economics, respectively.[9] Indeed, indirectly on this score, so concerned was the first generation of marginalists with not claiming too much explanatory power for their principles, especially against the weight of tradition supplied by classical political economy, that acceptance of general equilibrium was considerably delayed as opposed to partial equilibrium. For, there was considerable resistance to the idea, a corollary of general equilibrium, that distribution, as the prices of labour, capital and land, is little more than an application of price theory. It was only in the second half of the twentieth century that general equilibrium gained acceptance, its rise complementing the decline of distribution theory.[10]

The lingering commitment to the idea that distribution had something to do with classes or institutions, for example, as opposed to individuals and marginalism, is indicative of a more general reluctance to extend marginalist principles beyond the bounds of the market. The associated definition of the subject matter of economics determined the boundaries between mainstream economics and the other social sciences, divisions reinforced by differences in methodologies. From a logical point of view, however, there is nothing in principle that constrains economics to be confined to a study of market relations. For its underlying principle of rationality as individual utility optimisation, and its raw materials of preferences, factor endowments, technology, and so on, are broadly applicable across all social and historical contexts.

In short, this highly stylised account of the history of economic thought just seeks to provide some reason for the marginalist revolution being responsible

---

9   For a full account, see Velthuis (1999). See also Connell (1997) for the argument that the "classical" sociology of Marx, Weber and Durkheim arose out of confrontation with the consequences of (economic) imperialism in practice as the colonies were experienced as "other". But such sociology only became classic once the discipline had been given respectability by Parsons. Significantly, by contrast, mainstream economics has always set aside the "market imperfections" associated with (economic) imperialism – the violence that accompanies the supposedly free market. See Perelman (2000).

10 See Fine (1982) for a fuller account and, in the context of economic imperialism, Fine (2000c). See also Chapters 1 to 3 of previous volume on economics imperialism.

for taking the social out of economics whilst retaining the capacity to reintroduce it. As Lazear hints, the associated economic imperialism that this makes possible has a longstanding presence.[11] But, especially in the work of Gary Becker, it is only over the last few decades that it has flourished. To a large extent, however, this has rested upon the prominence of human capital theory, a concept rather than an approach that, significantly, has been integrated more or less informally into other social sciences without unduly displaying alien assumptions from perspectives other than economics – the supply and use of education as if it were a product rather than a socially constructed process. This is not to deny the prominence of the more recent of Becker's contributions, for the household and crime for example. But these have been supported by a political and ideological climate of neo-liberalism in which it has been argued that the world should be made as far as possible like a market, the "as if" market basis on which Becker's work has primarily proceeded.[12] Significantly, little more than a decade ago, Becker's economic imperialism was being treated with some contempt by his fellow economists for seeking to extend analysis based on individual rationality to areas where it was simply inappropriate (Swedberg (ed.) 1990).

Further, the attempted extension of such methodological individualism or rational choice to other social sciences is not new. It has long been rejected by many for its unacceptable reductionism of the social to the aggregate of individuals and crude optimising behaviour. This all suggests there is more to the social in the social sciences than is acknowledged as legitimate by Lazear. Failure to recognise this deepens the explanatory silence over the ebb and flow between economics and other social sciences as overlapping disciplines, on which see below.

The current success of economic imperialism, and its more general chronology, cannot be explained, then, as is implicit in Lazear's account, simply by virtue of its presumed scientific superiority. What Lazear tends to overlook are recent developments within the discipline that have both prompted its external push and made economics more acceptable to other social sciences.

---

11   As cited in Fine (1999a). Swedberg (1990, p. 14) traces the notion of economic imperialism back to the early 1930s. However, even as late as 1984, Stigler (1984, p. 12–13) concludes his discussion in terms of colonisation being prospective rather than achieved: "Heinrich Gossen, a high priest of the theory of utility-maximizing behaviour, compared the scope of that theory to Copernicus' theory of the movement of the heavenly bodies. Heavenly bodies are better behaved than human bodies but it is conceivable that his fantasy will be approached through the spread of the economists' theory of the behaviour to the entire domain of the social sciences".
12   See Carrier and Miller (eds) (1998).

In brief, the new micro-foundations or information-theoretic economics is able to explain, not to assume, market imperfections on the basis of individual optimisation, and to show how these lead not only to economic structures but also to non-economic structures. The world is to be interpreted as the economic and non-economic responses to market, especially informational, imperfections, endogenising economic and social structures and relations, including institutions, customs and norms. Such developments have opened up and appropriated the subject matter of the other social sciences in ways that are not possible through simple extension of the as if perfect market to non-market applications.

3 The Anomaly of Scope

In this light, a second anomaly arises through this refinement of Lazear's account. It concerns the, in part, understandable self-serving selectivity of the examples he has chosen. By way of contrast, the impact of economic imperialism, both in terms of timing and impetus, is well-illustrated in different ways by two applications that are not mentioned by him, although he does make much of finance that has been dominated by the new micro-foundations. One is the new development economics (and development studies more generally), in which developing countries are perceived to be particularly prone to market imperfections and associated deficiencies in economic and social structures and norms, etc. Specifically, with Joe Stiglitz in the vanguard, an attempt has been made to displace the Washington by the post Washington Consensus, with the full range of development issues being appropriated by economists.[13] This is an elementary example of how the new as opposed to the old economic imperialism is at the forefront taking, as its point of departure, the tradition associated with Akerlof (and his market for "lemons") as opposed to Becker (and his as if market for everything).[14] The new has different principles, those based on market *im*perfections, and is wider and deeper in colonising potential.

---

13 See Stiglitz (1998) for explicit launch of the post Washington Consensus, and Fine, Lapavitsas and Pincus (eds) (2001) for critique. Strangely, Lazear has no reference to the work of Stiglitz despite his prominence in the new financial economics. Note that in his study of socialism, Stiglitz (1994) manages over one hundred references to his own information-theoretic work making me look amateur by comparison.

14 As argued in Fine (2001a, Chapter 3), matters are not so simple since Becker (1996) has regained partial claim to a vanguard position by being in the lead amongst economists in deploying the notion of social capital.

The other example of interest not raised by Lazear is the new economic history or cliometrics. This had previously been based upon the old Becker-type economic imperialism. As such, it drove a wedge across the discipline, with dissidents rejecting the as if perfect market approach to economic history for neglect of institutions, culture and the like.[15] Even Douglass North, one of the discipline's founding fathers and, as such, Nobel prizewinner for economics, came to reject the approach for its narrowness. Now, however, a "new and improved" economic history is on offer, in which the sins and omissions of the past are confessed and prospectively rectified by drawing upon the new micro-foundations. Institutions and customs are, for example, incorporated and understood in terms of path dependence.

This discussion has already revealed that Lazear's coverage of economic imperialism is selective rather than comprehensive. Whilst this could be justified on illustrative grounds, the question remains of the directions and depth of penetration of economic imperialism. Of particular interest are the exceptions that both reveal and prove the rule, that is the no go areas for economics, which also serve as extreme examples of the uneven success of economic imperialism. One, ranging across all social science disciplines and a variety of objects of study, is provided by postmodernism. Initially, observe that (mainstream) economics is more or less unique in not having been influenced in any way whatsoever by postmodernism even though it has arguably been the most important development across the social sciences in the period of strengthening economic imperialism.[16] It follows that mainstream economics can only appropriate the subject matter of other social sciences by stripping them of any of the varied content associated with postmodernism. The reason why is relatively simple. For postmodernism is concerned with the social construction of the meaning of objects and activities even, *in extremis*, by denying that they are rooted in the material world given the subjectivity of individual interpretation and experience. This simply lies outside the domain of economics with its verities over the meaning of everything, albeit in the presence of informational imperfections. Significantly, Lazear mentions language and religion as examples of economic imperialism. But these are effectively understood purely in terms of "membership", incentives and transaction costs rather than the source and construction of meaning.[17] The absence of meaning in

---

15 See Lamoreaux (1998) and, for a critical assessment of the renewed assault of economics on economic or business history, Fine (2000b) and Fine and Milonakis (2000). See also forthcoming volume on (economics imperialism and) economic history.

16 See Cornwall (1997) for a heterodox contribution that reflects postmodern influences.

17 Lazear is modest in referencing his own claims as economic imperialist but does list his contribution in this vein to "Culture and Language" (Lazear 1999b).

economics is apparent in its abstract formalism in which mathematical symbols stand for variables that are related to one another through mechanical models.

Significantly, the importance of acknowledging the critical (re)construction of concepts has long been understood within the physical sciences that Lazear takes as his model for economics. Consider, for example, the position adopted by Thomas Kuhn, a central figure in debate over the nature of science even if often now by way of departure.[18] In positing the distinction between normal and revolutionary science, Kuhn (1970, p. 234) observes of Popper, and the attempt to defend a besieged notion of falsifiability, that:

> He and his followers share with more traditional philosophers of science the assumption that the problem of theory-choice can be resolved by techniques which are semantically neutral ... canons of rationality thus derive exclusively from those of logic and linguistic syntax.

He concludes that, p. 235:

> Philosophers of science will need to follow other contemporary philosophers in, examining, to a previously unprecedented depth, the manner in which language fits the world, asking how terms attach to nature, how those attachments are learned, and how they are transmitted from one generation to another by the members of a language community.

What is true of the natural world is surely even more apposite for the social world. As a result, the "science" and "rigour" on which Lazear, in part correctly, rests his explanation for the success of economic imperialism is paradoxical. For, across all other disciplines, and especially where methodology and the nature of science are explicitly addressed, the stance of economics in practice has long since been rejected.[19] Yet, it is its very simplicity and disregard of the

---

18 For economic imperialism in light of debate over Kuhnian revolution in (social) science, see Fine (2000d).

19 Falsifiability as such has long since been rendered redundant within discussions of economic methodology, leading to methodologies as diverse as McCloskey's (1986) rhetoric and Lawson's (1997) critical realism, on which see Boylan and O'Gorman (1995). The latter refer to a post-positivism phase as prevailing in economic methodology over the last quarter of a century whose desperate attempts to rescue falsifiability, and more, have proved futile, pp. 27 fwd.

issues raised by the problems attached to notions of science that allow it to sweep forward so effortlessly.

Such absences within economics, the unproblematic universalisation across time, space and context of its basic concepts, mean that, except in the limited way suggested, its imperialism cannot appropriate social science with a cultural content (unless understood as imperfect information). One result is that anthropology, with its traditions of ethnography, has not been subject to colonisation except in an economic anthropology that essentially extends neoclassical economics to non-market societies.[20] Another striking example, cutting across disciplines, is provided by consumption. Lazear in part organises his examples of economic imperialism under two broad headings Although one of these is consumer theory[21] and contains sub-headings for tastes, demography, discrimination, the family and social interactions, it bears no point of connection with postmodernism. This is despite what can only be described as an explosion of literature on consumption across the social sciences,[22] the vast majority of which is influenced to a greater or lesser extent by the need to address the meaning of consumption to consumers. It is not and cannot be touched by Lazear's economic imperialism.

---

20 For one exception, appropriating the gift, see Offer (1997) and Fine (2000f) for a critique.
21 This might be loosely thought of as the demand- as opposed to the supply-side factors examined under the theory of the firm.
22 The varied methods and theories of investigation of consumption both within and across the social sciences is evidenced by a number of surveys, which are often necessarily partial, specialised and rapidly dated in their coverage (Fine and Leopold 1993, Miller (ed.) 1995, Gabriel and Lang 1995, de Grazia, Furlough (eds) 1996, Holbrook (1995) and Fine et al (1996), for example). More recently, see Fine (2000f). The selective bibliography of Furlough in de Grazia and Furlough (eds) (1996) runs to twenty pages, including sections on conceptualizations; historical perspectives; distribution, retailing and shopping as sites of consumption; marketing and design; spectatorship and reception; production of representations; domesticity, household and the family: sexuality; bodies, clothing, and beauty as appearance; and politics and ideologies of consumption. On shopping alone, the brief history and selected literature of Hewer and Campbell in Falk and Campbell (eds) (1997), also of twenty pages, addresses typologizing, instrumental and recreational, gendering, economics, geography, history, literature, marketing, psychology, and sociology. The unlimited scope for the study of consumption, however, arises out of its being attached to the formation of identity – for which anything goes.

4 The Anomaly of Resistance

This all leads to a third limitation of Lazear's account. To parody, he provides a supply-side explanation – why and how economists are colonising other social sciences because of their superior "scientific" and "rigorous" production frontier for explanation. With minor exceptions, such as the suggestion that there is two-way traffic with non-economists appropriating economic analysis, he fails to examine the demand-side. To parody, to what extent do the corresponding developments within economics conform to existing tastes of non-economists or are the latter shifting their preferences? From Lazear's perspective, presumably some sort of diffusion model would be appropriate in which the preferences of non-economists, and the content of their work, gradually adjusts to acceptance of economic imperialism. This might, with some ingenuity, explain what is an uneven and complex, at times perverse lack of, spread of economic imperialism. A very different explanation is offered here.

First, Lazear's claims for the scientific status of economics relative to other social scientists is not accepted by them. Indeed, as already discussed, his notion of economics as scientific because of its commitment to falsifiability, and his understanding of the physical sciences in these terms is ante-diluvian from the perspective of all of those working within methodology and even from the perspective of those working on economics methodology. It is questionable whether economists actually engage in such forms of scientific endeavour, irrespective of their validity. Such insights have generally been accepted by those who study the matters seriously, despite many economists having false image of themselves, at least since the debate over Kuhn and normal science was open and closed, whether applied to the sciences, social sciences or economics.[23]

Second, the vast majority of social science continues to remain hostile to the methods and assumptions of economics as well as its methodology. Nor is this simply and primarily a matter of intimidation by mathematical and statistical technique (the economist's knee-jerk claim for own as science and others as lacking rigour). Individual optimisation, equilibrium and efficiency are alien to non-economists unless adopting a rational choice approach. Their preferred starting point is the social and the dynamics of change (or not), without necessarily focusing upon notions of efficiency that are questionable in a world of constructed meanings. And a powerful, if not overwhelming, case can

---

23   For discussion of Kuhn across the social sciences, see Gutting (ed.) (1980). For the continuing questioning of economists as upholding their (false) notion of science in practice, see Blaug (1980), McCloskey (1986) and Lawson (1997), for example.

be made in favour of the social as starting point since no individual ever sprang into action with fully formed preferences and a blank historical context.

Third, then, having knocked away Lazear's superior supply-side explanation for economic imperialism, both for its content and for its timing and incidence, what is to be put in its place? As already argued, there have been developments within economics that have made it more palatable to the other social sciences. With a shifting boundary between the exogenous and the endogenous, with the latter now including the social (such as institutions, customs and norms), common analytical terrain and language have been forged between economics and the other social sciences. Previously one ended where the other began, although Becker-type imperialism sought less successfully to conquer rather than to assimilate through the weapon of non-market as if market. In addition, as with human capital theory, considerable emphasis should be placed upon what is often the informalised incorporation of economics into other social sciences. The methods and assumptions upon which economic analysis is based tend thereby to be tempered and even transformed as they cross the great divide into other social sciences. This often leads to paradox and inconsistency with, for example, human capital sitting uncomfortably within a class analysis or, indeed, attached to any of the traditional variables of social theory!

One reason, then, for the increasing success of economic imperialism is that it has endogenised the social – as non-market responses to market imperfections. There have also been relevant internal developments within the other social sciences. At a general level, there is a retreat from the extremes of postmodernism, with its undue emphasis at times upon subjectivity as opposed to objectivity. In short, there is a wish to return to the examination of the impact of material factors, of which the economic is one. Social science is increasingly open to incorporation of an economic content. However, the influence of postmodernism across the social sciences has been uneven and, by the same token, so is its retreat. Consequently, the uneven success and content of economic imperialism results by virtue of the rhythm of influence of postmodernism as well as the internal structure, dynamics and traditions of recipient disciplines (and economics).

Such internal factors are complemented by the external intellectual and ideological environment. Becker-type economic imperialism was heavily conditioned by neo-liberalism. As with the post Washington Consensus for development, so there is now a reaction against neo-liberalism, with a desire to pick a path between it and the statism associated with the discredited socialist bloc. In this light, it is unfortunate that Lazear should have placed so little emphasis upon the new micro-foundations in his account.[24] For within economics itself, it provides for the revival of (a pale version of) Keynesianism as well as for an understanding of the economic and the non-economic in terms of market imperfections. Such perspectives are equally attractive to non-economists, seeking to complement economic with social analysis and engineering. In short, economics now provides social science with a rationale for (limited) economic and social interventions.

5 The Prospects for Radical Political Economy

With some exceptions, it is possible that Lazear would accept the comments offered here as enriching his own contribution. The picture that emerges so far is of a tripartite division between economics as such, a terrain of colonised social science, and an economics-free zone retreating into an exclusive concern with "culture" as the social construction of meaning. As Slater (2000) observes:

> The division between economic and socio-cultural analysis constitutes a kind of deep structure of modern western thought. While it has been a favourite pastime of critical thinking since early modernity to attack the formalism of economic theory, we have been less good at reflecting on how critical and cultural analysis has itself been structured by this opposition. Essentially, critical thought has generally accepted the same terms of engagement as does economics, in which culture and economy are seen as macro-structures operating on each other as externalities; each sees the other as a global force or potential impurity pressing on it from outside.

But this analytical landscape leaves aside an important element, not surprising in view of Lazear's own orthodox persuasion as an economist. This is heterodox economics or radical political economy as opposed to the new political economy, the latter serving as an example of economic imperialism based upon rational choice.

Here two points are of crucial significance. First, from within economics, radical political economy has itself been subject to a devastating pincer

---

24   This is surprising as much of Lazear's work is based on the problem of incentive compatibility in the context of imperfect information.

movement. On the one hand, in contrast to other social sciences, mainstream economics has been extraordinarily and increasingly intolerant of alternatives, especially in view of the Americanisation of the discipline.[25] On the other hand, radical political economy has itself been subject to economic imperialism. This is particularly pronounced, for example, in labour market analysis.[26] As a result, radical political economy has not been able to prosper within economics. Where it has been able to establish a marginal foothold, it is only at the expense of succumbing to the dubious charms of the mainstream – in concepts, techniques and method – whilst presenting itself as a fierce opponent.[27]

Second, then, radical political economy is liable to seek a home within other social sciences that are more tolerant of its approach. As social science seeks or is pressed to incorporate an economic content, there is liable to be debate over the middle zone. Economic imperialism will be contested both for its economics and for its imperialism, not least because social science other than economics is generally and traditionally more comfortable in method and assumptions with political economy than with mainstream economics. In addition, political economy offers the student of the real world certain attractions that are notably absent from the dismal science.

It is worth emphasising the virtues, certainly the distinctiveness of political economy, both as a means for understanding contemporary capitalism and for engaging in a genuine dialogue with other social sciences. The contrast is with a rampant economic imperialism that betrays little knowledge of, let alone respect for, empirical realities and methodologies that are not, respectively, reducible to statistical data and mathematical modelling.[28]

First, political economy is holistic, attempting a systemic analysis of the workings of the economy as a whole and independent of the otherwise isolated individuals who comprise it. Second, it takes social and economic structures and relations as its starting point, thereby placing emphasis upon class

---

25 See especially Coats (ed.) (1996), Hodgson and Rothman (1999), Lee and Harley (1998), King (2000) and Bernstein (1999).

26 This is most evident in segmented labour market theory. Little more than a decade ago, it was considered unacceptable by the mainstream. Now, it is part of the mainstream. See Fine (1998a) and also Spencer (1998). Further, as evidenced by Lazear's own work, industrial relations has been transformed into human resource development, personnel economics or the like and, as such, reduced to problems of incentive compatibility and transaction costs, etc.

27 An exemplary illustration is provided by Bowles and Gintis (2000).

28 Blaug (1998, p. 11) reports a US survey finding a lack of interest in the real world on the part of elite graduate economics students as opposed to their highly tuned knowledge of econometrics and mathematical economics.

and stratification more generally. Third, by the same token, notions of power and conflict come to the fore, how they are forged and how they are exercised, not least through the state and internationally. Fourth, economic categories are subject to critical examination and reconstruction in meaning as opposed to a closed and ahistorical understanding of the economy as inputs and outputs, production and utility, etc, with a corresponding need to divide variables into exogenous and endogenous even if the boundary between the two shifts in favour of the latter as economic imperialism proceeds. Last, systemic tendencies and processes, such as globalisation, monopolisation, and uneven development, are explained on the basis of the imperatives of profitability and capital accumulation as opposed to more or less harmonious and efficient market (and non-market) coordination of aggregated individual optimising strategies.

In short, Lazear's apparent prognosis of an increasingly triumphant economic imperialism is not only to be regretted but also to be questioned. For the outcome of the intellectual conflicts around the place and sort of economics within social science is far from pre-determined. A variety of outcomes are foreseeable across disciplines and topics. These depend upon the extent both of the revival of political economy outside economics and of the genuinely cultural or social content incorporated into the middle zone where debate over the economy as a social system, dominated by capitalism, is liable to be to the fore. By way of summary and strategic implications for those engaging in radical political economy, a number of points are posited:

- Across the social sciences, there is currently an intellectual retreat from the excesses of both postmodernism and neo-liberalism, although their presence and especially their continuing influence remain strong.
- Economics as a discipline is dominated by an increasingly esoteric and intellectually bankrupt technicism that is absolutely intolerant of alternatives and only allows for them to survive on its margins. Despite its fragilities, there is no sign that this situation is liable to change as a result of "implosion" through internal developments or critique within the mainstream.
- Paradoxically, though, the influence of economics on other social sciences in terms of methodology, concepts and approach is stronger than at any time in the post-war period. The depth, extent and nature of its influence by topic and discipline are diverse, not least in light of continuing traditions and content of other social sciences.
- Much of the current influence of mainstream economics arises out of the new information-theoretic economics through which both the

economic and the social (treated as mutually exclusive opposites) are perceived as the response to market, especially informational, imperfections. This involves, on the one hand, an extraordinary reductionism of the social to informational imperfections while, on the other, considerable scope for inscribing (bringing back in) the social by plunder of concepts and insights from other social sciences (ranging from trust and customs to institutions, etc).
- In the realm of methodology, the social sciences remain generally hostile to the methods and postures of mainstream economics, when they are explicitly confronted rather than informally incorporated. Nevertheless, rational choice adherents have made much headway in sociology, political science, history, and elsewhere.
- Within mainstream economics itself, despite the absolute dominance of methodological individualism in its current form and the widespread belief in the harmonious and potentially optimal, if at times flawed, properties of free market capitalism, there is no unified ideology comparable to post-war Keynesianism or mid nineteenth-century Ricardianism. Orthodoxy is more a matter of adhering to technique and adopting a certain approach in resolving theoretical and empirical problems. The diffuse nature of the new orthodoxy – its postures are contingent on the incidence and nature of market imperfections – makes challenges to it more difficult and less influential (unlike the challenge to neo-liberalism). Equally, there is a weakened appeal as far as other disciplines are concerned where the social and the systemic are taken as starting points.
- The prospects for political economy are not positive within economics as a discipline. They look far more encouraging as social theory addresses and embraces the need for an economic content. Political economy has the potential to compete successfully with mainstream economics across the social sciences in view of its more acceptable methods and theory to them. Nonetheless, social theory remains marked by the bifurcation between the social and the economic. Knowledge and use of political economy is fragmented and mixed, as well as arbitrary and ill-informed. There is a need for a renewal of core material from political economy, both targeting social sciences as a whole and specific issues and disciplines. In short, the battle for political economy and for how the economy is to be understood is liable to be situated outside economics as a discipline and more across the other social sciences where, if appropriately engaged, political economy has great potential to prosper.

References

Bailly F. (2022) "When Mainstream Economics Does Human Resource Management: a Critique of Personnel Economics' Prescriptive Ambition", *PSL Quarterly Review*, vol 75, no 301, pp. 103–17.

Becker, G. (1990) "Gary S. Becker", in Swedberg (ed.) (1990), pp. 27–46.

Becker, G. (1996) *Accounting for Tastes*, Cambridge: Harvard University Press.

Bernstein, M. (1999) "Economic Knowledge, Professional Authority, and the State: the Case of American Economics During and After World War II", in Garnett (ed.) (1999), pp. 103–23.

Blaug, M. (1980) *The Methodology of Economics: or How Economists Explain*, Cambridge: Cambridge University Press.

Blaug, M. (1998) "Disturbing Currents in Modern Economics", *Challenge*, vol 41, no 3, pp. 11–34.

Bowden, S. and A. Offer (1994) "Household Appliances and the Use of Time: the United States and Britain since the 1920s", *Economic History Review*, vol XLVII, no 4, pp. 725–48. See Chapter 4.

Bowden, S. and A. Offer (1996) "The Technological Revolution that Never Was: Gender, Class, and the Diffusion of Household Appliances in Interwar England", in de Grazia and Furlough (eds) (1996), pp. 244–74.

Bowden, S. and A. Offer (1999) "Household Appliances and 'Systems of Provision' – A Reply", *Economic History Review*, vol LII, no 3, pp. 563–67.

Bowles, S. and H. Gintis (2000) "Walrasian Economics in Retrospect", *Quarterly Journal of Economics*, vol 115, no 4, pp. 1411–1439.

Boylan, T. and P. O'Gorman (1995) *Beyond Rhetoric and Realism in Economics: Towards a Reformulation of Economic Methodology*, London: Routledge.

Carrier, J. and D. Miller (eds) (1998) *Virtualism: the New Political Economy*, London: Berg.

Coats, A. (ed.) (1996) *The Post-1945 Internationalization of Economics*, History of Political Economy, vol 28, Supplement.

Connell, R. (1997) "Why Is Classical Theory Classical?", *American Journal of Sociology*, vol 102, no 6, pp. 1511–57.

Cornwall, R. (1997) "Deconstructing Silence: the Queer Political Economy of the Social Allocation of Desire", *Review of Radical Political Economics*, vol 29, no 1, pp. 1–130.

de Grazia, V. and E. Furlough (eds) (1996) *The Sex of Things: Gender and Consumption in Historical Perspective*, London: University of California Press.

du Gay, P. and M. Pryke (eds) (2002) *Cultural Economy: Cultural Analysis and Commercial Life*, London: Sage.

Economist (1998) "New Economists: Journey Beyond the Stars", *Economist*, December 19th, pp. 143–46.

Falk, P. and C. Campbell (eds) (1997) *The Shopping Experience*, London: Sage.

Fine, B. (1982) *Theories of the Capitalist Economy*, London: Edward Arnold.

Fine, B. (1997a) "The New Revolution in Economics", *Capital and Class*, no 61, Spring, pp. 143–48.

Fine, B. (1997b) "Entitlement Failure?", *Development and Change*, vol 28, no 4, pp. 617–47.

Fine, B. (1998a) *Labour Market Theory: a Constructive Reassessment*, London: Routledge.

Fine, B. (1998b) "The Triumph of Economics: Or 'Rationality' Can Be Dangerous to Your Reasoning", in Carrier and Miller (eds), pp. 49–73.

Fine, B. (1999a) "From Becker to Bourdieu: Economics Confronts the Social Sciences", *International Papers in Political Economy*, vol 5, no 3, pp. 1–43.

Fine, B. (1999b) "A Question of Economics: Is It Colonising the Social Sciences?", *Economy and Society*, vol 28, no 3, pp. 403–25.

Fine, B. (1999c) "'Household Appliances and the Use of Time: the United States and Britain since the 1920s' – A Comment", *Economic History Review*, vol LII, no 3, pp. 552–62. See Chapter 4.

Fine, B. (1999d) "The Developmental State Is Dead – Long Live Social Capital?", *Development and Change*, vol 30, no 1, pp. 1–19.

Fine, B. (2000a) "Endogenous Growth Theory: a Critical Assessment", *Cambridge Journal of Economics*, vol 24, no 2, pp. 245–65, a shortened and amended version of identically titled, SOAS Working Paper no 80, February 1998.

Fine, B. (2000b) "New and Improved: Economics' Contribution to Business History", SOAS Working Paper in Economics, no 93.

Fine, B. (2000c) "Bringing the Social back into Economics: Progress or Reductionism?", *History of Economics Review*, vol 32, no 1, pp. 10–35, amended version of Department of Economics Research Paper no 731, University of Melbourne.

Fine, B. (2000d) "Economic Imperialism as Kuhnian Revolution", Paper presented to METU Annual Economics Conference, Ankara, September.

Fine, B. (2000e) "Whither the Welfare State: Public versus Private Consumption?", SOAS Working Paper in Economics, no 92.

Fine, B. (2000f) "Consumption for Historians: an Economist's Gaze", SOAS Working Paper in Economics, no 90.

Fine, B. (2001a) *Social Capital versus Social Theory: Political Economy and Social Science at the Turn of the Millennium*, London: Routledge.

Fine, B. (2001b) "Neither Washington nor Post-Washington Consensus: an Introduction", in Fine et al (eds) (2001), pp. 1–27.

Fine, B. (2002) "'Economic Imperialism': a View from the Periphery", *Review of Radical Political Economics*, vol 34, no 2, pp. 187–201.

Fine, B. (2004) "Addressing the Critical and the Real in Critical Realism", in Lewis (ed.) (2004), pp. 202–26.

Fine, B., M. Heasman, and J. Wright (1996) *Consumption in the Age of Affluence: the World of Food*, London: Routledge.

Fine, B. and C. Lapavitsas (2000) "Markets and Money in Social Theory: What Role for Economics?", *Economic and Society*, vol 29, no 3, pp. 357–82.

Fine, B., C. Lapavitsas and J. Pincus (eds) (2001) *Development Policy in the Twenty-First Century: Beyond the Post-Washington Consensus*, London: Routledge.

Fine, B. and E. Leopold (1993) *The World of Consumption*, London: Routledge.

Fine, B. and D. Milonakis (2000) "From New to Newest: the Economic History of Douglass North", mimeo, published in revised parts as "From Principle of Pricing to Pricing of Principle: Rationality and Irrationality in the Economic History of Douglass North", with D. Milonakis, *Comparative Studies in Society and History*, vol 45, no 3, pp. 120–44, 2003, and "Douglass North's Remaking of Economic History: a Critical Appraisal", *Review of Radical Political Economics*, with D. Milonakis, vol 39, no 1, pp. 27–57, 2007.

Fine, B. and D. Milonakis (2009) *From Economics Imperialism to Freakonomics: the Shifting Boundaries between Economics and Other Social Sciences*, London: Routledge.

Gabriel, Y. and T. Lang (1995) *The Unmanageable Consumer: Contemporary Consumption and Its Fragmentation*, London: Sage.

Garnett, R. (ed.) (1999) *What Do Economists Know?: New Economics of Knowledge*, London: Routledge.

Gutting, G. (ed.) (1980) *Paradigms and Revolutions: Applications and Appraisals of Thomas Kuhn's Philosophy of Science*, Notre Dame: Notre Dame University Press.

Hennessey, K. and E. Lazear (2013) *Observations on the Financial Crisis*, Stanford: Hoover Institution Press.

Hodgson, G. and H. Rothman (1999) "The Editors and Authors of Economics Journals: a Case of Institutional Oligopoly?", *Economic Journal*, 109, no 453, pp. F165–F186.

Holbrook, M. (1995) *Consumer Research: Introspective Essays on the Study of Consumption*, London: Sage.

King, J. (2000) "Has There Been Progress in Post-Keynesian Economics?", Paper to the conference of the European Society for the History of Economic Thought (ESHET), Graz, February, appearing in King (2002).

King, J. (2002) *The History of Post-Keynesian Economics, 1936–2000*, Cheltenham: Edward Elgar.

Kuhn, T. (1970) *The Structure of Scientific Revolutions*, Chicago: Chicago University Press, second edition with postscript, original of 1962.

Lamoreaux, N. (1998) "Economic History and the Cliometric Revolution", in Molho and Wood (eds) (1998), pp 59–84.

Lawson, T. (1997) *Economics and Reality*, London: Routledge.

Lazear, E. (1995) *Personnel Economics*, Cambridge: MIT Press.

Lazear, E. (1998) *Personnel Economics for Managers*, New York: Wiley.

Lazear, E. (1999a) "Personnel Economics: Past Lessons and Future Directions", *Journal of Labor Economics*, vol 17, no 2, pp. 199–236.

Lazear, E. (1999b) "Culture and Language", *Journal of Political Economy*, vol 107, no 6:2, pp. 95–126, previously National Bureau of Economic Research, Working Paper no 5249, 1995.

Lazear, E. (2000a) "Economic Imperialism", *Quarterly Journal of Economics*, vol 115, no 1, pp. 99–146, previously National Bureau of Economic Research, Working Paper no 7300, 1999.

Lazear, E. (2000b) "The Power of Incentives", *American Economic Review*, vol 90, no 2, pp. 410–14.

Lee, F. and S. Harley (1998) "Peer Review, the Research Assessment Exercise and the Demise of Non-Mainstream Economics", *Capital and Class*, no 66, pp. 23–51.

Lewis, P. (ed.) (2004) *Transforming Economics: Perspectives on the Critical Realist Project*, London: Routledge.

McCloskey, D. (1986) *The Rhetoric of Economics*, Brighton: Wheatsheaf.

Miller, D. (ed.) (1995) *Acknowledging Consumption*, London: Routledge.

Milonakis, D. and B. Fine (2009) *From Political Economy to Economics: Method, the Social and the Historical in the Evolution of Economic Theory*, London: Routledge.

Molho, A. and G. Wood (eds) (1998) *Imagined Histories: American Historians Interpret the Past*, Princeton: Princeton University Press.

Offer, A. (1997) "Between the Gift and the Market: the Economy of Regard", *Economic History Review*, vol L, no 3, pp. 450–76.

Olson, M. and S. Kähkönen (2000) "Introduction: the Broader View", in Olson and Kähkönen (eds) (2000), pp. 1–36.

Olson, M. and S. Kähkönen (eds) (2000) *A Not-So-Dismal Science: a Broader View of Economies and Societies*, Oxford: Oxford University Press.

Perelman, M. (2000) *The Invention of Capitalism: Classical Political Economy and the Secret History of Primitive Accumulation*, Durham: Duke University Press.

Slater, D. (2000) "Capturing Markets from the Economists", Paper for Cultural Economics Conference, Open University, UK, January, but see Chapter 3 in du Gay and Pryke (eds) (2002).

Spencer, D. (1998) *Economic Analysis and the Theory of Production: a Critical Appraisal*, unpublished Phd thesis, University of Leeds.

Stigler, G. (1984) "Economics – The Imperial Science", *Scandinavian Journal of Economics*, vol 86, no 3, pp. 301–13.

Stiglitz, J. (1994) *Whither Socialism?*, Cambridge: MIT Press.

Stiglitz, J. (1998) "More Instruments and Broader Goals: Moving Toward the Post-Washington Consensus", the 1998 WIDER Annual Lecture, January 7th, Helsinki.

Swedberg, R. (1990) "Introduction", in Swedberg (ed.) (1990), pp. 3–26.

Swedberg, R. (ed.) (1990) *Economics and Sociology, Redefining Their Boundaries: Conversations with Economists and Sociologists*, Princeton: Princeton University Press.

Thompson, G. (1997) "Where Goes Economics and the Economies", *Economy and Society*, vol 26, no 4, pp. 599–610.

Thompson, G. (1999) "How Far Should We Be Afraid of Conventional Economics? A Response to Ben Fine", *Economy and Society*, vol 28, no 3, 426–433.

Velthuis, O. (1999) "The Changing Relationship between Economic Sociology and Institutional Economics: from Talcott Parsons to Mark Granovetter", *American Journal of Economics and Sociology*, vol 58, no 4, pp. 629–49.

Zelizer, V. (2000) "Fine-Tuning the Zelizer View", *Economy and Society*, vol 29, no 3, pp. 383–89.

CHAPTER 4

"Household Appliances and the Use of Time: The United States and Britain since the 1920s" – A Comment

Postscript as Personal Preamble

By the end of the 1990s, I was well into policing economics imperialism, targeting the associates of each of Becker and Stiglitz, as leading representatives of its old and new phases, respectively, subject to particular vigilance. As chance would have it, my own work, both before and after I got the economics imperialism bug, had covered consumption (beginning with consumer durables), female labour market participation, Marxist value theory and its application to the domestic labour debate, and both the new economic history and new institutional economics. Across all of these, I had engaged in both theoretical and empirical work, often in tandem.[1]

As a result, it is hardly surprising that the contributions of Bowden and Offer, B&O hereafter, criticised in this published comment should get my goat, especially as they drew upon Becker to frame appliances as domestic labour time-saving, leading both to their diffusion and to greater female labour market participation.[2] Indeed, my work on consumer durables and female labour market participation was specifically designed not so much to address such hypotheses as to find them tautologous if not vacuous – as whatever happened could be explained by allowing underlying preferences and so derived choices to "explain" allocation of time according to income and substitution effects for leisure and income, if mediated by the role of labour-saving devices and lower pay for women than for men in labour markets.[3]

A related but separate point is that the Becker framework (and the explanation of shifting female labour market participation in response to incentives around availability and cost of supposedly labour-saving devices and female labour market access and rewards) is ahistorical and asocial, as well as being

---

1   For details see Volume 1, Chapter 1.
2   See also Fine (1995) for critique of Kotz (1994) on similar grounds.
3   To be honest, as is transparent, there was also an ulterior motive over and above policing economics imperialism, and that was to promote the system of provision approach to consumption, Fine and Leopold (1993), Fine (2002) and, most recently, Bayliss and Fine (2021a).

individualistic, but that the rise of domestic appliances and female waged labour is not. As a result, it is necessary to locate the rise of appliances and female labour market participation in historical context, not only in terms of how much of each but what they are and what they mean. And exactly the same applies to the various categories of time, whether it be spent in waged or (own-home) domestic labour, leisure or entertainment. There are different logics and meanings to different times, and they shift over historical time itself.

Presumably, and commendably, this was understood by those who allowed my comment on B&O to be published in the *Economic History Review*, the leading British journal for the discipline. Surely, this is as it should be for historians, especially in the wake of postmodernism. But, as is apparent from their response to my critique,[4] B&O (1999) are not sensible to these issues. Indeed, they begin their response to me with the suggestion that my "strictures are not always easy to follow", p. 565.[5] It is, however, easy to see, and immediately, why it should not be easy for them to follow my "strictures" – an at least implicit attempt to designate me as authoritarian, dogmatic or whatever as opposed to their own commitment to neoclassical headbanging. For they claim:[6]

> Economic categories (and the economic notions of rationality and motivation) are indeed timeless, but not in the sense that they stand outside historical time. Rather, economists assume that they apply throughout historical time. This is merely a way of saying that human nature remains constant in history, while environments, prices, and cultures change. Our critic may dislike this premise, but he presents no arguments in refutation. It is, of course, accepted widely in the social sciences, and we make no apologies.

This is simply bizarre, highly questionable empirically as far as human nature and the social sciences are concerned, and bordering on the self-contradictory, not least as any historian knows that prices, in particular, do not simply

---

4 And this is my first chance to respond to their response.
5 Bear in mind, the original response was probably restricted to 4000 words or so.
6 In their response, simple asocial/ahistorical propositions are taken for granted, such as, "In fact (like most economists and psychologists), we assume that stimulation delivers diminishing returns", p. 565. Ironically, by this time, work on the diseases of affluence and the epidemic of obesity (currently, there are now more over-than under-nourished in the world and the covid pandemic has intensified its consequences), had been completed. See Fine et al (1996), Fine (1998) and, most recently, Bayliss and Fine (2021a and b). In other words, we make our assumptions, and the world must fit, rather than vice-versa, or be made to fit in the ideology of neoliberal policy, Carrier and Miller (eds) (1998).

change, they may not even be present as markets are far from universally present throughout human history.⁷

Indeed, this passage begins to go to the heart of the differences between us for it sets aside any consideration of the historical and social nature of the categories we deploy. This is evident in how they continue:

> Fine makes a distinction between employment, where time is governed primarily by commercial consideration, and domestic labour, where there is no corresponding discipline. This 'is evident from the domestic labour debate', referring to a 30-page passage in his previous work. But there is no evidence contained there, only a discussion of a debate on value.

Once again, this is highly significant for revealing our differences. The domestic labour and corresponding debate on value is precisely about the differences between the two forms of labour, and whether each does or does not produce value – my position being that domestic labour does not precisely because it is not subject to direct and directly imposed commercial logics. And, it is worth adding, this follows in part because value itself is a historically and socially specific category within political economy associated with commercial, i.e. capitalist, society alone. Whilst there is a strand in the domestic labour debate that does treat all labour of whatever sort as equally creating (exploitable) value, this involves setting aside that it is governed by very different logics than those attached to commerce – with the result that what counts as value-creating, and how much, is indeterminate (as opposed to value creation under the direct control of capital which is subject to socially-determined market valuation as exchange value).

To some degree, B&O seek to use my own argument against me as they quote me to the effect that, "in the household 'a discipline of time is neither enforced nor liable to be adopted'", p. 564. But this is taken out of context. For, earlier in the same paragraph of my piece, it is made clear that, there is no "*corresponding* discipline governing time spent outside work". As a result, they mock me by suggesting I believe in some unworldly fashion that there are no time constraints outside of commerce – "Tell a mother trying to get her children to school, or preparing dinner for a household on several different timetables", p. 563. This is not the issue at all as opposed to the differences in the nature of

---

7   Note that Becker (1996) ultimately rests on biologically given preferences, albeit "extended" to allow for learning and experience and, thereby, to explain why our preferences do not remain the same, Fine (1997b) for a critique.

timekeeping and, as a result, of the time constraints themselves – no mother was sacked or lost wages for not keeping to time other than in the workplace.[8]

The result is a dialogue of the deaf, except that I hear them, being bilingual, but they are not, self-confessedly, fully fluent in the language of the social and historical. In short, in conformity to their Becker framing and appeal to universal categories (with Becker himself forced to rely upon an unchanging, biologically determined human nature), B&O understandably fail to understand my strictures. These, without going into further detail, derive from criticising their ahistorical conceptualisations, which mean that not only time-saving and time-using categories and the like, but also the notions of (domestic) appliance and durables become open to question. At methodological and theoretical levels, this is not only to open the door to economics imperialism, it is to rush through it. And, as I was already aware from my own empirical work on consumer durables, it was also to misunderstand the material and cultural causes and consequences of consumer durable diffusion, Bayliss and Fine (2021a) for a retrospective account.

Finally, on a chronological criterion, this piece appeared well before the peak of the watershed, as both the old Becker phase of economics imperialism gave way to the new Stiglitz phase of market imperfections and as explicit contestation against economics imperialism, as defined strictly only by its old phase, went into decline. So, why does this chapter appear in this second volume, as opposed to the first? Or why does it not appear in the third volume on economic history? Well, it could have appeared in any of the three volumes. Its appearance in this volume, as well as the previous chapter which is also to a large degree pre-watershed by criterion of content alone, is an explicit recognition of the murky nature, at least temporarily, of the watershed across and through its pre- and post- periods which are, nonetheless remarkably short in time in the great scheme of things. More specifically, despite being placed in a volume ahead of its time by virtue of being an example of the old economics imperialism, it does contain elements of what lay ahead for two reasons. On the one hand, it is a contribution to economic history. On the other, it deals in consumption. Each of these, and both together, tend to dull and dilute the pure application of the crudest forms of neoclassical economics as a result of both subject matter and disciplinary imperatives as is apparent from the trials and tribulations of the first phase of the new economic history itself as an example

---

8 And, of course, it is not just labour that is subject to different logics, given considerable significance of time in determining rates of return through speed of turnover, for which as fast as possible is imperative (unlike many household chores/pleasures which can afford to be leisurely without penalty, even with casual disregard for time within limits).

of old-style economics imperialism, see forthcoming volume on (economics imperialism and) economic history.

1 Introduction[9]

Elsewhere, I have argued that a revolution is currently under way in or, more exactly, around economics (Fine 1997a, 1998a, 1999a and b). Briefly, far from abandoning its well-established mode and content of reasoning, economics is vigorously seeking to colonise other social sciences through the extension of its methodology based on optimising agents. Much progress has already been made by way of cliometrics, although quantitative economic history does not logically entail reliance upon neoclassical orthodoxy. Further the creeping influence of economics is often piecemeal. Its concepts are deployed without examining overall conceptual consistency other than through eclecticism. The notion of human capital is the leading example. Significantly, it derives its widespread use from the popularisation of the notion by Gary Becker, a leading economist seeking to universalise standard economic methodology. He has also "inspired" the work of B&O (1994 and 1996). This comment demonstrates how this leads to an arbitrary content to their work and points to an alternative approach.

2 A False Economy of Time?

B&O's reliance on Becker only draws upon his work on the family and the use of time.[10] Time is particularly important for B&O since they do not refer to personal and social capital, although these form the generalisation of human capital within what Becker terms "the economic approach". Instead, B&O proxy such capitals in two different ways – as time itself and as the materialised productivity of time or physically durable (consumer) equipment.

Significantly, both concepts are ahistorical, although used to explain historically-specific outcomes – diffusion of household appliances in the twentieth century. Inevitably, the historical content – in both the use and meaning

---

9   Thanks to referees and others for comments on earlier drafts.
10 Becker (1975 and 1991). See also Becker (1993) for treatment of human capital, and Becker (1996) for an overview of all of his work, especially other than for human capital and the new household economics. For a critique of Becker in the context of consumption, see Fine (1997b, 1998a and 1999a).

of goods – has to be added on, potentially in arbitrary and inconsistent ways. For time, a distinction is drawn between that spent on work or domestic obligations and discretionary time. This is so that B&O can distinguish between those household appliances that are *time-saving* in enhancing the productivity of housework, so allowing for more discretionary time, and those that are *time-using* in requiring discretionary time in consumption. The duality between time-saving and time-using is seen as corresponding to producing and consuming within the household, the latter as a source of entertainment. Representative goods are the vacuum cleaner and the television, respectively.

The distinction between these different times has resonance with an extrapolation from the world of capitalist work, where time is sold and, in employment, is governed primarily by commercial considerations. As is evident from the domestic labour debate (Fine 1992, Appendix), there is no corresponding discipline governing time spent outside work. Consequently, distinguishing between time-saving and time-using appliances has limited systematic social basis. Nor is it even rooted in individual decision-making. B&O admit, "it is sometimes difficult to disentangle the time-saving and time-using attributes of goods", p.743, referring to television, motor cars and bicycles. Inverting their own definitional logic and descriptive hypothesis, for example, they classify the telephone as a time-saving appliance because its diffusion follows the pattern that is typical for them of the appliances delineated as time-saving, p. 744.[11] In short, whether derived by analogy with employment or not, the distinction between time-saving and time-using does not apply readily to the household where a discipline of time is neither enforced nor liable to be universally and tightly adopted.

Ambiguity also arises in addressing time devoted to *housework*. As B&O observe, this has stagnated until falling slightly in the recent period of greater female labour market participation. How is this possible given the adoption, however slowly, of *time-saving* appliances? The answer is in the shifting relative weight of household standards, productivity and other demands on time. Yet, if standards increase above home productivity, in cleaning and washing for example, raising time devoted to them, this is indistinguishable other than in name of activity, from time-using for entertainment through use of leisure appliances. Explanation has become tautologous in attaching time-saving and time-using to housework and leisure/entertainment, respectively. Why do we

---

11 For some discussion of the shifting meaning attached to the telephone, see Fine et al (1992).

not say that the standards of domestic entertainment have risen rather than that the appliances involved are time-using? For B&O, p. 728:

> "Time-saving" goods reduce the time required to complete a specific household task. An electric washing machine reduces the time required to clean a tubful of laundry, compared with manual methods ... Time-saving goods can increase the quantity of discretionary time, whereas time-using goods enhance its perceived quality.

But redefining time-using as enhancing the quality of time does not offer a resolution. Is not the *time* spent in cleaner houses or clothes of higher quality, at least subjectively? How do we distinguish between the quality of time as opposed to the quality of the appliances or their output?

There are two possibilities, leaving aside the availability of entirely novel services. Either an appliance saves time per unit of output, but may be used to provide a proportionately higher or lower level of output so that the actual time commanded can be higher or lower than before. If the household introduces an appliance that is not time-saving in this sense, it would appear to be behaving inefficiently, since it is paying for a durable without increased labour productivity. Or, scarcely addressed by B&O, the appliance can be a source of utility in and of itself without the use of time at all, as acknowledged for cars, p. 743/4. The most important example, however, is household accommodation. Presumably the same applies to furniture which is intriguingly associated with appliances because of their close income elasticities of demand, p. 733:[12]

> The priority for acquiring time-saving durables was similar to that of furnishing a home, and indeed it is likely that the two activities were related.

But are housing and furnishing time-saving, time-using or time-enhancing? These ahistorical categories create more conundrums than they resolve!

3 From Time to Demand

The preceding section suggests, within the Becker framework itself, that the simple division of time between using and saving is fractured by a variety of

---

[12] See Fine et al (1996, Chapter 7) for the argument, in the context of food, that the calculation of such elasticities is highly questionable both theoretically and empirically.

complications that undermine corresponding categorisation of household appliances. In addition, attention has shifted to demand, equally complex, on which B&O introduce two further influences. One is the low value placed upon women, whether as consumers or as workers. Their priorities as consumers are deemed to be low for time-saving appliances compared with what are deemed to be non-gendered appliances such as lighting and radio. Leaving aside ambiguity in the gendering of goods as male or female – would food be considered non-gendered because all have to eat? – such an argument is insufficiently tight. Even within a patriarchal framework, appliances that save women's working time within the household could, subject to price, still be adopted. For they could be used efficiently to serve men indirectly in other ways, as is evident from the limited reductions in the amounts of female domestic labour when time-saving appliances are adopted.

As workers, women are deemed to be unable to command a sufficiently high wage in the formal economy to warrant substituting for their time in the domestic economy with bought-out appliances. As it is observed that women were often responsible for producing the very goods that could allow, or make it economically viable for, them to work,[13] some sort of balance is required in determining how much they worked out of the home to allow them to purchase the appliances that made waged work a viable and adopted choice. For, presumably, the lower are women's wages, the cheaper will be the appliances that they produce. Consequently, it is worth observing the way in which patriarchy, although never termed as such, is being used as a residual explanatory factor in an implicitly extensive way and one which is not necessarily consistent with the underlying neoclassical economics employed. For, treating women's time and needs as of low value involves complex issues of conflict between efficiency and distribution both within the household and between the household and the (male?) formal economy. Who controls and gains the advantage from women's work?

Once again, elements of tautologous reasoning appear to be involved, with patriarchy relied upon when required but otherwise set aside. Goods are labelled as gendered, or not, according to who might benefit from consuming them (B&O 1994, p. 740 and 1996, p. 245 and 261). But how, then, in a world of patriarchy are we to explain that women's, girls' and children's clothing accounted in the UK in 1936 for a larger share of consumer expenditure (37%) than that of men and boys (26%)?[14] A separate point in the context of clothing

---

13   As recognised by B&O (1996, p. 247).
14   As reported in B&O (1996, p. 257).

is that the virtues of a washing machine depend upon having sufficient material to wash to make it worthwhile. If the fabric of household consumption, including hardware and hollowware as well as clothing, have yet to be purchased in sufficient quantities, it is hardly surprising that appliances that use them as raw materials are less attractive.

The other factor influencing demand is what can be called *access*. This has two components. On the one hand, differential access to household appliances is dependent on public policy, not least on whether and on what conditions electricity and gas are provided, for example. On the other hand, capacity to purchase, over and above income and price, depends upon availability of credit to smooth expenditure. There is a tendency to see credit as promoting diffusion; it makes possible in advance what would otherwise be impossible by outright purchase for, "Desire is stoked by advertising and facilitated by credit" (B&O 1996, p. 246).

This may be so for individuals *ceteris paribus*, i.e. for manipulable preferences and given cash prices for goods. But, as is apparent, purchase on credit is extremely expensive when taking account of the excessive levels of interest payments.[15] Consequently, the particular conditions governing the availability of credit can also be considered to have *impeded* the diffusion of ownership by virtue of the high prices effectively charged. In addition, the targeting of advertising to those elite households which could more readily purchase appliances can have an impact upon the quality of the goods made available, making them unduly costly at the expense of higher volume lower quality, or less heavily designed, products serving uniform mass markets (Atkinson 1995).[16]

Much of the foregoing is concerned with critical discussion of the factors that *influence* demand without, as yet, breaking fundamentally with the chosen inspiration provided by Becker. But what exactly is *demand* itself? This has essentially been taken for granted by B&O, with one exception provided by their discussion of "arousal", in which the natural preferences for goods is moved back one step biologically from utility (B&O 1994, p. 735 forward). The demand for time-using entertainment appliances is explained in terms of the natural human need attached to sensual stimuli, the ease with which these can be consumed, and the pace of technological progress in providing them cheaply. It is even argued by B&O that television viewing has addictive power.

---

15   As recognised by B&O (1994, p. 742/3) and B&O (1996, p. 254).
16   See Atkinson, 'Capabilities, Exclusion, and the Supply of Goods', for such an argument. See also Fine and Leopold (1990) and Fine et al (1996, Chapter 7) for the view that such elite consumption obstructed rather than promoted a putative consumer revolution in the eighteenth century.

Significantly, Becker's own theory of consumption is similarly based on biological considerations, presuming that all individuals have the same underlying preferences but that they learn differently what to enjoy through the differential accumulation of personal and social consumer capital. Consequently, for Becker, consumption paths, including addiction, are chosen in order to optimise.[17] Having surveyed the options, we would choose to be a telly addict or not. Consequently, it becomes arbitrary, if not again tautologous, to explain TV viewing as irrational, especially when it is considered as a deliberate pre-commitment to pay excessive credit charges to become addicted to it, p. 742.

The demand for TV suggests a further illustration of extrapolating from the discipline of time imposed by waged employment, for which time is usually seen as one-dimensional and activities are mutually exclusive of one another. In contrast, within the home, one is not at work or at play. In terms of the radio, for example, women are liable to have been listening whilst doing the housework and, indeed, programmes have been so designed. Similarly, the TV (and video) are essential for time-saving as far as childcare is concerned.[18] In some respects, the TV and radio can be considered as comparable to lighting, liable to household multiple ownership and to be on as long as someone is in the house.

In this light, note how tautologous the arguments become. Once a good, such as a TV, is purchased, even if on hire purchase, insatiable demand would suggest it would always be in use as running costs are extremely low. As this is not so, B&O introduce the value of time to explain the outcome. For TV watching is given up, once the individual's sensual capacities have been worked sufficiently far down the marginal utility curve:[19]

> Our explanation is cast in terms of the marginal cost of discretionary time, and its marginal utility. Consumers have apparently given greater priority to enhancing the quality of discretionary time than to increase its quantity. This reflects the uneven pace of technological change, which has found it easier to increase the attractions of leisure time than to reduce the burden of housework.

---

17 But, "'No one chooses to become an addict,' said Catherine, Princess of Wales", https://www.bbc.co.uk/news/uk-63440985.
18 As recognised by B&O (1994, p. 743, even if with some inconsistency, p. 739) and B&O (1996, p. 261). See also Seiter (1993).
19 B&O (1994, p. 732) and also elsewhere where equalities of marginal utilities are attached to the idea of equilibrium outcomes, a peculiarity in view of the wish to explain extensive economic and social change pp. 727, 738 and 744.

No doubt, with different empirical outcomes, the priorities would be judged to be otherwise, indicating that the analysis has no explanatory content.

4 The Appliance of Economic Science?

Apart from treating activities as mutually exclusive as far as time is concerned, a further deficiency in the account of demand by B&O is the notion of appliance itself. So far, the discussion here has been careful, with a few necessary exceptions, only to refer to (domestic and household) appliances, although B&O tend to alternate without thinking between the terms "appliance" and "durables". But the two are very different, although B&O probably intend the former to be a subset of the latter. Without wishing to be pedantic, a durable is simply something that lasts for what is an ill-defined length of time. It is a universal category without historical content. The household enjoys a very wide range of durables, from plastic buckets, fixtures and fittings, clothing, food stores, other household effects, through to the putative categories of time-saving and time-using appliances themselves. An immediate issue is why B&O's approach should not apply to all of these durables.

Appliances, on the other hand, especially with the terms "domestic" or "household" appended, are a different kettle of fish. As a sub-category of durables they are socially and historically specific. They simply did not exist prior to the twentieth century – there were Elizabethan durables if not domestic appliances. The notion of appliances is a socially constructed category, not only in the sense that electricity and the white goods have to have been invented and made, but in what counts as an appliance in practice. This is variable – does it now include an electric kettle or an iron? – and, without going into detail, it depends upon how the goods concerned are designed, produced, sold, used and construed as objects – do antique carpets or old masters count as household durables?

Yet again, it is to be suspected that the notion of appliance as durable has been gleaned by extrapolation from the economic theory of the market economy. In this context, the parallel durable is fixed capital. As such, it is tied both conceptually and chronologically to a more precise, however satisfactory, definition. Fixed capital is durable in the sense that it cannot be changed in the short run during which employment and output decisions are presumed to be made. By the same token, it lasts beyond the period of a single cycle of production for output. For convenience, in constructing national and corporate accounts, fixed capital is also presumed to depreciate at a definite rate so that it lasts for a particular period of time.

Such considerations cannot apply to the household because, unlike the capitalist enterprise, it is not motivated by a profit *rate*, which is necessarily tied to time. What would constitute the length of time of the production period for the household beyond which an appliance qualifies as a durable? Should it be daily or annual, by the regularity of wage or other payment, or even intergenerational? There can be no answer and, as a result, a slightly separate consideration has been brought into play concerning how goods are purchased. Fixed capital and household appliances are both heavily associated with use of credit. Consequently, appliances usually constitute a high expenditure relative to income, with goods losing the status of appliance as income increases relative to their price. But this need not be the case, and how and whether goods are treated as appliances or not inevitably depends upon the commercial strategy of those providing them rather than exclusively upon their physical properties of durability and service to the optimising consumer.

5   Towards a Durable Alternative

The discussion has primarily focused on the difficulties that arise out of deploying neoclassical economics to create simple and general concepts to categorise and to explain diffusion of household durables/appliances. Is there an alternative for what is undoubtedly a significant area for economic and social research on the twentieth century as a consumer (durable) society?[20]

Elsewhere, it has been argued that a general theory of consumption is inappropriate (Fine et al 1996). More specifically, first, durables do not form a general category open to a common theory, as each is determined by a varied and complex interaction of underlying factors. There is the need for a theoretically-informed, interdisciplinary but product-specific consideration of consumption. Despite belonging to the same household, the video, the telephone, the car and the washing machine belong to very different worlds. Despite being allocated to the same category of durables, such goods differ considerably more by other determinants than they share the common property of lasting a long time – as does a book, and many other goods that are not considered durables.

Now, it is inevitable that certain goods, including durables, do share characteristics in common – in how they are used or how they are sold, giving rise to

---

20   Although this term is itself ambiguous and questionable, Fine and Leopold (1993, Chapter 6).

empirical generalities. Is it not possible to address such regularities analytically whether in the fashion of B&O or otherwise? As argued in Fine et al (1996), the potential for such interconnections across goods is almost unlimited at the level of consumption itself because of, for example, life-style packaging or the more pervasive potential for cultural linkages to be forged across goods. Consequently, the properties of goods as items of consumption cannot serve as the basis for a causal analysis. Rather, why certain goods become associated with one another has itself to be explained. To do so depends upon examining their provision prior to consumption. Should not only consumption but also provision be integrated across goods, then a more general but historically-specific category will be created – use of credit and dedicated stores in the case of household appliances for example. The latter category cannot be derived, as for B&O, from abstract, ahistorical principles.

Nor is this a recipe for abandoning theory altogether and resorting to historical and empirical contingency. For, second, the study of durables can move beyond household demand decisions alone to consider the more general processes and structures by which specific consumption is provided, through what has been termed integral *systems of provision*. Consumer choice should not be seen as the aggregated, even if market-coordinated, outcome of isolated and independent individuals or households. Rather, such choice is the consequence of definite socioeconomic processes, which are inevitably going to create uniformities across individuals, both in terms of the creation and exercising of their preferences. In other words, choice is as much about the action of socioeconomic processes on individuals as it is about the latter's independent and exogenous room for manoeuvre.

Consequently, consumer choice is liable to trace out definite patterns across the population, in which variables such as socioeconomic status and household composition in terms of gender and age will be of importance. The various patterns of consumption that do or do not arise by different socioeconomic classifications give rise to norms of consumption. Crucially, a consumption norm in this sense is not to be interpreted as a common level, whether some measure of average or not, although this is what one aspect of a norm can be. Rather, the norm is supposed to reflect the presence or not of patterns of consumption that differ systematically across the population. For some goods, a TV or a lottery ticket for example, consumption is so common as to represent a norm in the sense that more or less everybody has one. For other, luxury goods, the norm is for those to have them only if they are wealthy and of a particular socioeconomic class – as in a country estate. It is even possible to perceive the norm for a consumption good to be what might be termed null, one of random distribution across the population – speculatively, whether hair is short or long, for example.

In short, choice is to be interpreted as a social outcome whose systematic patterns must be identified in the form of consumption norms. Although this does not imply that income and prices are unimportant in determining consumer choice, it does place them more in the background relative to other determinants. Second, then, the latter have yet to be specified. The definition and, where possible, the empirical identification of consumption norms does not, in and of itself, explain why they should have arisen in the form that they have – including the possibility of null norms, for which analysis would need to explain why socioeconomic processes have not ground out systematic patterns of consumption. This leads to the hypothesis that the way in which social norms are constructed will differ from one consumption good to the next. Rather than relying upon a general theory, such as utility maximisation, that applies "horizontally" across all consumption goods, the latter should be differentiated from one another, and the explanation for their consumption rooted in a "vertical" analysis. By this is meant tracing their origins from production through to consumption, and the material culture surrounding them, incorporating the roles of technology, distribution, design, retailing, etc.

The focus must, then, be upon specific products and the chain of activities around them, rather than the imposition of general considerations across a range of consumption goods, as in the optimising consumer of neoclassical economics, or the extrapolation from specifics (as is often the conclusion drawn from case studies from Veblen onwards). From the perspective offered here, Coffin offers an exemplary commentary on what needs to be done as well as a case study for the sewing machine:[21]

> I deliberately bring together subjects that are usually treated separately: family incomes and credit payments, construction of femininity and methods of marketing, and advertising, sexology, and models of the female body.

More generally, the most important collections of case studies and essays provided by Brewer and Porter (eds) (1993) and de Grazia and Furlough (eds) (1996) can be interpreted along these lines. The thematic essays are either

---

21 See Coffin (1994, p. 751 and 1996, p. 113). Note that she observes how the sewing machine straddles both labour and product markets in the relations between the formal economy and the household (Coffin 1996, p. 140).

product-specific in practice and/or erroneous in generalising from specific products. De Grazia (1996, p. 4) correctly lays out the issues involved:

> Thus, consumption is discussed here in terms of processes of commodification, spectatorship, commercial exchanges, and social welfare reforms, processes that involve the desire for and sale, purchase, and use of durable and non-durable goods, collective services, and images.

Further, earlier work is criticised:[22]

> Such approaches have tended to discourage analysis of processes of signification in the light of varying historical legacies, such as might be shaped by diverse processes of state building, or by the relative power of the market, or by varying patterns of accumulation of ... "cultural capital" ... (S)uch interactions are central, for they may account for politically significant differences in the evolution of the responses to changes in consumption habits within and across societies, and the diverse play of institutions, state, market, and family.

The additional insight offered here is that such imperatives can only be legitimately operationalised on the basis of product-specific systems of provision. These are ground out and distinguished from one another historically and socially rather than reflecting an ahistorical and asocial economy of time, arousal or whatever.[23]

References

Atkinson, A. (1995) "Capabilities, Exclusion, and the Supply of Goods", in Basu et al (eds) (1995), pp. 17–31.

Auslander, L. (1996) "The Gendering of Consumer Practices in Nineteenth-Century France", in de Grazia and Furlough (eds) (1996), pp. 79–112.

---

22 de Grazia (1996, p. 7). See also Auslander (1996, p. 101).
23 See also Peiss (1996, p. 312/3): "Given the incipient state of the field, generalizations are not yet warranted. Buying a lipstick and buying a car, for instance, are different consumer acts occurring in distinct discursive and social contexts, although both involve, among other things, consumption, appearance, and identity". Note that a lipstick, like many other cosmetics, is a *durable of a sort*.

Basu, K., P. Pattanaik and K. Suzumura (eds.) (1995) *Choice, Welfare, and Development: a Festschrift in Honour of Amartya K. Sen*, Oxford: Clarendon Press.

Bayliss, K. and B. Fine (2021a) *A Guide to the Systems of Provision Approach: Who Gets What, How and Why*, Basingstoke: Palgrave MacMillan.

Bayliss, K. and B. Fine (2021b) "Food, Diet and the Pandemic", *Theory and Struggle*, vol 122, no 1, pp. 46–57.

Becker, G. (1975) "A Theory of the Allocation of Time", *Economic Journal*, vol 75, no 299, pp. 493–517.

Becker, G. (1991) *A Treatise on the Family*, Cambridge: Harvard University Press.

Becker, G. (1993) *Human Capital: a Theoretical and Empirical Analysis, with Special Reference to Education*, London: University of Chicago Press, third edition.

Becker, G. (1996) *Accounting for Tastes*, Cambridge: Harvard University Press.

Bowden, S. and A. Offer (1994) "Household Appliances and the Use of Time: the United States and Britain Since the 1920s", *Economic History Review*, vol XLVII, no 4, pp. 725–48.

Bowden, S. and A. Offer (1996) "The Technological Revolution that Never Was: Gender, Class, and the Diffusion of Household Appliances in Interwar England", in de Grazia and Furlough (eds) (1996), pp. 244–74.

Bowden, S. and A. Offer (1999) "Household Appliances and 'Systems of Provision' – A Reply", *Economic History Review*, vol LII, no 3, pp. 563–67.

Brewer, R. and R. Porter (eds) (1993) *Consumption and the World of Goods*, London: Routledge.

Carrier, J. and D. Miller (eds) (1998) *Virtualism: the New Political Economy*, London: Berg.

Coffin, J. (1994) "Credit, Consumption, and Images of Women's Desires: Selling the Sewing Machine in Nineteenth-Century France", *French Historical Studies*, vol 18, no 3, pp. 749–83.

Coffin, J. (1996) "Consumption, Production, and Gender: the Sewing Machine in Nineteenth Century France", in Frader and Rose (eds), pp. 111–41.

de Grazia, V. (1996) "Introduction", in de Grazia and Furlough (eds) (1996), pp. 1–10.

de Grazia, V. and E. Furlough (eds) (1996) *The Sex of Things: Gender and Consumption in Historical Perspective*, London: University of California Press.

Fine, B. (1992) *Women's Employment and the Capitalist Family*, London: Routledge, reprinted 2011/12.

Fine, B. (1995) "Reconsidering 'Household Labor, Wage Labor, and the Transformation of the Family'", *Review of Radical Political Economics*, vol 27, no 1, pp. 107–125.

Fine, B. (1997a) "The New Revolution in Economics", *Capital and Class*, no 61, Spring, pp. 143–48.

Fine, B. (1997b) "Playing the Consumption Game", *Consumption, Markets, Culture*, vol 1, no 1, pp. 7–29.

Fine, B. (1998a) "The Triumph of Economics: Or 'Rationality' Can Be Dangerous to Your Reasoning", in Carrier and Miller (eds) (1998), pp. 49–74.

Fine, B. (1998b) *The Political Economy of Diet, Health and Food Policy*, London: Routledge, reprinted 2013.

Fine, B. (1999a) "From Becker to Bourdieu: Economics Confronts the Social Sciences", *International Papers in Political Economy*, vol 5, no 3, pp. 1–43.

Fine, B. (1999b) "A Question of Economics: Is It Colonising the Social Sciences?", *Economy and Society*, vol 28, no 3, pp. 403–25.

Fine, B. (2002) *The World of Consumption: the Material and Cultural Revisited*, London: Routledge.

Fine, B., N. Foster, J. Simister and J. Wright (1992) "Access to Phones and Democracy in Personal Communication: Myth or Reality?", SOAS Working Papers in Economics, no 20.

Fine, B., M. Heasman and J. Wright (1996) *Consumption in the Age of Affluence: the World of Food*, London: Routledge.

Fine, B. and E. Leopold (1990) "Consumerism and the Industrial Revolution", *Social History*, vol 15, no 2, pp. 151–79.

Fine, B. and E. Leopold (1993) *The World of Consumption*, London: Routledge, revised edition, 2002.

Frader, L. and S. Rose (eds) (1996) *Gender and Class in Modern Europe*, Ithaca: Cornell University Press.

Kotz, D. (1994) "Household Labor, Wage Labor, and the Transformation of the Family", *Review of Radical Political Economics*, vol 26, no 2, pp. 24–56.

Peiss, K. (1996) "Making Up, Making Over: Cosmetics, Consumer Culture, and Women's Identity", in de Grazia and Furlough (eds), pp. 311–36.

Seiter, E. (1993) *Sold Separately: Children and Parents in Consumer Culture*, New Brunswick: Rutgers University Press.

CHAPTER 5

The Economics of Identity and the Identity of Economics?

> It's identity, stupid. Not cost and benefit.
> MCCLOSKEY (1999, p. 52)

∙∙∙

> But economists, whether conservative or radical, think the answer to a 'why' question is always 'some material advantage'.
> MCCLOSKEY (1999, p. 198)

∙∙
∙

Postscript as Personal Preamble

This chapter is based on an article that was drafted just prior to the Global Financial Crisis, although published just afterwards. It is correspondingly free of any reference to it whatsoever. Instead, it reflects the chronological midpoint in the trajectory of my work on economics imperialism (or the colonisation of other social sciences by mainstream economics) which began with Fine (1997), with Fine (2019a) as my most recent contribution,[1] although the watershed of interest in economics imperialism had already passed, see Chapter 2.

The paper itself has an interesting history. As is apparent, it is a response to Akerlof and Kranton (2000) who adopted the simple expedient of treating identity as if it were a variable in a utility function (with social identities corresponding to aggregated common choices over available identities abstractly defined without substance as such). By the standards of the huge, longstanding and diverse literatures on the nature and sources of identities, this is simply laughable, especially in light of postmodernist accounts and their spawns.

---

[1] See Fine (2019b) for a more rounded account in passing and, for economics imperialism at length, see Fine and Milonakis (2009).

In any case, there is the height of irony for explanations for identity to be based upon a technical apparatus of given utility functions for which "identity" is already necessarily assumed to be defined only in the narrowest of terms (of one goal, utility maximisation, on the basis of given preferences on objects which have predetermined, more or less physical, properties). One of my intentions was, however, to set aside these gargantuan weaknesses in the specification of identity and confine myself to two goals. The first was to address the mainstream (and Akerlof and Kranton in particular) on its own terms, as the thin end of an analytical wedge to expose how inappropriately identity was being conceived. Second was to be pragmatic in terms of meticulously exposing criticisms in substance and form in a way that might be comprehensible to, and unavoidable by, the mainstream. As a result, the contribution is mostly concerned with how treating identity à la Akerlof and Kranton does not get past first base of mainstream preference theory itself for, as is well-known, there are well-established technical conditions that must be met for preferences to be representable by a utility function at all. These are not liable to be met by choices over identities!

Despite such bending over backwards to accommodate the mainstream on its own terms, when the article was sent to the *Quarterly Journal of Economics*, where the original appeared, it was returned immediately without being refereed on the grounds of being of insufficient interest to the readership.[2] I also received no response from Akerlof and Kranton to whom the comment was sent although it was acknowledged by return if I remember correctly. This raises serious doubts, if ever this were questioned, over whether the mainstream is ready and willing, let alone capable, of debating its own content even on its own, narrowest of terms.[3] Eventually, the piece was published in the *Cambridge Journal of Economics*.

But that is not the whole story. With the summary rejection by the QJE, I was left high and dry as far as an academic comment on a contribution is concerned. If it will not be published, even considered to be blunt, where the original appeared, why would another journal take it on? Undeterred, I decided to try the *Journal of Economic Issues* and, after consultation with editor(s), amended the commentary to suit their purposes by adding more exposition and bringing in the relationship with institutional economics. The piece was

---

[2] The same happened to another piece on economics imperialism commenting on Lazear (2000), eventually published as Fine (2002a).

[3] For similar experiences, with their own twists, at the hands of the World Bank, see Fine (2004 and 2010).

still not accepted.[4] But, for the purposes of the CJE, the article had to be revised once more to suit its referees, which involved taking out both the institutional stuff and the discussion of an alternative approach to identity (and material culture) around the 6Cs, now 10Cs, see below.

In the version here, the latter content has been restored to the published version together with some reorganisation. But the short, previously drafted discussion on institutional economics now follows albeit with minor revisions. The starting point is that it would inevitably, possibly not on second thoughts, come as a surprise to readers of the *Journal of Economic Issues* that A&K should claim to be bringing the question of identity into economic analysis as if it had previously been absent. The notion of identity has always been prominent in institutional economics, old and new. Indeed, the notion of institution itself, formal or informal, has been so widely understood that it necessarily incorporates some reference to the socially formed individual, as opposed to isolated economic rationality. A&K's suggestion, then, of bringing in identity anew involves omissions in relation to the heavy weight of earlier treatments – if not within the mainstream, but what else is there for A&K.

This is not so much true, however, of A&K with respect to the new institutional economics. Not only is there occasionally explicit reference to such work but also, as will be seen, A&K adopt a methodology that entirely conforms to its approach (and might be considered to be a contribution to it). Significantly, a later contribution, A&K (2005),[5] implicitly falls under the new institutional economics by virtue of its title let alone subject matter, "Identity and the Economics of Organizations". For, as Richter (2005, p. 171), himself the longstanding editor of the *Journal of Institutional and Theoretical Economics*, suggests the new institutional economics is primarily based upon mainstream, neoclassical economics:

> the foundation stones of the NIE are the same as those of neoclassical economics: methodological individualism and individual rational choice given a set of constraints. However, due to transactions or information costs, information is limited and thus institutions matter.

---

4 In looking through file copies to draft the version appearing here, I came across the JEI version and my correspondence to its editors. I had previously forgotten all about this, presuming I had gone straight from QJE to CJE!

5 This is a shorter version of A&K (2003) that is distinguished from the later by allowing one reference each to Ronald Coase and Oliver Williamson, the founding parents of new institutional economics, alongside Douglass North.

Yet, Richter is too extreme. The NIE does tend to have neoclassical economics at its core but it also adopts mixed or dirty approaches in which economic rationality is complemented by the irrational, or the individual by the social. This has been characteristic of Akerlof's research programme in general (Akerlof 1990, p. 61). And A&K's treatment of identity is equally designed to incorporate the insights from other social sciences.

As will be seen, such interdisciplinary ventures are, however, severely constrained since they are confined to those contributions to the economics of identity that are interpreted (falsely) to be or are compatible with neoclassical economics. It is not surprising, then, that A&K should overlook the major contributions from within heterodox economics that can be perceived to have addressed the economics of identity, those deriving from the old institutional economics in general and American Institutionalism in particular, quite apart from continuing contributions to these traditions.

For, for the old institutional economics, departure from *homo economicus* is something of an article of faith in two broad directions.[6] The first is to point to more rounded individuals with a broader set of motivations and capacities. The second is to locate these in the context of socially and historically determining factors. In short, individuals make their own identities but not in circumstances made by themselves. As Davis (2003) has argued, social science has offered two critiques of economic rationality, and these are germane to the issue of (individual) identity. How do the social influences impact upon the individual, and how does the individual internalise such influences. A&K do address these issues but, as observed, in ways severely constrained by their economic approach.

In contrast, for old institutionalism, Veblen's contributions are the starting point for a discussion of identity, ranging over conspicuous consumption (and emulation and distinction) and the tensions between business enterprise (search for profit) and the industrial process (innovative spirit), themselves derived from underlying human propensities. For Veblen, these and other factors are socially and historically specific and subject to evolutionary dynamics. Interestingly, Becker and Murphy (2000, p. 5) reveal in their study of the "social" that:

> We were surprised to discover, upon rereading Thorstein Veblen's influential *Theory of the Leisure Class* ... that he anticipated many of our results, although he does not make a systematic analysis.

---

6   And, much the same is true of, and from before, the "old" marginalism of Alfred Marshall.

Thus, there is some acknowledgement of the salient precedent set by Veblen but his analysis is reconstructed by Becker and Murphy systematically on the basis of a rational choice methodology that he had himself rejected. In case of A&K, however, Veblen simply does not figure.

This is despite, possibly because of, a more than usually heavy dependence upon literature other than mainstream economics, although this is primarily drawn from social sciences other than economics. One explanation, even excuse, for this might be the lack of explicit discussion of identity in heterodox economics literature. Remarkably, an electronic search over the term for available contributions from the *Journal of Economic Issues* only yielded seventeen items. In part, this is because inheritors of old institutionalism (those that reject mainstream economics) tend to take the rational *individual* as their point of departure and conduct analysis in such terms rather than by explicit reference to, and analysis of, *identity*.[7]

In the event, A&K and the economics of identity have not taken off. Even in the decade or so since this episode, the mainstream has moved on. Identity economics à la Akerlof and Kranton has made at most a minimal impact on the discipline. It has been trumped by randomised control trials and behavioural economics which had been hanging around and biding their time.[8] It may, though, have facilitated the shift to what I have characterised as the current phase of economics imperialism, one in which any factor, conceptual fragment or borrowed theory can be brought to bear (often ripped out, and plundered from, other social sciences) irrespective of the coherence or even consistency in doing so whilst the core dependence upon the utility-maximising individual, and more, remains sacrosanct.[9] This is so, even if the core is "suspended" as the sole assumption amongst many behavioural assumptions or as critical point of departure, or deviation, from normal behaviour. In this respect, the mainstream has a longstanding habit, as exemplified by identity economics, whereby the discipline's supposed superiority as social science in light of its mathematical rigour in fact takes second place (as does "realism") whenever it comes into conflict with substantive content.[10]

---

7   A major and continuing exception is to be found in the work of John Davis, cited below.
8   In context of development, see Bédécarrats et al (eds) (2020) and Fine et al (2016).
9   The mainstream still retains the simplest form of an uncontemplated positivism at its core, presuming an external world as given by data (its concession to realism) and to be studied through (statistical) models in lieu of theory if possibly derived, more or less securely or intuitively, from axiomatic mathematical methods that are perceived to represent rigour. Any of this can be suspended to suit inclusion of explanatory factors willy-nilly.
10 Of course, the most prominent example is the Cambridge Capital Controversy but this is just one amongst a legion of cases. See Fine (2023).

On a personal note, this paper would not have been possible without deep and extensive knowledge of the axiomatics of social choice theory and preference theory, with which I engaged within the first weeks of becoming a graduate student in economics having graduated in mathematics. From this I draw three lessons. The first is strength of criticism depends upon detailed knowledge of what is being criticised. Second, this is not necessarily a negative exercise but can inform the construction of alternatives by way of critical departure. Third, outcomes in terms of scholarly impact depend neither on the strength of criticism nor strength of alternatives but on the willingness to engage in dialogue and the opportunities for alternatives to prosper, however these might be determined.

And, on a final note of self-congratulation, in my first year as a graduate student in economics, 1969/1970, with first degree in mathematics, I had already tried to use neoclassical economics against itself. The very first paper I submitted for publication was entitled, "Action against the Expectations of Strikes".[11] It focused on the idea that bosses would pay higher wages not just in response to strikes but also in order to prevent them in advance. Although the first use of the theory of efficiency-wages is usually attributed to Alfred Marshall, it is apparent in retrospect, that my paper is an example, and formally a model, of efficiency wages, anticipating a literature to follow with those such as Stiglitz and Akerlof to the fore and contributing to a greater or lesser extent to their Nobel Prizes.

The paper was submitted to Oxford Economic Papers and its editor, John Flemming, ultimately Chief Economist at the Bank of England, took the trouble to meet with me to explain why it should not be published – I was not convinced he understood or accepted its implications. Unfortunately, I cannot find a copy of the paper to post, although I would never have thrown it away other than by accident. But, as chance would have it, I did show it to Stefan Szymanski who was working on such things at Birkbeck in the second half of the 1980s. He agreed that it did anticipate modern efficiency-wage theory. He went on to become a leading figure in sports economics.

---

11 My sister-in-law, Danny (Anne Fine), kindly typed it for me on a manual machine, such was the technology (and my own typing skills) at the time. She found better uses for her talents, especially those less mundane than typing, as a novelist, predominantly but not exclusively children's fiction, ultimately becoming the second Children's Laureate, holding the role between May 2001 and May 2003, Madame Doubtfire and all. Kit, now her ex-husband, also contributed to my publications – as the co-author of two classic contributions to social choice theory (Fine and Fine 1974a and b) now being applied to the rankings of wine and professional sports players, Barberà et al (2023) and Kondratev et al (2023), respectively.

1   Introduction[12]

It is appropriate that George Akerlof should have co-authored an article, "Economics and Identity" (Akerlof and Kranton 2000, A&K hereafter).[13] Thirty years earlier, his "Market for Lemons", Akerlof (1970), broadened the possibilities open to economics by incorporating non-economic issues into its analysis. "Economics imperialism" had previously relied upon Becker-style reduction of all economic and social phenomena to an as if market analysis, with individual optimisation, efficiency and equilibrium to the fore.[14] With the new information-theoretic economics, as it has been dubbed, emphasis is placed upon market, especially informational, imperfections and their consequences for market *and* non-market outcomes. Although these can be based upon motives other than utility maximisation, conformity to norms, altruism, the formation of formal and informal institutions more generally, and so on, can also be reduced to individual optimisation in response to endogenously-created, path-dependent market and non-market imperfections.

Such developments within economics have prodigiously extended the scope and palatability of economic analysis as far as the other social sciences are concerned, Fine and Milonakis (2009) for an extensive discussion of the logic, history and applications of this new phase of economics imperialism. That identity should now come within the orbit of economics is both symbolic of the previously shifting relations between the discipline and the other social sciences and a contribution to its continuing programme of colonisation of non-economic subject matter. As A&K put it, p. 716:[15]

> Because of its explanatory power, numerous scholars in psychology, sociology, political science, anthropology, and history have adopted identity as a central concept. This paper shows how identity can be brought into economic analysis, allowing a new view of many economic problems.

---

12   Originally published as Fine (2009a) but see preamble. Also translated into Turkish, with English introduction from which some part of the preamble is taken (Fine 2021).
13   Reference is to A&K (2000) unless otherwise indicated. See also A&K (2002, 2003 and 2005) and the section on "Economic Consequences of Social Identity", *American Economic Review*, Papers and Proceedings, vol 96, no 2, pp. 206–21, these P&Ps being overseen by Akerlof himself.
14   See Lazear (2000) for an account of the triumph of Becker-style economics imperialism, and Fine (2002a) for a critical assessment of his claims.
15   See also A&K (2003, p. 45, and 2005, p. 27).

If economics now addresses identity, it surely has the capacity to address more or less everything across the social sciences since identity, however understood and determined, underpins all action.

This chapter proceeds at three different levels. The first is an *internal* critique, offering a close scrutiny on its own terms of the notion of identity that is used by A&K. In section 2, this is done by exploring the relationship between preferences over identity and their possible representation by utility functions, the procedure adopted by A&K. This is followed in section 3 by noting and deploying a parallel between the economics of identity and social choice theory. A similar conclusion can be drawn across both sections – the uncertainty of outcome as far as the definition and/or determination of identity is concerned in contrast to A&K's own reduction of identity to a logic of choice. In other words, the results or needs of neoclassical economics can be turned against itself if it attempts to incorporate identity in the way attempted by A&K.[16]

To a large extent, at this first level, discussion works within the framework adopted by A&K, drawing out its intrinsic contradictory implications, much like Cambridge capital theory and its consequences for aggregate capital and the production function for example. These present problems that cannot be resolved within the approach adopted and that has created them. In short, Sections 2 and 3 informally draw upon technical results within mainstream economics, concerning preference representation and social (as identity) choice theory, to question the viability of A&K's approach to identity. In Section 4, moving to a different level, this provides the basis on which to address what has been omitted from A&K's treatment, precisely because it is an *economics* of identity, especially from the perspective of the other social sciences. In part, this is because of A&K's exclusive reliance upon the choice and distribution of *given* identities (or identity possibilities) rather than the *creation* of identity by reflecting subjects. Whilst this still focuses upon identity as a consequence of individual practice, it points to the need for a systemic understanding of identity that is far from compatible with an economic approach to identity unless the most important *social* determinants are, surely unacceptably, taken as exogenous to the individuals, taken alone or in aggregation.

In Section 5, the discussion moves to a further level, that of the nature of economics itself. Why has economics addressed identity now and in the way that it has? This raises a number of issues around the implications for the discipline of its trespassing into what has traditionally been the subject matter

---

16   See Fine (2023).

of other disciplines. Is this liable to reform or even to fracture the orthodoxy? Or, as argued here, is it more of the same blundering across a wider terrain of subject matter and influence without regard to the technical and conceptual incoherence that results? In short, as suggested in the concluding remarks, the literature on the economics of identity exposes the intellectual limitations and fragility of orthodoxy without disturbing its stranglehold over the discipline in the slightest.

2   Identity as Individual Choice

From a technical point of view, A&K define identity in a complex manner. Subject to constraints, individuals can choose actions and attributes that affect their own identity *and* the identity of others. This means that identity is not like other goods as it is necessarily subject to "a new type of externality", p. 717. In short, identity is a common attribute across individuals and can only emerge from some degree of uniformity across some individuals in practice. Thus, for example, masculinity might be defined as what males do and is an aggregated outcome based on what males choose. But individuals are not entirely free to choose their own identity given that it may be imposed upon them in light of others' behaviours and perceptions – to be female without wishing to be feminine. Others may attribute an identity to others, and behave towards them accordingly, in light of the implicit identity signalled by given or chosen characteristics for example, For simplicity for the moment, the potentially complex structure determining identity will be set aside, and identity will be considered only as a matter of choice, leaving aside intermediate links between action, reaction and outcomes. At most this is to leave aside the constraints endogenously imposed on individual free choice of identity. It may not be possible for a male to choose to be female or vice-versa in some sense for example.

In formal terms, an *i*th individual's utility is given by $u^i(x, I_i, I)$ where x is a vector of goods, I_i an identity chosen by individual i, and I the vector of social identities to which I_i marginally contributes alongside all other individuals. Thus, individual choice ranges over states of the world in which group identities emerge and constrain what can be chosen (whether to conform or not to the choices of others). This sort of interaction between micro and macro is, of course, standard in economic theory in which all options are laid out for the individual before they are constrained by exogenous (technology, endowments) or endogenous factors (others' aggregated actions). This is so for the micro-foundations of macro, for example, and its explanation for demand-constrained unemployment.[17] For, A&K, though, p. 717:

> Because identity is fundamental to behavior, choice of identity may be the most important "economic" decision people make. Individuals may – more or less consciously – choose who they want to be. Limits on this choice may also be the most important determinant of an individual's economic well-being.

More explicitly, and specifically in case of schooling, A&K (2002, p. 1168) use:

> a model where students maximize utility by making two choices. They choose their social category, and they choose effort in school.

And just as identity conforms to the logic of choice, so that logic is attached to utility because, for workers, "identity is a component in a worker's utility" (A&K 2005, p. 22).

Possibly unconsciously, A&K *incorporate* what are given notions of identity into their economic analysis in at least two separate ways that might be presumed to be, but which are not, equivalent.[18] One is to enter an identity variable into a *utility* function. The other is to present a set of two alternatives, red and green for example, over which there are *preferences*. Each of these approaches is more general than the other in one respect. In principle, the utility function is capable of varying over a continuous set and vector of identity variables, certainly more than two. On the other hand, the *ordering* of identity across (two) alternative options is not dependent on a utility function and corresponding numerical assignment of utility to outcomes.

Of course, this is elementary from the theory of representation of preferences by utility functions from within mainstream economics. And the most general formulation, incorporating each of the two options adopted as special cases, is for the individual to order a set of identities without presuming that these can be represented by a utility function unless certain conditions are satisfied.

---

17 See Akerlof (2006) for the reconstruction of Keynesian macroeconomics on the basis of the economics of identity.
18 To avoid confusion, it should be emphasised that this subtle distinction between two different but closely related ways of incorporating *given* notions of identity is itself different from the two different ways, equally subtle, of *defining* identity attached to A&K, and discussed below in Section 4 in light of Russell's paradoxes.

But can this more general formulation make sense in the context of identity as understood by A&K? The answer is surely in the affirmative. Taking the red and green, two-option case, it is reasonable to presume that these are not necessarily mutually exclusive and exhaustive. An individual may prefer to be red *and* green and not just red *or* green. Or preferred identity may be one of a little bit red and a lot green. In other words, red-green identities fill out a two-dimensional space, although each variable might be normalised to a range between zero and one, or between minus one and plus one.

Consequently, representing preferences over identity is potentially analogous to representing preferences over the commodity space in standard consumer theory. But, then, are the axioms for revealed preferences as a utility function reasonable when applied to identity? It will be shown that the answer is negative although the reasons for this draw upon what are liable to be unfamiliar, even esoteric, results from the fundamentals of the logic of choice. Economists are so habituated to making whatever assumptions are necessary to allow the application of utility functions and the like that these assumptions tend to escape critical scrutiny in those applications. This is surely why A&K seamlessly plug the variables for identity into a utility function without a backward glance at the conditions necessary to do so.

Thus, one necessary condition for the existence of a corresponding utility function is that the preferences be continuous, with lexicographic orderings being the most obvious example breaching this condition. Yet, such discontinuity is highly likely in case of identity where, for example, commitment to being a little bit redder takes precedence over being any degree of green.[19] Indeed, it can be argued that the construction of identity is lexicographical by its nature, as you are a criminal, for example, once transgressing as opposed to approaching a boundary defined by law (Hill 2005).

This signals a warning against the use of utility functions, and continuity, in addressing (the economics of) identity. However, there are other conditions apart from continuity, necessary for a preference ordering to be representable by a utility function. Transitivity, often taken for granted, is problematic. Elsewhere, I have addressed three reasons why transitivity might be violated for preference orderings, fully exploring the set-theoretic logic of the choice sets that are involved (Fine 1995a). Each of these reasons, and its relevance for identity, are discussed below, drawing as briefly as possible upon the technical results from the earlier paper.

---

19   For simplicity of presentation, it will be assumed on occasion, without loss of generality, that orderings of red and green, etc are monotonically increasing in depth of colour.

One rationale for breach of transitivity is because of *finite perception*.[20] In case of greenness for example, there can be different shades, potentially ordered in sequence of darkness and lightness, but for which individual distinction is only possible if there is sufficient depth of difference between shades. We may wish to be as green as possible but not always know that or when a little more is indeed more. Further, such a possibility carries over to being green as identity for which shades of difference in political stance are far from transparent or necessarily open to expression (except, interestingly, at the extremes where sectarianism and holier than thou tend to reign supreme as minor differences in vegetarianism or degrees of commitment to political correctness can run riot).[21]

If finite perception is a problem in expressing preferences, then those preferences do satisfy *quasi*-transitivity, that is transitivity of *strict* preference but not necessarily of indifference. If x is noticeably greener than y, y of z, then x is of z. But if x is not noticeably greener than y, and similarly of y for z, x can still be noticeably greener than z. This is if the difference in greenness between x and z is sufficient to distinguish them, and each of the differences between x and y and y and z is less than sufficient but greater than half the difference.

It is possible to show that a quasi-transitive ordering is not necessarily due to finite perception.[22] Indeed, finite perception orderings are precisely a subset of quasi-orderings known as semi-orders.[23] For semi-orders, it is intuitively apparent that choices can be broken down into a series of overlapping, or thick (by degree of perception), indifference sets or curves. Distinct choice of identity can be made *between* these indifference sets but not *within* them. In other words, there is a potential boundary of uncertainty around presenting and choosing one's own identity as well as in interpreting those of others (in order to be able to "belong" or not). In other words, identity is fuzzy.

---

20   I have two neat, but very different examples, from my experience of finite perception. The thread to my car tyre pump became worn and slipped off the connectors. So I added two connectors in tandem, one to smaller fitting before going back to the original fitting which then did not slip. It worked meaning the fittings were not transitive but were sharing the wear sufficiently to overcome it. More serious is the observation that with brain degeneration, we cannot see change from day to day but can see it over a longer period.

21   Fine (1995a) explores the implications of difference, rather than constancy, in degree of finite perception as an ordering ranges over alternatives.

22   At least of fixed or additive perceptive difference. Without this, the degree of perception might vary in each pair-wise comparison so that perception across a transitive chain does not carry over reducing the ordering to quasi-transitivity alone.

23   Results stated here depend occasionally on the set of alternatives being finite, or at least countable. Where they are not, as in two, or more, dimensional space, this worsens the problems highlighted as there is a countable subset of alternative identities to order.

To a large extent, a second reason why transitivity might be violated, incomplete expression, can be seen as the mathematical dual of finite perception. For the latter, there are too many *indifferences* between alternatives as a result of being unable to distinguish between them. Incomplete expression arises when there are too many *strict* preferences (too few indifferences) expressed because only one choice is needed, or is possible, in practice. I may, for example, be indifferent between being red and green but I do want a pure identity, so choosing one or the other – indistinguishable from being truly red (green) and not green (red) at all. Unlike finite perception, incomplete expression is a complete pain to interpret in practice, although transparent in principle. This is because any choice of identity is consistent with complete indifference across all identities! At most, it is possible to determine indifferences that *must* hold between identities, if I switch between red and green for example, or most generally if each of two identities is shown to be directly or indirectly preferred to the other. Otherwise, there is a band of uncertainty between those necessary indifferences over identity and total indifference across all identities.

A third reason for violation of transitivity is the presence of *multiple* criteria.[24] My choice of identity might be to be as green and as red as possible. In this case, an identity of redness-greenness only dominates another if it is darker in both respects. Unless one of two identities dominates the other, they will be treated as equivalent. It is readily shown that each multiple criteria ordering satisfies quasi-transitivity (as a result of transitivity of vector dominance) but also that each quasi-transitive order is equivalent to an appropriately defined (multiple) criteria ordering. In other words, quasi-transitivity and criteria orderings are essentially equivalent to one another and, as previously suggested, more general than finite perception orderings. Quasi-transitive orderings are also equivalent to satisfying dominance by every finite ranking rule (assigning progressively lower scores to lower order elements in the ranking of identity and ordering identities by overall score), Fine and Fine (1974a and b) for a comprehensive derivation. Once again, this carries with it a natural interpretation of uncertainty over identity. In general, full transitivity can only be guaranteed by restricting the class of all finite ranking rules to just one through which definite judgement can be reached. In other words, by how much do I weigh redness against greenness, etc, Fine (1996) for a full discussion.

---

24   A&K accept that, "an individual may be mapped into several social categories (e.g., individual j is both a 'woman' and a 'professional')", p. 718. They do not consider whether there are continuities in being both! Multiple identities are emphasised by Amartya Sen in critique both of the disregard of identity and its reduction to singularity. And, failure to acknowledge and deploy multiple identities is conducive to violence (Sen 2006).

In short, the logic of choice by the individual alone over a set of available identities suggests that it is unreasonable to expect to be able to represent identity by choice attached to a utility function. Yet, as emphasised, this is something that is done more or less automatically by A&K, without question, and hardly surprising in view of the way in which utility functions are a standard tool in the economist's toolkit.

3   Identity as Social Choice

By focusing on the problems associated with translating choice over identity into a utility function, especially in the context of violation of transitivity, the previous section has revealed the uncertainty, possibly the ambiguity, that surrounds choice of identity in case of finite perception, incomplete expression and multiple criteria. Significantly, the formal results deployed, and informally utilised, have been previously derived from an apparently different literature – that of social choice theory.

In this respect, two different aspects are involved. First, as just covered, there is the logical structure of (individual) choice itself in case of violation of transitivity. This has been of concern within social choice theory because, for example, of the wish to weaken the form taken by social choice from full transitivity in light of the impossibility theorems attached to social choice.

Second, though, the problem of choosing identity has a close, formal and informal, parallel with the problems of social choice theory. Essentially, I observe the ordering by all other individuals of the available identities (equivalent to social alternatives in social choice theory), and decide on my own ordering of those identities (equivalent to being the social choice theorist). In short, I wish to choose my identity in view of those available to me but also by incorporating the identities chosen (or ordered) by others. This raises two problems. One is common at the core of social choice (theory) itself – how to choose an identity (alternative) out of the identities (alternatives) chosen or ranked by others. As is commonly observed in social choice theory, this is subject to impossibility theorems so that questions remain over the capacity to make such choices (let alone represent them by a utility function) unless some of the corresponding axioms associated with social choice are weakened. As the choice of identity (out of the preferences of others for identity) is formally equivalent to social choice theory, all of the impossibility theorems associated with social choice theory apply equally to A&K's approach to identity. Individuals cannot choose an identity to satisfy reasonable conditions, quite apart from whether it can be represented by a utility function or not.

The second problem arising out of the parallel between social choice theory and choice of identity has been relatively marginal within the social choice literature but is essential to identity. This is that individual and social choice are subject both to interdependent preferences (I will be green if you will be) and/or game-theoretic strategic choice (ditto). As I have shown in interpretation of Sen's Paretian liberal, this means the simultaneous determination of both (interdependent) preferences and outcomes (Fine 1975). Interestingly, A&K make passing reference to the problems posed by the Paretian liberal (but not the impossibility theorem derived by Sen) but only in the narrow context of interdependent *outcomes* (through externalities), p. 731.[25] If this is extended to preferences themselves over identity – each individual wants to be like the others and, at most, has preferences over what the others' preferences would ideally be – then there is a danger of infinite regress over the definition of identity itself and its interaction with outcomes. Something must be taken as exogenous, or as a fixed starting point, or any configuration of preferences and outcomes is possible. So, it is hardly surprising that A&K reach the conclusion that they can derive predictions, "that are different from those of existing economic models", p. 716. This is inevitable given that there is the potential for multiple equilibria in which each equilibrium corresponds to a set of mutually supportive preferences or identities that is not fixed. In short, if everybody wants to be like everybody else, we have no idea what the outcome will be (or there has to be a first mover or the like).

Just to belabour the point, suppose that my preference, like that of all others, is to be as like everybody else as possible and that this takes precedence over my secondary criteria of being as green as possible. Then, each level of greenness is an equilibrium. Of course, the parallel with price determination for Bertrand oligopoly (repeated game) is striking, a point revisited below.[26]

4   Identity and the Social

The difficulties revealed in the previous sections are derived by developing the implications for identity of the approach adopted by A&K. Essentially, it involves adding identity to the pre-existing apparatus of neoclassical economics, most notably through its incorporation as an argument into a utility

---

25   But A&K do acknowledge such interdependence, see footnote 5, p. 719.
26   Note that if everyone wants to be different from others as first criterion (but as green as possible as second) we all jostle for being pure green without ever settling there, a little like Hotelling's ice-cream sellers at the centre of the beach.

function. From a formal point of view, on its own terms, this has been shown to be problematic. Individuals will have considerable difficulty in identifying let alone in choosing their own identity and that of others as they seek to handle the problems associated with finite perception, incomplete expression, multiple criteria, social choice, impossibility theorems, interdependent preferences, multiple equilibria and strategic decisionmaking.

No doubt, as with A&K, one way of proceeding is simply to overlook or ignore these fundamental conundrums, as is common across neoclassical theory when its own mathematical rigour, on the basis of given techniques, yields unpalatable results, not least, for example, Arrow's impossibility theorem in case of social choice theory.[27] Technique tends to take precedence over mathematical rigour when the two are incompatible (Moscati 2005 and Fine and Milonakis 2009). An alternative, though, is to abandon the attempt to construct a social category, such as identity, on the basis of the aggregated (optimising) behaviour of individuals. As shown by Fine (2011), this is even a logical requirement in the sense that the social cannot be derived from the aggregated individual without the risk of running into logical, that is mathematical inconsistencies.

This is all a consequence of Bertrand Russell's paradoxes in investigating the set-theoretic foundations of mathematics. It is easy enough to tie these to the issue of identity. If, for example, we define identity in terms of a property that a set of individuals share in common, then what about those that wish not to have an identity (counter-culture as it were). This is self-contradictory in so far as those not wishing to have an identity have that identity (just as being unfashionable can become a fashion)! Lest this be considered some sort of linguistic trick, it is precisely such conundrums that needed to be resolved in order to provide mathematics with rigorous foundations. It would be bizarre for a discipline that prided itself on its mathematical rigour to overlook the pre-conditions for that mathematics itself to be rigorous. And, as shown in Fine (2011), the solutions to be found in mathematics are essentially to abandon the hope of deriving the social from the individual or to require the individual to conform to the social rather than vice-versa.

More specifically, A&K essentially *define* the notion of identity in two distinct ways, quite apart from deploying it in two distinct ways as previously discussed (within utility functions and as an ordering). One is set-theoretic by appeal to set membership, as in gathering together each person who is, or

---

27   For which Arrow's theorem is not as great an obstacle as first appears, Fine and Fine (1974a and b), and Fine and Mendes Loureiro (2021).

considers self to be, green or whatever. The other is set-theoretic in terms of a relational property, notably greenness. The latter is what we generally mean by identity, what it is to be French for example, as a series of characteristics to which individuals are attached to a greater or lesser extent.[28] A&K appear simply and unconsciously to presume that these two ways of defining identity are either the same or at least mutually compatible. But, in general, they are not. Indeed, it is because of this that Russell's paradox arises and the foundations of mathematics were in need of careful reformulation. To avoid inconsistencies, it is necessary to place restrictions either on the membership or the relational definition of sets (or both). There are ways of doing this that preserve consistency and the properties of mathematics that we use in daily life, primarily by restricting the relational properties that are allowed to define sets.[29] But, as was also realised, such restrictions are entirely arbitrary in terms of the *application* of mathematics to the *non-mathematical*, to identity for example. These would require restrictions specific to the object of inquiry itself. And, as identity is first and foremost a relational property, this should serve as starting point, and with which individual membership should conform rather than vice-versa, Fine (2011) for fuller discussion.

This casts doubt on the methods employed by A&K irrespective of the problems revealed on the basis of techniques used *within* that method to define and use identity. In this respect, a starting point for an alternative is the observation that the uncertainty around identity already revealed previously on individualistic terms is compounded, if not dominated, by a factor yet to be considered, both here and by A&K.

This is that identity is reflexive, and not simply chosen, imposed or induced. Identity, as has been unduly emphasised to the extreme by certain currents within postmodernism, is invented, worked upon, practised and speculatively developed by those that adopt it, consciously or otherwise.[30] Even with a simple dualism between red and green, it is possible to go far beyond different shades and mixtures of each to embrace shapes and patterns of infinite variety (not least national flags and so on).

So analysis of identity should move beyond *identification* (with what is given) that seems to encapsulate the identity in the utility function approach

---

28 As opposed to a "German" definition that might be considered to be more membership-oriented as those individuals who are contained within particular territories.
29 Although as Gödel showed, there remain problems of decidability.
30 A&K accept that identity may be chosen unconsciously, when "maximizing a utility function", p. 719, but our conscious and unconscious do much more than choose! And, by the same token, identity is more than "a person's sense of self", p. 715, it is also *creation* of self.

adopted by A&K for whom the emergence of new identities, as opposed to identification with those already potentially available, is precluded. A&K do refer to identification as a critical part of an "internalization process", p. 728. But internalization should not be confined to passive receipt of given identities but incorporate the reworking of these into self-identity.

Thus, for example, in a model of schooling, A&K explicitly follow the lead given by Coleman (1961), with a number of stereotypes taken as given to which students choose to attach themselves or not – nerds, jocks, leading crowd, burnouts, etc. Significantly, Coleman's own analysis of educational achievement has been thoroughly discredited, and, by chance, he has been a leading light in the promotion of rational choice sociology at the University of Chicago, having run a seminar with Gary Becker and established the journal *Rationality and Society*.[31] Such guilt by association aside, what is crucial here methodologically is that identities have to be taken as given externally in order that the whole technical apparatus of the economic approach to identity can be adopted. Individuals choose their identity from those available in light of external constraints that might themselves at most be endogenously created by the overall actions of all individuals.

This means that A&K's approach depends upon a sharp division between identity as chosen by the individual and the external influences on those choices (whether exogenous or endogenously the product of those individual choices). Such, for example, is the way in which Burawoy's study of work norms and efforts is interpreted by A&K. It leads to the idea that employers would do better to appeal to, and nurture, workers' loyalty and cooperation rather than to their cash nexus. But there is far more to worker identity than this for their loyalties and cooperation can reside outside as well as inside the firm, to a trade union for example with broader economic, political and ideological goals. It is all very well for employers to encourage cooperation (trade unions) but, by doing so, there is no presumption that the change in identity will be confined within the firm and to greater effort on its behalf. The decisive analytical point is that the technical apparatus of neoclassical economics, when turned upon identity, illegitimately constructs it as a relationship of choice between the individual and a given environment. In contrast, at the very least, the individual alone is able to change that environment (and by joining a trade union, this becomes internal to the firm as well and not just external).

---

31 For detailed commentary on Coleman, see Fine (2001), in the context of his leading role in promoting the notion of social capital, on which see below. See also Fine (2010).

Nor is this purely an academic matter as is obvious from the fierce battles that have been fought over trade union recognition. Such conflicts do not arise out of a logic of individual choice of identity but over the way in which broader social categories will be internalised. What I am as a worker may follow a logic of internal norms and work effort but, equally, it can be about identification with broader goals and organisations. There is no neat separation between the internal and the external, the given and the chosen identities.

Of course, raising subjective development of self-identity in this way reinforces rather than resolves the problems associated with identity as identification. This is because the relationships between social symbols (the image of class for example) and equally social outcomes (the reality of class) cannot be resolved through an analysis that builds up from individuals (with given identities from which to choose). At the very least, it is necessary to adopt a stance on what are the relevant social categories to be taken as exogenous or at least as analytically prior (whether it be class, race or gender), whilst recognising that these have been historically and symbolically determined themselves. A&K's notion of identity as choice (and derived utility) either overlooks such social categories or arbitrarily takes them as given, usually either as superficial stereotypes in practice, the nerd, or as ideal abstractions, red versus green.

Traditionally, the social is a starting point for most *social* science other than economics, not least in its treatment of identity. It reflects a preference, common if not universal given rational choice theory, for systemic analysis over the methodological individualism of a special type (utility maximisation) deployed by mainstream economics. Whilst the latter might extend its techniques beyond the market to address the non-economic, including identity, it does so at the danger and expense of exposing its continuing methodological and, it should be added, technical inadequacies on its own terms as previously exposed in Sections 2 and 3.

These remarks can be illustrated and reinforced by considering identity in the context of the consumer. Whilst, conceptually, consumer theory has stagnated within economics since the marginalist revolution, it has experienced explosive development across the social sciences, especially in the wake of postmodernism. Elsewhere, in critically assessing this literature, I have argued that the consumer can be understood in terms of six Cs (Fine 2002b and 2005).[32] And it is worth examining the extent to which A&K's approach is capable of incorporating these.

---

32   Dugger (1980, p. 901) addresses such issues to some extent, and somewhat obscurely and as a source of corporate power, through the notions of "subreption, contamination, emulation and mystification". For Earp (1996), it is a matter of circuits and networks of

First, consumer identity is Contextual. This is accepted by A&K, but only in a limited way, with identity associated with "who is matched with whom and in what context", recognising that different activities "have different meanings for different people", p. 731. But, as previously if implicitly suggested, this is an extremely narrow notion of context and, it should be added, of meaning, since it involves pre-determined as possibilities rather than subject to the inventive practices of consumers in making their own (not mish mash of old and given) identities.

Second, then, identity is Construed by the individual, reworked on the basis of the context, meanings and possibilities that are available. As much is recognised by those who seek to influence consumers, such as advertisers and politicians, possibly attempting to reinforce, combine or shift existing senses of identity but also forging *new* ones.

Third, consumer identity is Chaotic, shifting between different influences and practices that are often mutually inconsistent. This is because of the multiple identities adopted by consumers. These would appear to be impossible to reconcile with an approach based on (rational) utility maximisation.

Fourth, consumer identity is Constructed (and de- and re-constructed in the vernacular of postmodernism), by an interaction of material and cultural elements. This is in a sense accepted by A&K as identity and outcomes are mutually determined and determining. But this is once again a pale reflection of what construction of identity means in the wake of postmodernism (and before). The consumer lies at the end of a long line of economic and social structures and processes that impart a material and cultural content to those objects of consumption and the consumer – from fashion to life-style, from what it is to be a green product and consumer to the shifting nature of Coke as the "real thing".

---

commerce, state redistribution, and gifts. See Bayliss and Fine (2021) by which time the 6Cs have long been expanded to 10Cs, adding Collective and Closed in Fine (2009) in pursuit of the South African "Rainbow Nation", and Conforming and Commodified in Fine (2013). Note, this is where I bring the process of adding new Cs to an end, p. 226/7: "I have added two from before the conference, Commodified and Conforming, on my own initiative. Others were suggested such as Chimerical, Markus Walz; Communicative, Community-substituting, Colonising, Conquering, Corporate, Concealing, Catastrophic, Congressional, Conciliatory, Cathartic, Constricted, Alan Bradshaw; and Coercive, Conventional, and Commonsensical from myself. Even where these Cs are not Covered by, or the Consequences, of others, or not generally applicable to all cultural systems attached to systems of provision, I have to stop somewhere and ten Cs seems to round things off. Otherwise, subject to alphabetical limitations, there is a danger of reproducing all the elements that go into (the psychology) of marketing and more".

Fifth, consumer identity is Contradictory, not simply in the sense of chaotic suggested above, but in terms of the clash of social forces that interact with one another to give rise to more complex, shifting and uncertain outcomes. This is so, for example, for eating disorders (anorexia, bulimia, obesity), a peculiarly modern phenomenon, resulting from the interaction of the compulsions to eat and to diet that derive from the modern food system and the meanings that it generates alongside other aspects of identity concerning gender, body image and so on (Fine 1995b and 1998). Equilibrium outcomes on the basis of optimising individuals cannot handle such aspects adequately.

Sixth, the making of identity is conflictual or Contested. This is acknowledged by A&K in the sense that, "much conflict occurs because people with different prescriptions or identities come into contact", p. 731. But this scarcely begins to address the problem of how the conflicts over the meaning of identity are fought, consciously or otherwise, through each of the aspects covered and through the exercise of power. Consider, for example, the cases of female circumcision and sati cited by A&K as demonstrating how conformity to identity can enhance the utility of its victims (and hangers on). Eradicating these barbaric practices, however, and especially where they are not willingly embraced, involves structural shifts in power relations through conflict over them as well as the meanings associated with women, sexuality and so on. And conflict over the nature and meaning of identity can be or can be used as the cause of war, as evidenced by different ideas of nationality, as hinted at in earlier footnotes.

In their conclusion, A&K open the prospect of an expanding research agenda for the economics of identity, p. 749:

> Researchers, for example, could consider why notions of "class" or "race" vary across countries; why might gender and racial integration vary across industries; what might explain the rise and fall of ethnic tensions. Such comparative studies would be a fruitful way to explore the formation of identity-based preferences.

In the absence of the 6Cs or the like, it is doubtful how this goal can even be embarked upon. How can the differences in the nature and meaning of the identities themselves be explained, a major focus of the other social sciences, let alone be addressed, and why and how identities are formed and with what effects.

5 The Economics of Identity as Economics Imperialism

In this critical light, it is appropriate to comment on how the economics of identity literature has emerged and evolved. A&K are representative of one strand that is driven more by technique than by substance. It ranges as widely as possible over a subject matter that can be called identity only so long as the analysis can be fitted into a utility maximisation format (or some modification of it) with identity as a variable.[33] As chance would have it, the economics of identity has also emerged out of the work of Amartya Sen (2005 and 2006).[34] This has been more or less ignored by the identity as utility literature, although it has been taken up on the heterodox margins of economics in ways that expose the conceptual inadequacies and problems of the mainstream from a variety of perspectives in addition to those offered here.[35] This offers the opportunity to use the economics of identity to draw some broader and grander conclusions about the current nature and dynamics of economics.

First is the issue of whether initiatives such as the economics of identity represent an *incorporation* and influence of ideas from the social sciences or an appropriation by economics of the subject matter of other disciplines. Is economics colonising the other social sciences or is it vice-versa? And is this a welcome shift in economics or not as it becomes more rounded even if to a limited extent?

Whilst this might appear to be a judgement of whether a glass is half-empty or half-full, interpretation of economics as the aggressor is more appropriate. Consider, for example, for purposes of comparison, Daly's (1982, p. 308) critique of Becker and Tomes (1979) on sexual reproduction:

---

33 See Bénabou and Tirole (2005) for an overview of these approaches, ranging over altruism, greed and self-respect as motives, and across intrinsic, extrinsic and reputational influences.

34 Note that, whilst Sen emphasises multiplicity of identities and reasoned choice over them, he rejects identity as self-discovery. But by this what appears to be meant is learning what is your given but yet to be known identity. He is less open in his views over the discovery of identity through inventively remaking it. He also does not explicitly reject the A&K approach, although he has a long tradition of rejecting rationality as a sole explanatory device, as well as exhibiting a tension between focusing on individual and social determinants. See Fine (2004) for this in the context of Sen's ethics as well as his limited attempts to address the socially constructed meaning of categories of analysis. See also Fine (2018) and concluding remarks.

35 See, for example, the special issue of the *Journal of Economic Methodology*, vol 13, no 3, 2006.

The implications of these assumptions are then elaborated in 25 pages of algebra. Given the exceptionally heroic nature of the assumptions, one would expect a rather heroic, or at least interesting, conclusion. Nevertheless, their main conclusion is rigorously self-evident: "We have shown that the family is more important when the degree of inheritability and the propensity to invest [in children] are larger". One already knows that without making any assumptions or algebraic manipulations; how could it be otherwise? Despite the trivial result, the Becker and Tomes article is extremely interesting in that it reveals just how far some members of the Chicago School will go in amputating those limbs of human society that do not fit the Procrustean bed of individualistic utility maximisation.

Much the same would appear to be true of A&K, despite distance from Chicago. Blindingly obvious conclusions are to be drawn from highly selective and dubious assumptions. For them, for example, in the context of work relations, A&K (2003, p. 42):

> The model suggests at least five separate items that could impact workers' performance.
> (i) social categories/job assignments (the Insiders, Outsiders, or Group members in our models)
> (ii) the identity utility workers derive from a specific job
> (iii) the ideal behavior for jobholders
> (iv) their utility gain from conforming to that ideal
> (v) whether or not firms make investments to change workers' identities.

What is notably absent here, by reference both to the real world and to the world of other social sciences, are questions of conflict and power, in relation to production let alone society more generally. By contrast, as Dugger (1980, p. 897) puts it, "The problems of power and of individuality are intertwined in such a complex fashion that one cannot be understood without understanding the other". And, for Waller (2004, p. 1112), who could well have been anticipating A&K's economics of identity, "if choices are the only characteristics of atomistic individuals, the theory of the individual becomes so reductionist that it ceases to be about human beings".

This is because, second, as an example of economics imperialism more generally than with A&K, the extension of economic analysis to other subject matter is based upon a process of bringing back in what has previously been left out. This is more or less without regard to change in methodology and/or technique in response to the needs of newly introduced concepts and variables. To put it bluntly, from the marginalist revolution onwards, the issue of identity has been discarded in deference to the ill-defined utility-maximising individual. On this basis, a standard technical apparatus has been constructed, with utility and production functions to the fore. Rather than considering the nature of identity as such, on its own merits as it were, it is re-introduced to fit within the limits of that apparatus whatever its intrinsic quality in general and for the notion of identity in particular.

Thus, A&K (2003, p. 6) "build a principal-agent model where the agent could identify with the organization and her office within it", and the result is to seek positive-sum outcomes through non-market considerations such as identity. In the absence of any reference to power and conflict, they close with the unsurprising conclusion that, "the ability of economic institutions to instill loyalty in their employees, and for the employees to further the goals of forward-looking institutions, may be a key to economic growth", p. 48.

This bears more than a passing resemblance to the thrust of analysis based on social capital – anything can be better the more people know and trust one another – and A&K (2005, p. 29) even refer to the influence of identity as endowing firms with "motivational capital".[36] Significantly, not only Coleman but also Becker (1996) have already been heavily embroiled in this approach, with social capital having come to represent for economists any resource that is social by virtue of not being attached to an individual alone. So, implicitly at least, identity becomes a form of (capital), and might even be added to production functions as well as to utility functions. Becker has also, in his own way, endogenised preferences as a means of incorporating apparently non-rational behaviour, with current utility functions being derived from an exogenously given extended utility function that shifts through time with experience.[37] It seems that the commitment of A&K to the technical apparatus of neoclassical economics plus something more from other social sciences has driven them

---

36   This is the endpoint in the theory of organisations that begins with physical capital, and moves through human capital, contract and information theory, "Insofar as the firm can profitably motivate its employees … these investments should be considered as part of the capital of the organization, its *motivational capital*".

37   Fine (2001) for critique. Note that A&K (2003, p. 41) reveal again their partial view of economics as mainstream neoclassical in suggesting that, "Preferences, which are at the heart of our theory, are typically not an object of economic inquiry".

towards an affinity with the economics imperialism of Becker from whom Akerlof would otherwise have sought to depart, see below.

Third, this is all attached to and reflects a rolling programme of advance by economics across the social sciences, a prospect explicitly anticipated by A&K (2000, p. 749) in their closing sentences:

> Many standard psychological and sociological concepts – *self-image, ideal type, in-group and out-group, social category, identification, anxiety, self-destruction, self-realization, situation* – fit naturally in our framework, allowing an expanded analysis of economic outcomes. This framework is then perhaps one way to incorporate many different nonpecuniary motivations for behavior into economic reasoning, with considerable generality and a common theme.

Just where and how far this programme can prosper is a matter for speculation, with consequences for economics itself (will it become aware of, and act upon, the limitations of its existing methods and techniques) and for the other social sciences (how will they respond to the forward march of economics). These issues are taken up in the concluding remarks.

Fourth, as indicated in the last quote, the broad scope of the rolling programme, symbolised and consolidated by the economics of identity, is a consequence of its reliance upon abstract, universal categories of analysis – not least red and green for example, for a core model of identity without conceptual content or meaning to the identities deployed. Yet, possibly more than any other category of social analysis, identity is heavily contextual or situated in its content raising doubts over the applicability both of mathematical models and universal concepts. Significantly, as teased out in section 3, A&K's analysis of identity bears more than a family resemblance to the theory of discriminating oligopoly. This is not surprising as each individual is strategising around how to conform or to differentiate self from others. Yet, to treat identity as oligopoly is to expose, not surprising in view of the universal nature of the approach, a failure to grasp the specific aspects of identity itself.

Fifth, this is why, when working with A&K's framework in Sections 2 and 3, reference was made to the uncertainty surrounding individual choice of identity. The resonance with Frank Knight's distinction between risk (probabilities attached to knowable outcomes) and uncertainty (the unknowable as a result of invention, innovation and change) is deliberate given, as indicated, the extent to which A&K's treatment precludes the inventive creation or construction of identity. Pushing this further, the "vagueness" surrounding identity is a paramount feature both in reality and in analysis, just as Wittgenstein argued that the identity of, or what defines, a "game" is appropriately difficult to pin down in view of overlapping criteria that define them and the shifting meanings attached to language. Keynes became persuaded of the salience of this vagueness in the meaning of concepts and, accordingly, rejected the use of mathematics in economic modelling, like Marshall, other than as a guide to thought, Fine (2006) for a fuller discussion and references. And Talcott Parsons (1931, 1932 and 1934), in a series of articles in the *Quarterly Journal of Economics*, in part in critical response to Robbins' definition of economics as the allocation of scarce resources between competing ends, drew the conclusion that economics and sociology should go their separate ways.[38] Whilst they might address the same subject matter, they would offer different methodologies, individualistic as opposed to systemic.

This scattering of commentary from the 1930s indicates how limited was considered the scope of economics, as it was then and continues to be constructed. A division of subject matter, techniques and methods was established whose origins go back to debate in and around the marginalist revolution, Fine and Milonakis (2009) for much of the discussion here. Both within economics itself, and in its relationship with the other social sciences, it was accepted by all sides that universal, deductive theory was at most one part of the picture for one part of the subject matter. In a broader sense, the social sciences were struggling with the intellectual consequences of modernism – rationality, science and logic, on the one hand, and a reaction against that in the world of culture and, it should be added, identity from bohemianism onwards. As McCloskey (2001, p. 104) puts it:

> The two kinds of modernism were formed out of a Marriage of Modernism, which in its popular version left a mechanical notion of Science with one half of the culture and a romantic notion of Art with the other half.

Crudely, economics has remained rigidly attached to the rational, ordered side of modernism whilst the other social sciences, not least in addressing identity, have not only incorporated the cultural and romantic as well but have travelled beyond modernism and through postmodernism. The latter, and its pre-occupation with what meaning (of identity) is and how it is constructed, might just as well not exist as far as economics and the economics of identity are concerned.[39]

---

38 See also Parsons (1968).
39 Cullenberg et al (eds) (2001) for claims otherwise but more of an exception that proves the rule.

When Becker sought to do as much as he could with his own modernist version of economics imperialism, Akerlof (1990, p. 73) lampoons him in terms of Samuelson's image of Friedman's monetarism as having learnt how to spell banana but not knowing when to stop![40] But A&K's own approach to identity is far from incompatible with Becker's and, as seen especially for social capital, Becker seems to have more than anticipated Akerlof in some respects. It follows that, on its own canvas, A&K's discussion of identity attempts to take economics too far and, as such, is an implicit and, presumably, unconscious attempt to turn back the clock and rewrite the history of the relations between economics and the other social sciences. A&K seek to impose the century-old approach of analytical modernism on the concept of identity. But the latter essentially belongs at least to the cultural side of modernism if not to postmodernism. Ironically, the technical apparatus deployed by the economics of identity could only be established by stripping the individual of any identity through reduction to an ideal utility function. This has offered a blank page on which to bring identity back in but in a way that is heavily constrained by its corresponding notion of the atomistic individual within society.

6 Concluding Remarks

In a critique of A&K in the CJE, Davis (2007a) appropriately locates its economics of identity in relation to two themes. The first is that it relies exclusively upon a theory of *social* identity, itself reduced to the choice by an individual over those identities available. This is at the expense of consideration of *personal* identity, how individuals go about negotiating their own identity by reflecting upon and combining those that are available. In formal terms, Davis replaces the A&K utility function in which identity appears as a choice variable with one in which the utility function itself is chosen.[41] Second, Davis locates A&K in relation to developments within what he terms "recent economics". These involve the incorporation of non-standard material and variables, such as identity, currently on the fringes of the discipline but with the potential effect of either disturbing the "traditional framework" or not and, if disturbing, possibly heralding orthodoxy's dissolution and replacement by a

---

40 This can be extended to bananarama or even substituted for by taramasalata!
41 It is unfortunate, seemingly uncharacteristic and possibly to court an orthodox audience, that Davis casts this as "recommendations for treating the individual objective function as a production function" (Davis 2006b, p. 371), something entirely compatible with Becker for example.

new one (that might be pluralist). He suggests, though, that A&K conform to neither of these possibilities, within or against the current orthodoxy, representing an "ad hoc" outcome of their own.

With respect to the critique of A&K's concept and use of identity, this chapter is entirely complementary to Davis'.[42] It does, however, point to a different way of moving beyond the criticisms involved. For, whilst there is some affinity with Davis as far as the role of the reflexive and active individual is concerned, the emphasis here is on how identity involves socially created meaning as opposed to or, more exactly, in conjunction with individually chosen identity or utility function (if matters are to be expressed in this way). Thus, in a monetary economy for example, not only is our identity (self-perception and perception of us by others) as rich or poor constrained if not determined by level of income, but how we endow meaning to being rich or poor is also similarly constrained, something that would be impossible in a society without money. And the way in which social relations, structures and processes, etc, constrain and influence the meanings that can be attached to identity are multifarious and complex because identity is both multi-dimensional and, inevitably, bound to context.[43] Whilst Sen is right to emphasise that identities are chosen if not in circumstances chosen by ourselves, this has to be taken further to emphasise that the meanings that can be taken by those identities are also constrained or, more exactly, socially constructed.

In light of correspondence with Davis and his other published work, Davis (2003 and 2007b) for example, I suspect that this is not a point of disagreement between us. But there almost certainly is one reflecting difference not so much over the understanding of identity (and A&K's impoverished treatment of it) than how this fits into Davis' notion of "recent economics". As indicated, the issue is one of whether neoclassical economics is dead or dying and, following Colander (2000), whether those current developments at its fringes such as game theory and behavioural economics, represent the beginnings of a new orthodoxy (Davis 2006a and 2007b).[44] Significantly, little or no reference

---

42 It is accidental that the papers are complementary insofar as the first drafts of this one preceded any knowledge of Davis'. See also his introduction to the special issue on "The status of the concept of identity in economics" (Davis 2021).

43 Space does not allow this theme to be developed here but see Fine (2002b and 2005) for detailed discussion and framework for analysis in case of the identities of the consumer, and the meanings attached to the consumed. See also Fine (2013) and Bayliss and Fine (2021).

44 See Lawson (2006) for a similar view in order to be able to argue that the mainstream is characterised first and foremost by its social ontology as opposed to its varying theoretical substance, and Fine (2006) for dissent.

is made to the new information-theoretic and market imperfection economics that lies at the core of mainstream economics, has developed prodigiously over the past two decades, and is its most obvious progeny with respect to method, theory, technique and use of evidence (and so only departing traditional neoclassical economics if this is perceived to be based on perfectly working markets).

My view, by way of contrast, is that what is currently on the fringes is precisely that, and the mainstream continues to prevail if seen more appropriately as drawing upon a sacrosanct technical apparatus (utility and production functions, for example) that is liable to take precedence over any profound impact of disturbing elements (endogenising or incorporating this or that variable or technique). Where does this situate the economics of identity? This is exactly what is characteristic of A&K's approach. But it is interpreted otherwise as an "ad hoc" contribution by Davis, presumably because it does not, for him, fall neatly into core mainstream nor revolutionary fringe. Across the bigger picture, this difference of interpretation is in major part an empirical question over exactly what is happening within and at the borders of the mainstream and what is or is not contributing to major change within the discipline if such is in process. In case of identity, though, in its methodology, failure to engage adequately with heterodoxy, interdisciplinarity and history of economic thought, and in its use of standard technical apparatus, A&K is not an example of ad hoc analysis but ideal application of the orthodoxy to pastures new. In this instance, at least, "recent economics" is not undermining itself as Davis concedes in assigning it to an ad hoc category of idiosyncrasy. But, further, A&K's pieces are far from ad hoc and say more about the contemporary identity of economics than they do about the economics of identity.

References

Akerlof, G. (1970) "The Market for 'Lemons': Quality Uncertainty and the Market Mechanism", *Quarterly Journal of Economics*, vol 84, no 3, pp. 488–500.
Akerlof, G. (1990) "George A. Akerlof", in Swedberg (ed.) (1990), pp. 61–77.
Akerlof, G. (2006) "The Missing Motivation in Macroeconomics", Preliminary Draft, American Economic Association, Presidential Draft, January 6th, 2007, Chicago, http://www.aeaweb.org/annual_mtg_papers/2007/0106_1640_0101.pdf.
Akerlof, G. and R. Kranton (2000) "Economics and Identity", *Quarterly Journal of Economics*, vol 115, no 3, pp. 715–53.
Akerlof, G. and R. Kranton (2002) "Identity and Schooling: Some Lessons for the Economics of Education", *Journal of Economic Literature*, vol XL, no 4, pp. 1167–1201.

Akerlof, G. and R. Kranton (2003) "Identity and the Economics of Organizations", mimeo, available at http://www.wam.umd.edu/~rkranton/identityandorganizations.pdf#search='Identity%20and%20the%20Economics%20of%20Organizations'.

Akerlof, G. and R. Kranton (2005) "Identity and the Economics of Organizations", *Journal of Economic Perspectives*, vol 19, no 1, pp. 9–32.

Barberà S., W. Bossert and J. Moreno-Ternero (2023) "Wine Rankings and the Borda Method", *Journal of Wine Economics*, forthcoming, doi:10.1017/jwe.2023.7.

Bayliss, K. and B. Fine (2021) *A Guide to the Systems of Provision Approach: Who Gets What, How and Why*, Basingstoke: Palgrave MacMillan.

Becker, G. (1996) *Accounting for Tastes*, Cambridge: Harvard University Press.

Becker, G. and K. Murphy (2000) *Social Economics: Market Behavior in a Social Environment*, Cambridge: Harvard University Press.

Becker, G. and N. Tomes (1979) "An Equilibrium Theory of the Distribution of Income and Intergenerational Mobility", *Journal of Political Economy*, vol 87, no 6, pp. 1153–89.

Bédécarrats, F., I. Guérin and F. Roubaud (eds.) (2020) *Randomized Control Trials in the Field of Development, a Critical Perspective*, Oxford: Oxford University Press.

Bénabou, R. and J. Tirole (2005) "Incentives and Prosocial Behavior", Institute for the Study of Labour, IZA, Discussion Paper, no 1695, Bonn.

Colander, D. (2000) "The Death of Neoclassical Economics", *Journal of the History of Economic Thought*, vol 22, no 2, pp. 127–44, reproduced in Colander (2001), pp. 46–62.

Colander, D. (2001) *The Lost Art of Economics*, Cheltenham: Edward Elgar.

Coleman, J. (1961) *The Adolescent Society: the Social Life of the Teenager and Its Impact on Education*, New York: The Free Press.

Cullenberg, S., J. Amariglio, and D. Ruccio (eds) (2001) *Postmodernism, Economics and Knowledge*, London: Routledge.

Daly, H. (1982) "Chicago School Individualism versus Sexual Reproduction: a Critique of Becker and Tomes", *Journal of Economic Issues*, vol 16, no 1, pp. 307–12.

Davis, J. (2003) *The Theory of the Individual in Economics: Identity and Value*, London: Routledge.

Davis, J. (2006a) "The Turn in Economics: Neoclassical Dominance to Mainstream Pluralism?", *Journal of Institutional Economics*, vol 2, no 1, pp. 1–20.

Davis, J. (2006b) "Social Identity Strategies in Recent Economics", *Journal of Economic Methodology*, vol 13, no 3, pp. 371–90.

Davis, J. (2007a) "Akerlof and Kranton on Identity in Economics: Inverting the Analysis", *Cambridge Journal of Economics*, vol 31, no 3, pp. 349–362.

Davis, J. (2007b) "Postmodernism and the Individual as a Process: Comment on Ruccio and Amariglio", *Review of Social Economy*, vol 65, no 2, pp. 203–8.

Davis, J. (2021) "The Status of the Concept of Identity in Economics", *Forum for Social Economics*, vol 50, no 1, pp. 1–9.

Dugger, W. (1980) "Power: an Institutional Framework of Analysis", *Journal of Economic Issues*, vol XIV, no 4, pp. 897–907.

Earp, F. (1996) "Transactions, Circuits, and Identity: Proposing a Conceptual Framework", *Journal of Economic Issues*, vol XXX, no 2, pp. 407–12.

Fine, B. (1975) "Individual Liberalism in a Paretian Society", *Journal of Political Economy*, vol 83, no 6, pp. 1277–81.

Fine, B. (1995a) "On the Relationship between True Preference and Actual Choice", *Social Choice and Welfare*, vol 12, no 2, pp. 353–61.

Fine, B. (1995b) "Towards a Political Economy of Anorexia?", *Appetite*, vol 24, no 3, pp. 231–42.

Fine, B. (1996) "Reconciling Interpersonal Comparability and the Intensity of Preference for the Utility Sum Rule", *Social Choice and Welfare*, no 13, no 2, pp. 319–25.

Fine, B. (1997) "The New Revolution in Economics", *Capital and Class*, no 61, Spring, pp. 143–48.

Fine, B. (1998) *The Political Economy of Diet, Health and Food Policy*, London: Routledge, reprinted 2013.

Fine, B. (2001) *Social Capital versus Social Theory: Political Economy and Social Science at the Turn of the Millennium*, London: Routledge.

Fine, B. (2002a) "'Economic Imperialism': a View from the Periphery", *Review of Radical Political Economics*, vol 34, no 2, pp. 187–201. See Chapter 3.

Fine, B. (2002b) *The World of Consumption: the Material and Cultural Revisited*, London: Routledge.

Fine, B. (2004) "Economics and Ethics: Amartya Sen as Point of Departure", World Bank ABCDE Conference, Oslo, June, 2002, published in *The New School Economic Review*, vol 1, no 1, pp. 151–62, http://www.newschooljournal.com/files/NSER01/95-104.pdf.

Fine, B. (2005) "Addressing the Consumer", in Trentmann (ed.) (2005), pp. 291–312.

Fine, B. (2006) "Debating Critical Realism in Economics", *Capital and Class*, no 89, June, pp. 121–29.

Fine, B. (2009a) "The Economics of Identity and the Identity of Economics?", *Cambridge Journal of Economics*, vol 33, no 2, pp. 175–91.

Fine, B. (2009b) "Political Economy for the Rainbow Nation: Dividing the Spectrum?", Keynote Speech for "Making Sense of Borders: Identity, Citizenship and Power in South Africa", South African Sociological Association, Annual Conference, June/July, 2009, Johannesburg, available at https://eprints.soas.ac.uk/7972/1/sasa_benfine.pdf.

Fine, B. (2010) *Theories of Social Capital: Researchers Behaving Badly*, London: Pluto.

Fine, B. (2011) "The General Impossibility of Neoclassical Economics", *Ensayos Revista de Economía*, vol 30, no 1, pp. 1–22.

Fine, B. (2013) "Consumption Matters", *Ephemera*, vol 13, no 2, pp. 217–48, http://www.ephemerajournal.org/contribution/consumption-matters.

Fine, B. (2018) "*Collective Choice and Social Welfare*: Economics Imperialism in Action and Inaction", *Ethics and Social Welfare*, vol 12, no 4, pp. 393–399. See Chapter 6.

Fine, B. (2019a) "Economics and Interdisciplinarity: One Step Forward, N Steps Back?" *Revista Crítica de Ciências Sociais*, no 119, pp. 131–48. See also Chapter 10.

Fine, B. (2019b) "Post-Truth: an Alumni Economist's Perspective", *International Review of Applied Economics*, vol 33, no 4, pp. 542–567, revised and shortened from "Post-Truth: An Alumni Economist's Perspective", SOAS Department of Economics Working Paper No. 219, 2019, https://www.soas.ac.uk/economics/research/workingpapers/file139489.pdf.

Fine, B. (2021) "Introduction to, and Turkish Translation of, 'The Economics of Identity and the Identity of Economics?'", *Yıldız Social Science Review*, vol 7, no 1, pp. 1–14.

Fine, B. (2023) "Mathematical Economics as Aid or Obstacle to Heterodox Economists?: a Personal Experience", *The New School Economic Review*, vol 12, no 1, forthcoming.

Fine, B. and K. Fine (1974a) "Social Choice and Individual Ranking", Part I, *Review of Economic Studies*, vol 41, no 127, pp. 303–322.

Fine, B. and K. Fine (1974b) "Social Choice and Individual Ranking", Part II, *Review of Economic Studies*, vol 41, no 128, pp. 459–475.

Fine, B., D. Johnson, A. Santos and E. Van Waeyenberge (2016) "Nudging or Fudging: the World Development Report 2015", *Development and Change*, vol 47, no 4, pp. 640–63.

Fine, B. and P. Mendes Loureiro (2021) "From Social Choice to Inequality-Decomposition: in the Spirit of Arrow and Atkinson by Way of Sen and Shorrocks", *International Review of Applied Economics*, vol 35, no 1, pp. 765–91.

Fine, B. and D. Milonakis (2009) *From Economics Imperialism to Freakonomics: the Shifting Boundaries between Economics and Other Social Sciences*, London: Routledge.

Hill, C. (2005) "What the New Economics of Identity Has to Say to Legal Scholarship", University of Minnesota Legal Studies Research Paper, no 05-46.

Kondratev, A., E. Ianovski and A. Nesterov (2023) "How Should We Score Athletes and Candidates: Geometric Scoring Rules", Operations Research, forthcoming, https://doi.org/10.1287/opre.2023.2473.

Lawson, T. (2006) "The Nature of Heterodox Economics", *Cambridge Journal of Economics*, vol 30, no 4, pp. 483–505.

Lazear, E. (2000) "Economic Imperialism", *Quarterly Journal of Economics*, vol 115, no 1, pp. 99–146.

McCloskey, D. (1999) *Crossing: a Memoir*, Chicago: Chicago University Press.

McCloskey, D. (2001) "The Genealogy of Postmodernism: an Economist's Guide", in Cullenberg et al. (eds) (2001), pp. 102–128.

Moscati, I. (2005) "History of Consumer Demand Theory 1871–1971: a Neo-Kantian Rational Reconstruction", Università Bocconi, Milan, mimeo.

Parsons, T. (1931) "Wants and Activities in Marshall", *Quarterly Journal of Economics,* vol 46, no 1, pp. 101–40.

Parsons, T. (1932) "Economics and Sociology: Marshall in Relation to the Thought of His Time", *Quarterly Journal of Economics,* vol 46, no 2, pp. 316–47.

Parsons, T. (1934) "Some Reflections on 'The Nature and Significance of Economics'", *Quarterly Journal of Economics,* vol 48, no 3, pp. 511–45.

Parsons, T. (1968) *The Structure of Social Action: a Study in Social Theory with Special Reference to a Group of Recent European Writers,* Volumes I and II, New York: The Free Press, first edition of 1937.

Richter, R. (2005) "The New Institutional Economics: Its Starts, Its Meanings, Its Prospects", *European Business Organization Law Review,* vol 6, no 2, pp. 161–200.

Sen, A. (2005) *Writings on Indian History, Culture and Identity,* London: Allen Lane.

Sen, A. (2006) *Identity and Violence: the Illusion of Destiny,* London: Allen Lane.

Swedberg, R. (ed.) (1990) *Economics and Sociology, Redefining Their Boundaries: Conversations with Economists and Sociologists,* Princeton: Princeton University Press.

Trentmann, F. (ed.) (2005) *The Making of the Consumer: Knowledge, Power and Identity in the Modern World,* Oxford: Berg.

Waller, W. (2004) "Review of Davis (2003)", *Journal of Economic Issues,* vol 38, no 4, pp. 1112–14.

CHAPTER 6

Collective Choice and Social Welfare: Economics Imperialism in Action and Inaction

Postscript as Personal Preamble

I was asked out of the blue to contribute a short symposium review article on Amartya Sen's (1970/2017) revised edition of his classic contribution to social choice theory. The review was for the journal *Ethics and Social Welfare*. In part, it describes its aims and scope in the following terms:

> [The journal] publishes articles of a critical and reflective nature concerned with the ethical issues surrounding social welfare practice and policy. It has a particular focus on social work (including practice with individuals, families and small groups), social care, youth and community work and related professions.
>
> The aim of the journal is to encourage dialogue and debate across social, intercultural and international boundaries on the serious ethical issues relating to professional interventions into social life. Through this we hope to contribute towards deepening understandings and further ethical practice in the field of social welfare.

As a result, the invitation brought together a number of concerns, some personal, some intellectual and some the intersection of these. Sen had been my PhD supervisor on social choice theory and had supported me as referee in some of the few jobs or other such ventures for which I had applied. Like many others, I followed his work closely, extending far beyond social choice theory to many aspects of development economics and philosophical and ethical issues (especially around famine, entitlements and capabilities). Sen both commanded respect from mainstream economics, and had been awarded the Nobel Prize for economics, but was clearly not a mainstream economist albeit fully engaged with, if not against, the mainstream, see below.

In addition, I felt more than usually obliged to respond to the invitation to contribute given the journal's ethos as I have a special needs son, then in his eighteenth year. Given the extent to which special needs often finds itself at the rough end of policy, especially in times of (neoliberal) austerity, I felt I could bring some practical experience from the coalface to the ethical issues involved. I do mention my son in the piece in passing, but it is telling that social choice theory, as in much economics more generally, is based upon a methodological individualism in which, perversely, the nature of individuals remains entirely abstract/ideal (signified by mathematical symbols) so there is limited space for specific differences, whether special needs or otherwise, except at most as an afterthought. It has no interest in why needs are the way they are, and why preferences are the way they are (except as the basis for choices made), nor what those needs and preferences mean to the individuals concerned. Nor that individuals may have difficulty in identifying their self-interest, let alone meeting them equitably. This is hardly the basis on which to broach either welfare itself or its ethics.

At this time, I was also acutely sensitive intellectually to issues not only of economics imperialism but also of social policy. My starting point for the latter had been the failure of the literature to take fully into account the role that financialisation was playing in social policy, as a defining characteristic of neoliberalism (as opposed to more or less austerity and more or less privatisation). Through the FESSUD research programme (with work on housing, water and pensions in particular), the relationship between financialisation and social policy was linked to shifting norms of provision within economic and social reproduction.[1]

But none of this finds its way into this piece which is more concerned to bring out to its likely audience the ways in which economics imperialism might impact upon their ways of thinking. In a sense, it highlights the extent to which the economics discipline treats Sen, and everything else, as its plaything – to be picked up or dropped according to its own evolving practices and postures.

I am, however, inclined to tar at least some heterodoxy with the same brush. From a Lawsonesque, critical social ontology perspective, Ragkousis (2022) has designated Sen as a neoclassical economist albeit, from his perspective in Veblenesque terms of Sen having been inconsistently caught between being both deterministic (neoclassical as everyone else understands it from perspectives other than social ontology alone) and evolutionary in his methodology.

I do not doubt that there is some truth in this characterisation, and it is implicit in my critique of Sen's entitlement approach (Fine 1997) and in the substance of this chapter, but it reduces the complexities and range of Sen's work with a broad brush that does not allow for its grand constructions and designs nor for its subtleties in detail and motivation. In Monty Python vein, no one expects the social ontology, if not Spanish, inquisition to which should

---

[1] See https://fessud.org/working-papers/#WP5 and Fine (2020) and Bayliss and Fine (2021).

be added, only a select if significant few have taken any notice of it, while its powers of punishment to effect change towards what might be taken to be a non-neoclassical economics, if only neoclassical could be deemed to exist, seem to have been limited.[2]

In this light, my own tentative assessment of Sen is as follows. First and foremost, he is an intellectual who delights in engaging with ideas at the highest levels of scholarship. Second, he is very good at and enjoys it,[3] alongside remarkable skills in formulating and presenting his ideas. Third, he is an economist by initial training, with an Indian background concerned with the practical and ethical issues of development, not least in light of inequality, famine and ethnic and other conflicts – matters of life and death. Fourth, his milieu early on was the Cambridge common room and its economics, to which he sought both to contribute and to persuade – these are your ideas, I can do better and different.[4] Fifth, the rest is the history of his remarkable endeavours, reflecting his qualified acceptance by, not of, the mainstream and his equally more or less qualified adoption by much heterodoxy, and disciplines other than economics, with consequences that are not necessarily of his own making but, contextually, broadly positive and progressive whatever criticisms are and have been levelled. Sixth, as suggested in this piece, what is more important than how Sen is specified as such (ranging across much more and much more significant than his ontology) is how he has been received. The focus here is upon economics, with the conclusion that his rise and fall within the discipline reflects to a large degree the trajectories of economics imperialism and its inability, and hence unwillingness, to engage, indeed its increasing disengagement, with the substance of the intellectual journey he has himself

---

2   Although, as a stone-thrower myself in the greenhouse, I should be sensitive to my own lack of impact. I have critically assessed Critical Realism in Economics and its later view that neoclassical economics no longer exists, in Fine (2004, 2006, 2007 and 2015) and scattered in numbers of places across forthcoming volumes, especially the one on heterodoxy, but also, of most relevance here, see first volume on economics imperialism, Chapter 2. To be explicit, I am essentially strongly in favour of the ontological critique of the mainstream but feel the need to move on to a substantive theoretical specification and critique, not least in terms of economics imperialism, its foundations and its trajectories.
3   It never ceases to disappoint me how little the beauty of mathematical results is appreciated by those who do not pursue them.
4   Elsewhere, I have argued that critical pragmatism, within economics and whether for researching or teaching, can take the mainstream as critical point of departure and deploy its own methods (including mathematics and modelling) as the basis for both persuading and constructing alternatives (Fine 2023). To some degree, this chapter offers an example – this is the best social choice theory can do and this is what has to be done to do better – and it is a lot and it is different.

taken. Seventh, my one enduring disappointment is that Sen did not deploy his considerable powers to engage in more popular and wide-ranging persuasion although he can hardly be faulted for the extent of his influence within academia and its milieux. Had he but conformed to the imperatives of the social ontology police, he may even have lost this latter level of influence and engagement.

1 Disciplinary and Personal Beginnings[5]

Arrow's (1951) slim volume initiated the field of social choice, within economics, and Sen (1970/2017) founded its subsequent classic form and content, testimony for which derives from the first edition of this book and its second edition published nearly forty years later with an additional three hundred pages or so on top of the original two hundred or more. Self-mockingly, I penned "Bible" on my copy of Sen's original book just I had done the same for my undergraduate (Mendelson 1964). My own introduction to social choice theory came in 1969, the very first week in which I began studying economics immediately after graduating in pure mathematics. Having done an optional paper in formal logic, I realised that the problem of social choice was equivalent to intuitionistic logic and truth tables (with true and false or third middle value, corresponding to strict preference in favour and against, or indifference for individual and social choice) although, unbeknownst, Murakami (1968) independently got there just before me. Within a few years, I had completed a PhD in social choice theory in record time (Fine 1974) under Sen's supervision at the LSE (with Frank Hahn as external examiner, himself situated in general equilibrium just below Arrow and Debreu, for which they were awarded the Nobel Prize for Economics). My thesis consisted of just one hundred pages of mathematics and one page of references, and it also allowed for publications in the major journals of economics and to gain an academic post, choosing Birkbeck College over the London School of Economics because of a commitment to offering mature students the chance to study for a part-time degree.

This self-indulgent narrative serves the purpose of highlighting the nature of social choice theory as it derived from Arrow nearly seventy years ago. It was profoundly mathematical. This explains to some extent why, surely somewhat inappropriately given its original focus on voting systems, it should be an economist who came to provide the classic contribution to the field, as opposed to

---

[5] Initially published and revised from Fine (2018).

a political scientist. At this point, economics was about to enter what has been termed a formalist revolution, one in which mathematical reasoning (and an increasingly deductive methodology) begins to dominate.

In this sense, that social choice was located within economics was accidental, but it was an accident waiting to happen for other reasons. After the marginalist revolution of the 1870s – establishing the conceptual apparatus of mainstream economics as we know it today as opposed to the classical political economy of Smith, Ricardo, Mill and Marx – and with the emergence of microeconomics in the 1930s (alongside Keynesian macroeconomics), mainstream economics was wont to frame any issue in terms of given individual preferences (aka utility functions) or given capacity to supply (aka production functions). Significantly, to organise economic analysis around the individual and corresponding utility and production functions, an intellectual process of what I have termed implosion was required, casting aside the social, the historical, complex motivations of the individual and the nature of goods, even externalities and interdependencies at the individual level (and, it might be added, that such framings offered the pretence of being ethically free).[6]

Thus, having thrown out all of these considerations to establish a technical apparatus around the individual and utility and production functions, somewhat perversely, and on the basis of its mathematical methods, mainstream economics began to extend the scale and scope of what it had created beyond the narrow confines of the self-interested market behaviour of individuals. In the mid-1950s, we have the remarkable reduction of (national) production to a single simple process combining all available resources (capital and labour), the Solow production function and its use to measure technical progress.[7] Is it surprising that it should be complemented by the parallel attempt to create an as if individual preference function for society, p.271 for Sen's acknowledgement of this. Or, to put it in extreme form, Milonakis (2017, p. 1380), "Rational choice economics found its prime mathematical expression in Arrow's *Social Choice and Individual Values*", see also p. 1385.

This is where Arrow's genius arises in attempting to deal with the problem of how to derive social choice by aggregating over individual values (or choices/ preferences) over the available alternatives. Ultimately, he came up with what was taken to be a devastatingly negative result, an impossibility theorem. The goal of establishing social choice seemed to be floundering on the basis of his

---

6 As Tsakalotos (2005, p. 896) observes, "Abandoning the terrain of values is a position that is value-laden to the core". See Fine (2002 and 2012) for a critique of economics on ethics.

7 Although shown and accepted to be invalid in the 1960s, the aggregate production function remains a staple of mainstream economics, Fine (2016, Chapter 5) for an account.

four commandments (or axioms/assumptions), to continue the biblical metaphor, as he establishes his impossibility theorem from which the field of social choice has evolved, either negatively by establishing further impossibilities, or positively by weakening the axioms.

For the latter, as Sen eloquently establishes, the impossibility result can be approached from the opposite direction. Start with a much weaker set of axioms and proceed with the addition of more commandments (possibly intersecting with but necessarily weaker than Arrow's as a whole) until we approach but do not exceed impossibility, pp. 7–9. In this respect, at least in the first instance, a major thrust in Sen's work has been to allow for *interpersonal* comparisons (trade off one person's choices against others, otherwise any person would potentially prevail over any other whatever the issue and strengths of preferences). This is related to the economists' much beloved Pareto criterion – one state of the world cannot be judged superior to another unless no one is made worse off. So, a billionaire's extra piece of cheesecake cannot be sacrificed to keep a billion people alive. My own work in part became focused upon taking account of the dual problem of the *intrapersonal* intensity of preferences[8] – that I prefer to be alive rather than dead might be assigned greater weight than choice between cheesecake or tart for pudding.

Significantly, Arrow's impossibility theorem did not allow either for inter- or intrapersonal comparisons (primarily because choice is binary, or pairwise, and no distinctions are drawn between who has what preferences over what things). Be this as it may, Arrow planted the social choice seed within economics and, it proved fertile terrain for mathematically-oriented economists, keen to exercise their technical skills around utility functions (or, more exactly, the more general preference orderings) that served as a core concept, with Sen himself seduced as an undergraduate and beyond, pp. xiv and xv.

2   Bringing Back in (BBI) as Analytical Context

Somewhat unkindly, Mirowski (2007) dubs Arrow the "Cowles poster boy" of economics, with his popularity within the profession reflecting the irony of repudiating at one time or another each of the mainstream advances that he was himself making across a whole range of fields. Across economics more generally, this process is part and parcel of what I have termed economics

---

8 For a recent contribution in this vein, offering an account of, and contributing to, the relationship between social choice and measurement of inequality, see Fine and Mendes Loureiro (2021).

imperialism in which concepts, theories, factors, methods and so on, which were left out to establish the mainstream's technical apparatus (including utility functions), have been selectively and partially reintroduced on the basis of the framing that could only be established by excluding them. This has involved an explosion of mainstream economics in narrow terms across the discipline itself (a sort of internal colonisation) as well as in colonising, with whatever success, the subject matter of other disciplines and fields.[9]

Social choice theory offers an ideal and early example of such economics imperialism, and the process can be traced through the trajectory of Sen's own contributions. I hesitate, given my personal and intellectual debts to him, to dub him poster boy alongside Mirowski's Arrow. But it is convenient to situate his contributions in these terms especially if social choice is to be situated in relation to the trajectory of economics more generally and not only on its own terms. Interestingly, Sen spends little time more broadly contextualising social choice as a field within economics, apart from its history with Condorcet (for discovering the voting paradox) and Borda (for proposing a voting rule) and the like, although he mentions the Cold War environment at its emergence, p. xii.[10] But his contributions can be roughly classified into two types – those that BBI in ways that are acceptable to economics as a discipline and those that are not, with corresponding implications for the evolution of the reception and location of his own work.

More specifically, there are two features which tend or tended to make social choice theory acceptable to mainstream economists. One is the deployment of mathematics in its own right (with social choice theory an early example of what is now commonplace, economics is mathematics without too much regard to what is its subject matter) – for Sen, mathematics is necessary but not sufficient, p. xxxiii, but bear in mind only the last of his old and new chapters are not the informal equivalent of a formal/mathematical chapter. Hence, for the economics of social choice, there is a love for (im)possibility results on the basis of axiomatic deduction. And, corresponding exactly to its origins with Arrow, the other central aspect of the economic approach to social choice theory is the framing around individuals and correspondingly derived social orderings as if those of an individual – we want to be able to reduce society to an as if individual.[11]

---

9 For this, and earlier discussion, in the context of economics and ethics, see Fine (2013), and Milonakis and Fine (2009) and Fine and Milonakis (2009) for fuller accounts.

10 We know that game theory was established to frame Cold War nuclear strategy, and a social welfare function (state as individual) is needed to define objectives.

11 My own work on/within social choice theory has revolved around rejecting the axiom of irrelevance of independent alternatives (making choice binary between pairs of

Let me bring this down to earth and to the personal, with relevance to this journal's readership. I am father to a severely brain-damaged son with corresponding learning difficulties. As he transitioned to adult services, he was subject to a test of his abilities, with varieties of questions whose answers were scored numerically. These were aggregated into a total against which funding could be allocated or, as was the case, further reviewed in light of severity of his condition. In principle, this is exactly like social choice, with individuals to be ranked in relation to one another as more or less disabled by virtue of the vectors of their capacities.

Apart from being a demeaning experience, there are two major issues involved here. One is the reduction of complex disabilities to an index without regard to multiple contexts and meanings – ability to appreciate danger, spending fifteen minutes arguing if that should be 2 or 3, for example. Fair enough, then, but mathematical reasoning is an aid but insufficient although it does, or can, involve a three-step procedure of quantifying the unquantifiable, valuing the invaluable, and prioritising the essential. Well, I slipped the last one in there around the second issue, which is that such technically constructed metrics can, if not of necessity, be deployed as an instrument of limiting support to those with special needs. Indeed, that is why it has been adopted. In short, treating social choice through social choice theory, even partially, can have deleterious consequences in underpinning deprivation rather than alleviating it.[12]

In this vein, Sen brings back in interpersonal comparisons, as mentioned, and incomplete social orderings – it is not essential that every alternative be ordered in relation to every other to give an optimal as opposed to a maximal outcome (none can be deemed to be better for the latter but not all others can be adjudged to be inferior). Significantly, Sen accepts that social choice need not be complete orders in all circumstances but with arguments that still render them as if individual orderings, p. xxv, and individuals can justifiably have incomplete orderings in case they exercise multiple and incommensurable criteria.[13]

---

alternatives without regard to preferences over other alternatives). The axiom prevents perfectly symmetrical (isomorphic) preferences across individuals and alternatives from guaranteeing total indifference (as should be the case for the voting paradox). Fine and Fine (1974a and b) for the liberating consequences!

12   A similar point about treating sexual assault as if an economic crime, subject to compensation for injury received, is made by Radin (1996) with, interestingly, a response by Arrow (1997).

13   My own work has shown how incomplete orderings might reflect too little choice (due to limited perception of differences) and too much choice (in case conflicting multiple criteria are treated as indifference); see Fine (1995) as a delayed dalliance out of doctoral

Interestingly, Sen implicitly accepts that, starting with Arrow, a BBI is essential to come to social choice in ways that go beyond these formalities. On the one hand, he sees social choice as needing to be something more than *voting* on anonymous alternatives (by individuals). On the other hand, relying upon voting data alone is perceived to constitute *"informational* penury", pp. 15–16. Indeed, there is a section headed, "INCORPORATING MORE *INFORMATION* IN SOCIAL DECISIONS", p. 18, bold added. So, information about individuals and alternatives begins to compensate for the narrow terms on which Arrovian social choice theory was first set up, with the result that interpersonal comparison can become informationally rich, p. xxvi.

I suspect the confinement in this account to terms such as voting and information as far as social choice theory is concerned is too narrow but it is indicative of what is acceptable to the mainstream insofar as it can be formalised. Sen's own work, though, subsequently, goes far beyond this even if rooted to whatever lingering extent in these origins. Just a minimal list would include the normative, personal liberties (as with the impossibility of the Paretian liberal), the entitlement and capabilities approaches, rights, basic needs and the roles of democracy and public reasoning, quite apart from a free press to guarantee against famine.[14]

What these factors share in common is the, more or less, loosest of connections to social choice theory as it was originally formulated and, to be blunt, at most a significant if partial remedying by BBI without going much further than this. First, more often in examples than in full discussion, there is the relative absence of context. It makes sense only to make social choice when we know what are the choices involved, what they mean to those making those choices and why they have made those choices – Sen acknowledges this when observing those deprived can be more contented because of reduced aspirations, p. 24.[15] Second, this opens up issues of causation for which the social tends to be most notable for its absence within social choice theory, in conformity to the thrust of mainstream economics – where is the power, the class, the conflict, the social relations, and so on. And, third, there is the interaction of context

---

thesis, although arising out of empirical application of social choice theory to preferences over acquisition of consumer durables (Fine and Simister 1995) – do we vote for dishwashers or not as a social choice (aka consumption norm)!

14   See Fine (1997) for a discussion of tensions with the entitlement approach to famine along the lines discussed here.
15   See the classic, and relatively early, Sen (1977) for similar thrust, although it remains primarily side-lined by mainstream economics other than for opportunistic purposes of bringing back in this, that or the other.

and causation, the dialectic between how social choices are determined and how we interpret and render them with meaning as a result. Consider, whether someone deserves housing benefit depends upon complex understandings of how housing and benefits are provided, why, with what forms, conditions and ethos of such provisioning, quite apart from how this is all normatively interpreted.

3 Economics and Social Choice: Marriage and Divorce

With economics initiating social choice theory on its own and conducive terms, it rapidly became a leading field amongst the upper echelons of researchers, if not for students as too technically demanding and marginal in substantive importance. Indeed, it was commonplace to hear Arrow referred to as having proved that a social welfare function is impossible, something obviously false, but a "truth" being shamelessly deployed, and ignored as an inconvenience, in any case. For a golden period, contributions to social choice were published in the leading journals, with Sen to the fore or often setting the lead on which others piggybacked, especially from (the first edition of) the volume under review.

But this could not be sustained for two reasons. The first is that, as the formalist revolution took hold, the scope for applying its (mathematical and other peculiar microeconomic) methods across many other fields was equally expanding, thereby eroding any initial advantage that had been gained by social choice theory. Increasingly, social choice theory became confined to the specialist journals that were set up in the wake of its initial success. For example, a casual glance at the list of Sen's own publications in the new volume displays a shift away from a presence in the mainstream journals from within economics.

Second, though, this also reflects the boundaries around which social choice negotiates economics. As indicated, social choice can prosper within economics as long as it primarily remains confined to formal methods, and on its own terms that do not stretch much beyond the "voting" to incorporate the "informational". But, as soon as social choice moves beyond such confines, then economics tends to lose interest. Unsurprisingly, as Sen has moved to expand the scope of social choice theory beyond what is acceptable to its home discipline, so he has engaged much more with those situated within the disciplines of philosophy, political theory, and development studies (where he has a prominent status for other reasons than for social choice alone as a prominent development economist in his own right).

4   Interpreting the History of Social Choice Theory in Reverse?

It is certainly possible to read the evolution of social choice theory, as Sen appears to do, as having been founded by Arrow and, then, having expanded in scale and scope from such humble beginnings to its current position as "Reasoning and Social Decisions", in which Sen's contributions are monumental, Fine (2002) for an earlier appreciation. His volume remains primarily a chronology of steps taken towards the present, with the new chapters succeeding and not rewriting the earlier ones. As covered here, but scarcely mentioned in Sen's own account although implicit, this neglects the changing constituencies involved in social choice of this broader type, and the different disciplinary and broader contexts within which they operate (other disciplines and styles of theorists rule social choice theory, Cold War is over, neoliberalism rules supreme despite a Global Financial Crisis, apparently without remedy, certainly from our economists). Social choice theory would surely command limited interest from the readers of this journal if confined to a calculus of voting mechanisms. The interest derives from the way in which Sen has taken social choice theory forward, and his wider contributions however much they may have been tied to social choice theory in his personal and their intellectual origins.

Such observations raise the issue of what is the continuing presence of social choice theory, and its origins and trajectory in continuing discourses that have been inspired by Sen, and even to question whether it is positive rather than negative and constraining. Certainly, Sen in language and conceptualisation does have a continuing influence; the axiomatic methods and their pursuit primarily through economics are less so if not negligible or non-existent. Sen's own attachment to the significance of the history of how we got here would be understandable given his role within them, and that it forms such a major part of his own intellectual history and of the corresponding conceptualisations. But it is arguable that much of (his) current framings derive primarily from traditions other than, and even in opposition to the thrust of social choice, rather than simply complementing it, not least as we are dealing in longstanding issues such as rights, freedoms, democracy, distributional equity, and so on. The current situation is, in part, put very well by Cherrier and Fleury (2016, p. 23):[16]

---

16 They continue as follows, possibly indicating how economics imperialism continues to exert its influence even after it has been decolonised as it were: "Those questions were taken up (or back) by scholars from political science, social psychology, law, philosophy and the new policy science that emerged in the 1960s … [T]he publication of Rawls's

The study of collective decisions may well have stabilized in the 1980s, but the topic remained quite elusive and never really became central to economic theory. The only field explicitly concerned with the positive and normative analysis of collective decisions, namely social choice, was marginalized. Public choice economists expanded their interests in a large number of directions, but only a few of them explicitly framed their field and its core concepts – free-riding, public goods, constitutions, rent-seeking – as dealing with the collective decisions made necessary by living in society and by so-called market failures. While acknowledging the development of social and public choice, public economists largely endorsed models in which the objectives embodied in the government's social welfare function were considered exogenous, while aggregation problems were solved with the use of representative agent models, thereby suppressing the preferences of individuals other than the hypothetical representative agent. What happened in the 1980s was not so much that the new theories and tools developed by economists ceased to be relevant to the study of collective decision making. It was, rather, that theoretical and applied investigations of revelation, coordination and allocation mechanisms ceased to be framed as studies of collective decisions because economists were not asked, by their clients, to answer questions such as "whose preferences and values do this policy reflect, or should reflect?"

In this light, I am particularly mindful of the way in which the systemic, the causal and the contextual are absented or reduced by social choice's origins in mathematical methods and methodological individualism, especially where economists are concerned, with comparable implications for the social, the public, the collective and the political.

References

Arrow, K. (1951) *Social Choice and Individual Values*, New Haven: Yale University Press.

Theory of Justice in 1971 put an end to a century without grand political philosophy synthesis. And the language it was couched in, that of analytical philosophy, as well as philosophers' development of axiomatization and the dissemination of game theoretic tools among political scientists, enabled them all to converse and compete with economists, and reclaim collective decision expertise".

Arrow, K. (1997) "Invaluable Goods", *Journal of Economic Literature*, vol 35, no 2, pp. 757–65.

Bayliss, K. and B. Fine (2021) *A Guide to the Systems of Provision Approach: Who Gets What, How and Why*, Basingstoke: Palgrave MacMillan.

Cherrier, B. and J.-B. Fleury (2016) "Economists' Interest in Collective Decision After World War II: A History", Available at SSRN: https://ssrn.com/abstract=2786400 or http://dx.doi.org/10.2139/ssrn.2786400.

Fine, B. (1974) Individual Decisions and Social Choice, London School of Economics, unpublished University of London, Phd thesis.

Fine, B. (1995) "On the Relationship between True Preference and Actual Choice", *Social Choice and Welfare*, vol 12, no 2, pp. 353–61.

Fine, B. (1997) "Entitlement Failure?", *Development and Change*, vol 28, no 4, p. 617–47.

Fine, B. (2002) "Economics and Ethics: Amartya Sen as Point of Departure", World Bank ABCDE Conference, Oslo, June, 2002, published in *The New School Economic Review*, vol 1, no 1, Fall, 2004, pp. 151–62, http://www.newschooljournal.com/files/NSER01/95-104.pdf.

Fine, B. (2004) "Addressing the Critical and the Real in Critical Realism", in Lewis (ed.) (2004), pp. 202–26.

Fine, B. (2006) "Debating Critical Realism in Economics", *Capital and*, no 89, June, pp. 121–29.

Fine, B. (2007) "Rethinking Critical Realism: Labour Markets or Capitalism?", *Capital and Class*, vol 31, no 1, pp. 125–29.

Fine, B. (2013) "Economics – Unfit for Purpose: the Director's Cut", SOAS Department of Economics Working Paper Series, no 176, http://www.soas.ac.uk/economics/research/workingpapers/file81476.pdf, revised and shortened to appear as, "Economics: Unfit for Purpose", *Review of Social Economy*, vol LXXI, no 3, 2013, pp. 373–89.

Fine, B. (2015) "Neoclassical Economics: an Elephant Is Not a Chimera But Is a Chimera Real?", in Morgan (ed.) (2015), pp. 180–99.

Fine, B. (2016) *Microeconomics: a Critical Companion*, London: Pluto.

Fine, B. (2018) "*Collective Choice and Social Welfare*: Economics Imperialism in Action and Inaction", *Ethics and Social Welfare*, vol 12, no 4, pp. 393–399.

Fine, B. (2020) "Framing Social Reproduction in the Age of Financialisation" in Santos and Teles (eds) (2020), pp. 257–72.

Fine, B. (2023) "Mathematical Economics as Aid or Obstacle to Heterodox Economists?: a Personal Experience", *The New School Economic Review*, vol 12, no 1, forthcoming.

Fine, B. and D. Milonakis (2009) *From Economics Imperialism to Freakonomics: the Shifting Boundaries Between Economics and Other Social Sciences*, London: Routledge.

Fine, B. and J. Simister (1995) "Consumption Durables: Exploring the Order of Acquisition", *Applied Economics*, vol 27, no 11, pp. 1049–57.

Fine, B. and K. Fine (1974a) "Social Choice and Individual Ranking, Part I", *Review of Economic Studies*, vol 41, no 3, pp. 303–322.

Fine, B. and K. Fine (1974b) "Social Choice and Individual Ranking, Part II", *Review of Economic Studies*, vol 41, no 4, pp. 459–475.

Fine, B. and P. Mendes Loureiro (2021) "From Social Choice to Inequality-Decomposition: in the Spirit of Arrow and Atkinson by Way of Sen and Shorrocks", *International Review of Applied Economics*, vol 35, no 1, pp. 765–91.

Lewis, P. (ed.) (2004) *Transforming Economics: Perspectives on the Critical Realist Project*, London: Routledge.

Mendelson, E. (1964) *Introduction to Mathematical Logic*, London: Chapman and Hall.

Milonakis, D. (2017) "Formalising Economics: Social Change, Values, Mechanics and Mathematics in Economic Discourse", *Cambridge Journal of Economics*, vol 41, no 5, pp. 1367–90.

Milonakis, D. and B. Fine (2009) *From Political Economy to Economics: Method, the Social and the Historical in the Evolution of Economic Theory*, London: Routledge.

Mirowski, P. (2007) "The Mirage of an Economics of Knowledge", https://pdfs.semanticscholar.org/117c/1f5f7de592604322b2f01f7fbf8c86783fad.pdf?_ga=2.160268090.643385654.1519070492-620705970.1519070492.

Morgan, J. (ed.) (2015) *What Is This 'School' Called Neoclassical Economics?: Debating the Origins, Meaning and Significance*, London: Routledge.

Murakami, Y. (1968) *Logic and Social Choice*, London: Routledge & Kegan Paul.

Radin, M. (1996) *Contested Commodities*, Cambridge: Harvard University Press.

Ragkousis, A. (2022) "Amartya Sen as a Neoclassical Economist", *Journal of Economic Issues*, forthcoming.

Santos, A. and N. Teles (eds) (2020) *Financialisation in the European Periphery: Work and Social Reproduction in Portugal*, London: Routledge.

Sen, A. (1970/2017) *Collective Choice and Social Welfare*, London: Penguin for second edition.

Sen, A. (1977) "Rational Fools: a Critique of the Behavioral Foundations of Economic Theory", *Philosophy and Public Affairs*, vol 6, no 4, pp. 317–44.

Tsakalotos, E. (2005) "Homo Economicus and the Reconstruction of Political Economy: Six Theses on the Role of Values in Economics", *Cambridge Journal of Economics*, vol 29, no 6, pp. 893–908.

CHAPTER 7

From Freakonomics to Political Economy

Postscript as Personal Preamble

In 2019, Dimitris Milonakis and I published two books (Milonakis and Fine 2009, and Fine and Milonakis 2019). These represented the culmination of almost a decade of cooperation between the two of us, although we had worked together on other topics previously. The main title of the second book, *From Economics Imperialism to Freakonomics*, could not have signalled more explicitly what was its subject matter, especially as the subtitle banged home the message, *The Shifting Boundaries between Economics and Other Social Sciences*. In retrospect, if already implicit in the text, Freakonomics can be seen to have anticipated a third phase of economics imperialism, one in which the mainstream's market imperfection economics is supplemented by whatever other considerations take the analysis's fancy, drawing from across social science as a whole.

In short, economics imperialism was on *our* agenda, big time. The first book's title, *From Political Economy to Economics: Method, the Social and the Historical in the Evolution of Economic Theory*, is less obviously about economics imperialism as such. But there is no mistaking its intent. If economics is colonising the other social sciences from an initial position of separation, then it must have been created or separated from other disciplines in the past. As classical political economy is, not least by virtue of its name, heavily embroiled in the non-economic, the separation is something that occurred in the past given it was not a founding original sin. Accordingly, the first book addresses how economics became constituted as a separate discipline with limited overlap with others. And the focus is upon how that separation was realised in theory through the presence, or not, of particular methods and the historical and the social. In short, at least in major part, the first book was concerned with the pre-history of economics imperialism.

The two books were received with some favourable attention by our peers. Each was awarded a book prize, the Myrdal for the first and the Deutscher for the second.[1] Further, what follows is our response to a symposium on the books

---

1 The Gunnar Myrdal Prize is awarded biennially by the European Association for Evolutionary Political Economy on a theme broadly in accord with the EAEPE Theoretical Perspectives, https://eaepe.org/?page=awards; its name was changed to the Joan Robinson Prize in 2021,

published in *Historical Materialism*, also signalling the seriousness with which the books were being treated (by both editors and contributors), not least as three of the four reviewers were not Marxists, despite the journal's orientation, and one was the leading British historian of economic thought. Geoff Hodgson (2011 and 2012), a leading figure in EAEPE and founding editor of the *Journal of Institutional Economics*, mysteriously eschewed the chance to contribute to the symposium and published his response, subsequently in debate with us, Milonakis and Fine (2012), in the *Review of Social Economics*.

In short, economics imperialism seemed to have been on the agenda, big time. But the signs were already present within the symposium that this was not the case. The symposium did represent a high point in the critical exposure of economics imperialism, but it also symbolised a watershed, or at least a subsequent gentle decline in significance of economics imperialism within the literature. Symbolically and substantively, discussion of the second book, and of economics imperialism as such, was mooted. Instead, commentators were more interested in related and relevant, but separate, issues, such as methodology, history of economic thought, the role of internal and external factors in the evolution of economic thought (and the social sciences), the origins and history of disciplines, the natures of mainstream and heterodox economics, and how to strategise in relation to them. Our plea, in this longer, if not the published, version seems to have fallen on hearing-impaired ears across the topics covered and all others:

> In case of economics imperialism, the diverse cases of industrial relations, management, labour economics and economic history are of interest and significance, and we would welcome contributions including our own but especially those from others.

The reasons for the failure to answer this call are interrogated in more detail in Chapter 2 of this volume. They include:

a) Precisely because economics imperialism straddles the intersection of so many controversial aspects, as listed just above the previous quotation, it can be contested, reasonably or not, as a result of a difference of opinion over any one of the corresponding issues. You got the nature of the mainstream wrong, or the history of thought, or

---

in view of alleged sexual offences by Myrdal (who died in 1987). The Isaac and Tamara Deutscher Prize is awarded annually "for a book which exemplifies the best and most innovative new writing in or about the Marxist tradition", http://www.deutscherprize.org.uk/wp/.

methodology, and so you are wrong about economics imperialism too. Even if we accept it as such, it could represent "reverse imperialism" in which the social sciences are favourably influencing economics rather than vice-versa and negatively, with the mainstream beginning to disintegrate from the outside in.

b) By the same token, with focus upon one or other of these aspects, or upon a particular topic, economics imperialism in general seems to be of lesser relevance especially, as argued, the extent, incidence and nature of economics imperialism is itself variegated across topics and disciplines.

c) The drafting of the book occurred primarily before the Global Financial Crisis of 2007/8 but the symposium appeared after it. At least temporarily, mainstream economics seemed to be in a crisis of legitimacy given its failure to be able to predict, let alone explain, the crisis, nor to do much about it policy-wise. In addition, finance (or, more exactly, "financialisation") was taking off across the social sciences, with the notable exception of where it was needed most, economics. As a result, although mainstream economics had internally colonised financial economics (moving its approach from being market perfect to being market imperfect), it was to prove totally irrelevant for the burgeoning "financialisation" of social science.

d) To hold fast to economics imperialism is to adopt an uncompromisingly critical attitude towards the mainstream, one that is highly unfavourable to professional progress as an economist. Intersecting with this is the heavy pressure to specialise both between and within disciplines – so that economics imperialism as the bigger picture gets lost in smaller contributions and expertises both for heterodox economists and for those sympathetic to political economy within other disciplines. Further, in its first market perfect phase, economics imperialism had been proudly promoted by Gary Becker and admiring followers, inviting critical response from heterodoxy. By contrast, the second phase of market imperfections economics saw itself in opposition to the first phase and, inevitably, positively relating to other social sciences and not imperialistic, thereby dulling the flame drawing heterodox critique.

e) Last, and least, Dimitri and I had reached some sort of limits to our cooperation, if not in absolute terms.[2] Projected volumes on (the

---

[2] Each of us was involved in other academic endeavours but our major joint energies became focused upon founding and developing the International Initiative for Promoting Political

new and newer) economic history, although much drafted alongside the two books, never materialised.³ I do not doubt that had economics imperialism gained more of a purchase, we would have done more by way of, and encouraged by, collective endeavour.

This is not supposed to be a big whinge – look, we offered the gift of economics imperialism and you failed to make proper use of it – not least as there may have been more important things to do. And the example of financialisation suggests so, not least as it has proven to be a highly fruitful avenue for political economy across the social sciences (Fine 2022, and see also Mader et al (eds) 2020).

But, of course, financialisation is precisely a topic in which, for whatever reason to date, economics imperialism has made at most limited inroads. Yet, there are other examples which speak with a different voice in two respects. On the one hand, social capital has remained a leading aspect of economics imperialism, albeit with its own characteristics. It does not originate within economics, but it has allowed economics to incorporate the social without needing to question the asocial nature of its economics. It is an exemplary route for the third phase of economics imperialism, most notably leaving aside the power, conflict and contested relations of capital(ism) as an economic category and addressing its dysfunctions as market imperfections that can be readily remedied by appropriate self-help at some level of community organisation and pathologised if failing to do so. As it were, never mind the causes of poverty, say, you are to blame if you do not organise to make things better for yourself – self-help raised to the level of the collective.⁴

As chance would have it, just as Dimitri and I were suffering economics imperialism burn-out, so I was completing my second book on social capital, Fine (2001b) followed by Fine (2010c), with similar symptoms as a consequence. However, alongside financialisation, the increasingly prominent issue across the social sciences, and more, has been the environment. Natural resource economics was already an established mainstream field and, just as human and social capital presented no conceptual problems to its practitioners across the social sciences, so natural capital has come to prosper on a terrain wider than economics alone. It is even seen as offering a critique of the

---

Economy, iippe.org, which sought to promote heterodoxy, interdisciplinarity, informed criticism of the mainstream, Marxist political economy, and policy activism.
3 But see following volume on (economics imperialism and) economic history.
4 In the vanguard of such postures was the Grameen Bank initiative which simply imploded, even for its erstwhile leading proponents. See Bateman et al (2018) and Fine (2023) in the context of social capital.

mainstream in terms of its neglect and implicit waste of the environment and its capital.

Accordingly, the idea that the environment should be valued like other "things" gains purchase with a tendency to neglect, or only partially incorporate, the relations, structures, agencies and conflicts attached to capitalism and the imperatives that underpin global warming. As a result, environmental and ecological economics tends to score an own goal as far as economics imperialism is concerned. Nor is it a matter simply of mainstream economics lording it over the ecological and the environmental, the opportunity is lost to reflect back upon the weaknesses of mainstream economics on its own terrain of the economy and how it is theorised.[5] The interdisciplinary contestation against economics imperialism is a two-way affair, seeking to bring political economy to and from the social sciences. As this piece concluded, "the way forward is for political economy to be vigorously pursued collectively and critically across the social sciences" (Fine and Milonakis 2012, p. 95).

1 Introduction[6]

First and foremost, we would like to thank our commentators who took the trouble to read our books[7] and make such detailed and informed comments. It has to be acknowledged that, had we had the benefit of these comments before the final drafts, our books would have been much better. We would also like to thank the editors of HM and especially Sam Ashman (2012) who had the idea for this symposium.[8]

It is instructive to start our response with one very important observation: almost every single individual who takes part in this symposium draws his[9] main inspiration from a different school or schools of thought or trends

---

5   For critique of ecological/environmental economics, see Pirgmaier (2018) and Hofferberth (2022).
6   Originally published as Fine and Milonakis (2012). Note that in a footnote, it was promised, "We have drafted and intend to post a longer response at some point in the future", p. 108. This delivers on that promise.
7   Milonakis and Fine (2009), in what follows M&F, and Fine and Milonakis (2009), in what follows F&M.
8   We would also like to thank all those who, to our knowledge, took the trouble to read our books and offer comments or write reviews in other journals including Alex Callinicos (2011), Joseph Choonara (2010), David Colander (2010), Christopher Gunn (2012), Hardy Hanappi (2011), Tony Lawson, Alessandro Roncaglia (2009) and Hajime Sato (2012).
9   It is unfortunate that no woman was invited, or agreed, to take part in this symposium.

in economic theorising or is a well-known representative of that increasingly marginalised branch of economics known as history of economic thought or both.[10] This is a healthy sign of pluralism as far as political economy and heterodox economics are concerned.[11] We remind the readers that one of the aims of our books was exactly to promote pluralism in economic science.[12] To that extent the gathering together of this distinguished colloquium of people is both gratifying and reassuring as far as pluralism within non-mainstream economics is concerned. This lies at the extreme opposite of what is happening in economic science more generally where an increasingly entrenched orthodoxy is reluctant to engage with anything that lies outside its mode of thinking. This is (very) unhealthy.

It is normal in such symposia that the commentators concentrate on the differences between themselves and the contributions of the authors involved. And this is also the case with this symposium. Having said this, three of our commentators, McNally (2012, pp. 10–11), King (2012, p. 40), and Fleetwood (2012, pp. 61–2) are in general agreement with the main thrust of our argument which we consider significant because political economy needs some common ground between its practitioners on which to build. Staying at this general level, Backhouse (2012, p. 25) raises some general disagreements over our approach to the history of economic thought (HET). It is worth noting that, as far as the first book is concerned, most of our commentators focus almost exclusively on the classical figures in the history of economic thought such as Smith, Ricardo, the marginalists, Marshall and Keynes, and also on formalism, which together comprise less than one third of our first book. Given the significance of these classical figures in the evolution of economic thought this in itself is hardly surprising. What *is* surprising, however, is that they give no

---

10   In addition to the articles by Roger Backhouse, Steve Fleetwood, John King and David McNally, Geoff Hodgson has also written an extensive comment which was intended to be included in this symposium but in the event was published in the *Review of Social Economy* giving rise to a debate there between him and ourselves. In what follows reference will be made to the views expressed in this exchange with Hodgson but for a fuller account the reader is advised to consult the debate itself, Hodgson (2011 and 2012) and Milonakis and Fine (2012). See forthcoming volume on mainstream economics.
11   Recently a similar if more extensive symposium has taken place over Tony Lawson's *Reorienting Economics* and the critical realist project more generally (see Fullbrook (ed.) 2009).
12   More precisely one of our explicitly stated aims is to bring to the fore "how rich, diverse, multidimensional and pluralistic this science once was. And if this was once the case, then nothing can preclude the possibility that it could be so again. It is with this hope in mind that we embarked upon writing this book ... If our book adds a small stepping stone in this direction, then our task will have been accomplished", M&F, pp. 9–10.

attention whatsoever to what according to Backhouse represents the "welcome innovations" of our book, including attention to Weber and Schumpeter, the separation of economics from sociology, the Austrian school, the German and British historical schools, but also Mill and Marx. Are we right to assume that on the rest of individuals and schools there are no substantial disagreements between us otherwise, no wonder, they would have raised them?

At the same time, however, it has to be said that, although many of the comments are well taken, some others are simply based on different perspectives or different readings of the HET, while others are due to misinterpretation or misunderstanding stemming, no doubt, from us having laid our argument in less than clear fashion, as some commentators have been at pains to point out (King, Fleetwood, Hodgson). We hope to be able partly to redress these flaws and to clear away some of these misconceptions and misunderstandings in what follows. Granted all this, although the agreements between us are more than will be apparent from this exchange, there still remain some substantial differences with some (but by no means all) of our commentators. To do justice to all the points raised, we would need a response of at least equal length for each commentary. The space we have been granted here is hardly enough to do justice to comments coming from four knowledgeable and informed commentators. However, we will try to cover as much as possible saving space by grouping them together wherever possible and being brief on each of the issues raised. But our intention here is not to answer all objections and criticisms point by point, but to deploy the basic argument of our two books to situate and deal with several categories of concepts and criticisms. Thematically we categorise the comments into three according to whether they mostly deal with HET, methodological issues or other general issues, and in terms of their validity and weight we treat them either as valid, as based on some misconception, or simply wrong.

2   Economic Crisis and Economic Theory

These books were written before the onset of the present crisis, following the crash in the financial markets in September 2008. The crisis has brought to the fore another crisis that has been going on for very many years, and diagnosed as such by many, other than by most of its own practitioners. We refer to the crisis of (orthodox) economic theory. What better evidence is there for the existence of such a crisis than the fact that a scientific field with the adjective "economic" in front of it has failed so badly not only to predict the most catalytic economic event of almost the last century, but also to come to terms even in the most rudimentary way, let alone explain, why it happened. Indicative of this is that until the onset of the recent crisis a university graduate in economics could finish his/her degree without having heard once the word crisis, illustrating how remote mainstream economic theory has become from the realities of the world economy.[13]

The crisis has also brought to the fore in important ways both the significance of studying the history of economic thought, but also, and chiefly, the relative strengths of various forms of political economy and heterodox economics when it comes to analysing and explaining such immensely important phenomena such as the present crisis. Before the Second World War the concepts of crisis and of business cycles were very high on the agenda of the economics profession. Foremost amongst those who showed a keen interest in analysing and explaining economic crises was, of course, Karl Marx, with many of his followers expanding further and elaborating in different directions his unfinished work on this matter.

In the interwar period, business cycles and crisis feature prominently in the writings of some of the chief theoretical protagonists in economic affairs such as Keynes, Schumpeter and Hayek. Schumpeter devoted what he considered to be the locus classicus of his work on the question of business cycles, while Keynes' *General Theory*, as is well known, was prompted by the crisis of the 1930s, and in important ways should be seen as both an attempt at understanding and explaining it as well finding ways to cure it. More recently we have the example of Hyman Minsky and his attempt at explaining financial crises. All of these authors and the schools they represent have either been ignored or marginalised within the mainstream academic profession or else they have been reinterpreted beyond recognition in order to make their theories acceptable to the mainstream, as with Keynesianism and, even more so now, New Keynesianism.

3 The (General) Criticisms

One major difficulty that authors encounter in the sort of project addressed in our books is how to approach and how to present the subject matter. Given the huge intellectual terrain covered, the diverse nature of the readership which ranges from the uninitiated to the expert, this is an immensely difficult task. Given, however, that we identified as our chief readership advanced students

---

13   For a more thorough critique of this trend in economics, see Fine and Milonakis (2011).

and researchers in political economy and other social sciences interested in interdisciplinary approaches to economic phenomena, then our task became a little more focused. Even so, there is a further difficulty which has to do with the fact that the modern economist is relatively or totally uneducated relative to the main issues and themes of our books (be it the history of economic thought, methodological issues or the social and the historical dimensions of economic phenomena). Dealing with all these difficulties means that hard choices, and compromises, have to be made, which almost always come at a cost. The question is whether the cost is or is not worth paying. It seems that at some points we have got the right balance while at other points we could have done better.[14]

From the minute these two volumes were conceived we knew that they would be two highly controversial books on highly contested terrains.[15] At the same time, any account involving such a multidimensional project and covering such a vast terrain is bound to be partial and incomplete. Once the project was fully conceived, however, we tried (according to one commentator successfully, see Backhouse, p. 25), to delineate it as clearly as possible and to stick to it throughout. We have made the themes and aims of our books explicit both in our subtitles and in our respective prefaces and introductions.

Generally, as is natural, most of the points raised by our commentators stem from their own perspectives and areas of interest. On particular points, as far as the first book is concerned, our commentators complain that we have

---

14   Our intention was to introduce the subject at a relatively advanced level. To do so, though, we also aimed at avoiding intimidating our uninitiated readers. This is partly the reason why we decided not to include a chapter on methodology, King, p. 46. We thought that an introductory chapter (or two) on methodological issues might deter the uninitiated readers because of its abstract and (meta) theoretical nature. We opted instead for the option of introducing and explaining all methodological and conceptual issues as we moved along, as we encounter them in our narrative. The cost of this, for fear of interfering with the flow of the narrative, was that we simply stuck to simple definitions or descriptions of our concepts without entering any deeper into their meaning or into the debates around them. It now seems that including a chapter or two as appendices, rather than as introductory chapters, would have aided our (uninitiated) readers and would have entertained many of our commentators' complaints, such as lack of precision in the use of some of our concepts, etc (see King and Hodgson).

15   Our initial intent was to write a *single* volume detailing how the historical and social had been taken out of (mainstream) economics only for it to be restored through economics imperialism over the last fifty years. Economic history was to have served as a case study but became designated for two future volumes of their own. But see our work on the new and newer economic history, Fine (2003), Fine and Milonakis (2003) and Milonakis and Fine (2007), and the forthcoming volume on (economics imperialism and) economic history.

not spelt out clearly the meaning of some of our concepts such as methodological individualism, the social, the market (Hodgson), positivism (King) and abstraction (Fleetwood), that we have unduly demonised either Ricardo (King, for whom Menger and Marshall "escape relatively lightly", pp. 40–41), or Marshall (Hodgson, but see King, p. 41 for the opposite view) whose portrait as painted by us is, according to Backhouse, one-sided leaving out "his obsession with evolution and biological analogies" and that he was not a utilitarian, p. 29. We have, however, according to our commentators, given fuller accounts and treated fairly the institutionalists (Hodgson) and Keynes (Backhouse, but for King, p. 44, our "treatment of Keynes is sparse"). According to King, there are important omissions in our account such as the treatment of Marxism since Marx, Kalecki and macroeconomics since Keynes, post-Keynesianism and other heterodox schools. Fleetwood complains that we have not covered critical realism (his preferred approach) in any detail and McNally takes us to task for not making an attempt to offer an alternative political economy and for not having dealt with the question of finance. For Backhouse, our historical account of the evolution of economic thought fails to take into account adequately the political and social context, an omission that also causes King, p. 47–9, to wonder "what are the main causes of major changes in economic theory? Are they internal or external?".[16]

As far as the second volume is concerned only King, Fleetwood and McNally offer some comments. King regrets that we have not treated the incursion of economics into other social sciences such as political science (although we have),[17] or the non-incursion into yet more social sciences such as anthropology, and we have not considered behavioural economics as a possible case of a reverse form of imperialism from social psychology, and asks whether Akerlof's work is also such an example.[18] Fleetwood though thinks (wrongly, see below), that we have implied that information-theoretic economics may actually be able to explain institutions.

Last, on the related questions of the diagnoses and remedies of the current maladies of economic science, King, pp. 55–6, raises the question of "where is mainstream economics heading?", giving four possible scenarios: stasis, involution, fragmentation and revolution. And Backhouse takes us to task for not having proved why mainstream modeling and "prediction – conformity

---

16   Callinicos (2011) in his review of our first book makes a similar point.
17   See F&M, pp. 36–42 and below.
18   Ironic given the detailed treatment of Akerlof as establishing a Kuhnian exemplar for the second phase of economics imperialism as well as his theory of identity (with Kranton) subject to devastating critique on its own terms. See Fine (2001a, 2004a and 2009a).

of models with data – is [not] a better criterion than conformity with a prior belief that they should take into account something called the social?", p. 34.[19]

4 Clearing the Ground

Against these general consideration, let us start by clearing the ground of some misconceptions and misunderstandings. As we make clear in our introduction above, we did not attempt to write a history of economic thought, let alone to rewrite it. And we certainly had next to nothing to say about the history of the social sciences.[20] Rather, as explicitly stated on many occasions, not least in the subtitle of our first book, our aim in the latter was to investigate the trajectory of the social and the historical element in the evolution of economic thought, all set in a methodological context.[21] With political economy giving way to economics at the end of the nineteenth century and the beginning of the twentieth, this gradually became synonymous with the relationship between economics and other social sciences which, from the 1950s onwards, chiefly took (but not exclusively) the form of economics imperialism. The latter was the aim of the second volume, i.e. to explore the shifting boundaries between economics and other social science since the 1950s, *as seen from the confines of the dismal science*.[22] Our vantage point, reflecting our own interests, is also explicitly stated: political economy broadly conceived as the body of theory which tries to analyse economic processes set in a social and historical context (historical specificity). The ultimate aim of this whole exercise is to put political economy back on the agenda drawing on the rich traditions of the past. So, our clearly stated intention was to write an *intellectual* history focusing on three specific aspects – the social, the historical and the methodological.

Hence, our books should not be treated as histories of economic thought. Indeed, the readers will find very little by way of economic theory as such in our books. As stated in our introduction to M&F, p. 8, "there are also incursions into the elaboration of economic theory and political economy but those are

---

19 Hodgson believes we are wrong to place the roots of the malaise as far back as the marginalist revolution, opting instead to locate them exclusively in some adverse institutional developments since the Second World War, although in his response to our response he seems to have backtracked from his initial position (see Hodgson 2011 and 2012, and Milonakis and Fine 2012).
20 M&F, p. xiii, King, p. 40.
21 M&F, pp. 1, 2, 4, 9.
22 F&M, p. 1.

kept to a minimum (with references to fuller accounts) and motivated more by illustrating our arguments concerning the historical and the social content of the theory than providing exposition". In this sense, Backhouse, p. 24, captures the spirit of our books well: "A historical narrative is used to argue a case about modern economics – that the methods that have increasingly dominated the subject have led to the separation of the economic from the social. They thereby create a case against modern economics and in favour of a political economy that pays attention to the social". Similarly, our (much more limited) incursions into sociology, or economic history or social theory more generally, were done from the confines of developments within the dismal science in relation to these other disciplines.

To recap, no complete theory of economic thought, let alone sociological thought or social theory (which we hardly touch upon), is the intention of our books. Indeed, our exposition of actual economic theory and its relation to other social sciences is limited to illustrations related to our theme(s). Even so, however, the terrain covered remains immense, both in terms of the number of authors and schools covered, but chiefly in terms of identifiable themes and perspectives. As such it has always been, and still is a highly contested set of terrains, affording different interpretations from a number of different theoretical, epistemological and methodological perspectives and different approaches to HET. Hence, given the highly diverse backgrounds and perspectives of our commentators, which is welcome, it is natural that all these different interpretations have come to the fore.

5 Methodological Issues

"Why should economists not defend their methods by arguing that prediction – conformity of models with data – is better criterion than conformity with the prior belief that they should take into account of something called social?", asks Backhouse, p. 34. Just to deal with this question would require a book on its own. We will try to state our position very briefly. The reason we have made the social a central aspect of our inquiry is not some metaphysical prejudice about "something called social", but the reality that all economic processes involve social relationships between individuals, even when it appears otherwise.[23] So this social nature of economic processes has to be

---

23 The example of so-called "property rights" can help to illustrate the point. This is normally defined as a relationship between an individual (or a collectivity) and the thing over which this individual (or collectivity) is assigned these property rights. Such a

explicitly taken into account and treated as such. So what is this thing called "the social" and why bother with it?[24] We define the social in very broad terms to include all relationships between individuals through their participation in social entities such as social classes, institutions, organisations etc, which together form society's social structure. Culture, ideology, etc, are also deeply social in nature, but are derivative upon the structural societal factors, thus occurring at a different analytical plane providing in this way a liaison between structure and human agency which occurs at the level of social practices.[25] In our framework, while social structures, generally speaking, take analytical precedence over individual and collective agency, the latter is not fully determined but only *filtered through* and *conditioned by* these structures while also influencing them in decisive ways. As Marx (1972, p. 5) has put it, "men make their own history but they do not make it just as they please; they do not make it in circumstances chosen by themselves, but under circumstances directly encountered, given and transmitted from the past". But even at the structural level not all social relationships are of equal analytical importance. Social relations and institutions built around economic processes are constitutive of the subject matter of political economy, and as such take (analytical) precedence over other social relationships and institutions such as the state, law etc, which are built around political and legal processes (Milonakis and Fine 2012).

Why then is "conformity of models with data" not a better criterion in conducting economic research? This raises the huge question of what is the best way to conduct scientific research (and what is the best test of the scientific credentials of this research) in the social sciences in general and in economic inquiry in particular. The best we can do here is simply and briefly, express our own position on this hugely controversial topic. Before we do so, however, it has to be said that it is highly ironic that instrumentalism in economic

---

        definition, however, fails to capture the true essence of property which involves relations between individuals. Because property rights are assigned to some individual *in relation to* other individuals – for example in the case of private property rights – these rights are assigned to a given individual *to the exclusion* of all other individuals. *Private property* by an individual over an asset, in other words, implies *non-property* over this asset by every other individual. So, although property rights appear as relations between an individual and a thing, in essence they are relations between people. As such the concept of *property relations* is better placed to capture this social essence of the concept of property, see Milonakis and Meramveliotakis (2012).

24   See also Hodgson (2011, p. 373).
25   F&M, p. 154.

method, based on the criterion of prediction,[26] should be invoked in this specific conjuncture when mainstream economics has failed in the most blatant way to predict what is perhaps the most cataclysmic economic event of the past century, the recent global economic crisis. Is it not the case that by this criterion mainstream economics is an utter failure? Be that as it may, we do find Backhouse's drift to an instrumentalist method to be unfortunate – maybe neoclassical models work as well if not better than others (especially in prediction). This is an impoverished take on method both in terms of meaning and causation incorporated into theory but, more important, might reflect a disposition to accept the mainstream as correct unless proven otherwise, and even mounting and retreating to ever more refined arguments of which its own orthodox practitioners are blissfully unaware and uninterested. It is surely not accidental that debate over economic method (other than extremely narrowly) and methodology has been entirely abandoned by the mainstream as reflected in Samuelson's (2016, p. 64) dictum, "To paraphrase Shaw: Those who can, do science; those who can't prattle about its methodology". The forty year old defences of economic theory mounted by Friedman, Koopmans and Lipsey, which Backhouse cites, have been taken apart many times both as prototypes of better models and as predictors. It is the economic theory which demands reconstruction (and even, arguably, failing by its own criteria), not the arguments over method that might allow it to remain as it is.

We are at one with Fleetwood in emphasising the methodological chaos of mainstream economics, to which we would add innocence as ignorance and neglect and lack of rigour even on its own terms. We also suspect that Fleetwood is wrong about things being just as bad in other social disciplines for a number of reasons. Methodology is at least taught, as an established part of research, and is incorporated within the disciplines themselves. Although inevitably uneven by comparison, the absence of methodology from economics is extraordinarily marked. Similar to Fleetwood, p. 68, though, we are against scientism, a term which, following Hayek (1942–4), is taken to mean the doctrine of the (mis)application of scientific methods, used (or presumed to be used) in natural sciences, to the social sciences (M&F, p. 260). Fleetwood, p. 68, reproduces the definition of the *Collins Dictionary of Sociology* (1995) according to which scientism is "the doctrine or approach held to involve oversimplified conceptions and unreal expectations of science, and to misapply 'natural science' methods to the social science". Positivism in all its varieties

---

26   Instrumentalism in the context of economic science was first put forward by Milton Friedman in his famous essay "The Methodology of Positive Economics", published in 1953.

is one prime example of scientism. As King, p. 45–6, rightly points out, and we ourselves have emphasised, M&F, pp. 230–6, positivism is used in a variety of ways and has many different meanings. However, we did take care to clarify what we consider to be the essential elements that all forms of positivism share in common: "the conception of reality as consisting of what our senses perceive, the desire for the clearing of scientific thought from all forms of metaphysics, and the 'unity of science' dogma, or the belief that both physical and social sciences share common logical and methodological premises with strict distinction between facts and values".[27] The chief characteristic of logical positivism, on the other hand, is "the verifiability principle" or, in other words, the emphasis on the need for empirical confirmation of all theories, also raised by Backhouse.[28] It is in this broad sense that we have included both Friedman's instrumentalism and Samuelson's operationalism, in the (logical) positivist tradition. Despite their differences, what they share in common is the stress on the need to test against the evidence either the theory's predictions (Friedman) or its "operationally meaningful theorems", by which Samuelson (1947, p. 4) means theorems consisting of (empirically) refutable propositions.

In our view, because of the substantial differences in the nature of the subject matter between natural and social sciences (chief among them are the non-experimental nature of most of social sciences, the intentionality of human action, the fact that the investigators in social sciences are themselves part of the phenomenon under investigation, etc), social sciences *cannot* and should not try to imitate the methods of natural sciences. In very broad terms, the aim of any scientific endeavour should be the *explanation* (and *not* prediction) of some natural or social phenomenon through the identification of causal relations. The question is how can this be done successfully? It is our firm contention that any true science needs theory. The question, of special importance in the social sciences, is *what* theory (i.e. what method and what substance). Any successful theory must be grounded in reality. By this we do not mean any form of empiricism, i.e. what our senses perceive. Neither do we mean inductivism, i.e. starting from some observed regularities and, based on these, making theoretical generalisations. Instead the phrase "grounded in

---

27   M&F, p. 230. Two missing commas is the cause of the misunderstanding with King on Ricardo's method. Thus, the proper quote should be "Indeed, Ricardo's deductivism, *and* positivism, are taken to the limit in mainstream economics, as with Friedman's (1953) instrumentalist methodology", M&F, p. 69. As far as Ricardo's method is concerned, we have made our position abundantly clear on many occasions; we consider him as one of the first champions of pure deductivism.

28   See above and M&F, p. 231.

reality" is used in two different but related senses. First, as said already, the aim should be the explanation of some *real* social phenomenon, and second, that in doing so and reaching for the essence of the phenomenon in question, the investigator should go behind surface phenomena through the use of the force of abstraction. By the latter we mean *real* abstractions or abstractions *in accordance with material reality*. Through these abstractions the investigator tries to reach for explanations of surface phenomena by digging deeper into the structures and social relationships that form the template and have a causal influence on these surface phenomena. Although these structures and social relationships may be lacking immediate empirical reality and, as such, be unobservable to the casual observer, they are no less real than the surface phenomena under investigation. This is close to what Lawson[29] has called *retroduction* or *abduction* or what Marx called *analysis*.[30]

This definition of abstraction contrasts sharply with the "simplifying assumptions" (or *fictions* as Fleetwood, p. 74, calls them)[31] of neoclassical theory which take the form of perfect foresight, perfectly rational individuals, etc, most of which are *against* material reality. These types of fictional assumptions form an indispensable part of the deductive method used by neoclassical theory, i.e. building a theory by starting from assumed premises and a set of initial conditions, and arriving at conclusions that are pre-determined by these premises and initial conditions, M&F, p. 15. Our proposed method for political economy has nothing to do with either induction or deduction. Neither do we believe that some form of synthesis or complementary use of both according to the object under investigation and the questions asked, will salvage economic science. Rather, it is a matter of transcending this dichotomy through the method described above which could provide economic theorising with what it lacks right now: explanatory power in terms of causal relations and anchorage of theory in reality (what Fleetwood, p. 72, and others, has called *realisticness*).

---

29   Lawson (2003, p. 145).
30   Marx (1973, p. 100). Analysis as opposed to what Marx calls synthesis which describes the opposite mental route, going from previously derived abstract categories to more concrete ones, dubbed by Marx (1973, p. 101) "the scientifically correct method". We hope this discussion answers Callinicos' (2011, p. 268) accusation that in our books "we give the impression that right lay on the side of the inductivists" and that the latter underplays the role of theory in economic analysis. We fully agree with the latter, and it was certainly not our intention to side with the inductivists but to show the need to *transcend* this distinction in the ways suggested here.
31   See also Lawson (1997 and 2003).

In this respect we do strongly believe that both deduction and induction and the dichotomy between the two is unhelpful for the purposes of building the political economy of the future, and that the battles that have been fought over their relative merits represent no more than "wasted energies", to use Schumpeter's (1981, p. 782) expression (although pointing to the distinction can be part of a powerful critique of the deficiencies of mainstream economics and how it got to be that way). So, the fact that we used this dichotomy as one of the pillars on which the narrative of the first book is based, has nothing to do with the way we view these two methodological approaches. Instead, its use is instructive, or so we think, because of the role this division has played in the various twists and turns in the evolution of economic theory, and for the delineation of the conceptual differences and the understanding of the various clashes between different individuals and between different schools, especially in view of the themes of our books. These are two entirely different issues (see King's point 5).[32]

6   Questions of the History of Economic Thought

A few of the questions raised relate to our approach to HET. To begin with, some general comments and some clarifications, conceptual or otherwise are in order. First, both the form taken by our narrative and the decision on which individuals and schools of thought to include were functions chiefly of our themes, and to some extent our own interests and expertise. Our position is that in trying to explain developments in economic thought and in social sciences more generally, both factors internal to the discipline and external to it, relating to social, political and ideological developments, play a crucial role. Thus, any account of the evolution of economic thought that does not take into account both these sources of change is bound to be partial and

---

32   The same applies to a lot of other concepts and arguments we have used. Thus, for example, when we talk about Becker's approach as representing an "as if market" type of approach, or new information economics as having given rise to a more successful form of economics imperialism, we mean this *on their own terms*. In other words, the term "market" in this context is used in the "highly impoverished" way used by Becker, while by the success of the new form of economics imperialism we do not mean that new information theorists have managed to make any serious inroads into the true nature of the institutions and the social phenomena to which they have applied their limited models, but simply that they have been more successful, *on their own terms*, than their Becker-type predecessors, in making incursions into non-economic phenomena, see Fleetwood, pp. 53–54, and Hodgson (2011, pp. 367–70).

incomplete. In this regard we are at one with Backhouse. So, we are neither in favour of purely external explanations of the evolution of economic thought nor of purely internalist ones (see King).

As far as our account in concerned, however, there are two things that need to be borne in mind. First, to repeat, our intention was not to offer a HET. Thus, although at first sight Backhouse's claim that our very theme (the role of the social and the historical in economic theorising) should have made the inclusion of the role of social and political factors influencing the trajectory of economic ideas mandatory seems correct, there is another aspect of our narrative which can be invoked as a justification of the opposite thesis (i.e. the non-inclusion of such factors in our narrative). This is that our intention was to write an *intellectual* history of the shifting role of method, the historical and the social in the evolution of economic theory. Hence, the themes of our books are examined in a methodological or meta-theoretical context. This dictated (explains) the focus of our narrative mostly at the level of ideas rather than the social and political developments influencing them, without this implying an internalist position taken by us on the question of the evolution of economic theory.

Second, as King, pp. 41–2, notes, we have not left such factors out of considerations altogether. In our discussion of the *Methodenstreit*, the German historical school, Tarshis and the post war triumph of neoclassical (Keynesian) economics, and our discussion of the connection between neo-liberalism and mainstream economics, we have taken such factors into account. It is true, however, that, despite the methodological nature of our narrative, we could have made the role of such factors more explicit in our narrative even if we could not have fully integrated them into our analysis, given the nature of our books. Granted this, we consider, for example, Backhouse's claim to the effect that the French Revolution poses a dividing line in how economics is perceived and formed as absolutely valid. In the same spirit, who can doubt that Keynes' *General Theory of Employment, Interest and Money* was to a large extent the result of the Great Depression of the 1930s (the external) but also to the discrediting in conjunction with such external events of the classical notion of self-adjusting markets prevalent at the time?[33] Or that the ludicrous New Classical Economics of the 1970s, with its representative individuals holding rational expectations, perfectly working markets and ineffective states and the perceived collapse of Keynesianism (the internal), was prompted by the fiscal crisis of the state and the ensuing phenomenon of stagflation (the external),

---

33 See Fine and Milonakis (2011).

and hence being equally dependent upon the extrapolation of the orthodoxy to extremes in defiance of the external (as quasi-realism)? Significantly, the intellectual response to the current downturn cannot mirror that of the 1970s because it involves a loss of legitimacy of neo-liberalism as opposed to a monetarist counter-revolution against Keynesianism.

Our themes have also dictated in important ways the individuals and schools of thought dealt with in our books. As far as the first volume is concerned, our aim was to bring to the fore the main staging posts in the process of desocialisation and dehistoricisation of economic theorising, rather than provide a full account of all the individuals and intellectual currents of the corresponding period. This explains our non-inclusion of the important analyses in terms of the themes discussed, of many Marxists during this period (Hilferding, Luxemburg, Bukharin and others) and of Michel Kalecki and his important contributions to macroeconomics (King, pp. 41–2). However, we do believe that we have given fuller treatments to most non-neoclassical currents of this period including the German and British historical schools with their emphasis on the role of history and their crucial role in the genesis of economic history as a discipline, Weber, Schumpeter and Pareto and their role in the birth, or continuing evolution, of sociology and the separation of economics form sociology, the old institutionalists with their broad conception of economic science and their emphasis on evolutionary themes and institutions, and the Austrian school.

Our interpretation of the pivotal role of the marginalist revolution and of Alfred Marshall has also been a matter of dispute. In our view, the differences between classical political economy and neoclassical orthodoxy (acknowledging that each is itself diverse across time and contributor) are more marked than any other division between schools in the evolution of economic thought, if such things could be quantified. Having said this, McNally gives the impression that the transition was abrupt, understandably so given how little he spends on it. As we have argued in our first book, however, the transition involves a slow, painful and complex process, between the appearance of the first traces of neoclassical principles in the 1830s and 1840s, to its establishment as the main corpus of economic science following Marshall's treatise, culminating in its total dominance following the formalist revolution of the 1950s, with the marginalist revolution occupying a mid-way but crucial staging post in this process, M&F, p. 93. And there is much to learn by examining critically the processes by which these new principles were testily received, whether in acceptance or rejection, if only to carry on regardless.

As for Marshall's role, we do not recognize our account of Marshall as offered by Backhouse (and Hodgson) as purely a stepping stone to Robbins. It is interesting in this respect that King sees us as unduly benevolent to Marshall as opposed to Ricardo. What is incontrovertible of (our account of) Marshall is that, despite his undoubted roundedness as compared with the earlier marginalists, he deliberately and successfully sought to establish the foundations for the technical apparatus that has come to dominate the mainstream thereafter but that he himself saw this apparatus as at most a part of economics. That recent research, much cited by Backhouse, suggests that Marshall was even more rounded than we acknowledge is beside the (or even strengthening of our) point.

But it is not only with Marshall that we are charged with misinterpretation. King finds us unduly harsh on Ricardo for having highlighted his deductivism. The reason for doing so, however, is threefold: first, Ricardo was the first to apply this method with such force; second is the pivotal role deductivism has played both in the marginalist revolution and in subsequent developments in mainstream economics; and, last, but not least, is to allow for presentation of the debate between inductivism and deductivism itself of primary importance in our narrative (if not to us as such, see above). This was certainly taken to be serious at the time and symbolic of difference with marginalism from within the historical schools, as reflected in the *methodenstreit*. Further, there has been a false presumption that deductivism won the debate in principle as opposed to practice, whereas there was a general acceptance of both deductive and inductive methods. Last, Backhouse and King dispute our account of Keynes and, once again, this is more a matter of emphasis and opinion than fundamental disagreement, once accepting our goal of demonstrating how the foundations of Keynes' own economics, and their implications, were dissonant with what Keynesianism (and much more across the discipline) was to become. As suggested, if Keynes could not hold back what was to become the orthodoxy's roller coaster – who could?

Last, King accuses us of getting the history of sociology, especially the history of its emergence, wrong. According to him, the desocialisation of economics had nothing to do with the emergence of sociology as we argue. Drawing on the work of Giddens (1986) and Swingewood (2000), he points out that the origins of sociology go back to the French and the industrial revolutions and have roots in the works of Comte and Marx. King here confuses two different but interrelated things. First is the question of the origins of a scientific field and, second, is its actual emergence as a separate discipline. When we talk about the influence of the desocialisation of economics in the emergence of sociology we refer to the latter *as a separate discipline*. We make this absolutely clear when we say that "both the concepts of positivism and sociology were invented by the French nineteenth century philosopher Auguste Comte

(1798–1857) … However, although the origins of modern sociology can be traced back to Comte's vision of a new science of society which would become the "Queen of the Sciences" … it did not fully emerge as a separate discipline until the turn of the last century. Following the developments taking place around economic science, sociology played its part in filling out the gap left by the desocialisation of economic science. As a separate discipline, sociology was to concern itself with the "social", defined negatively as the "non-economic", or more exactly, non-economics", M&F, pp. 216–7. We see absolutely no contradiction between our account and those of Giddens and Swingewood. What is novel in our account is the emphasis on the developments in economic science as an extra factor in the emergence of sociology as a separate discipline, a point illustrated at length in our first book with reference to the works of Max Weber, Vilfredo Pareto and Talcott Parsons, each of whom, to a larger or lesser extent, played a decisive role in this process. This is natural given that in our books we approach the developments in other social sciences *as seen from the confines of the dismal science.*

7   Economics Imperialism and the Role of Finance

In case of economics imperialism, the diverse cases of industrial relations, management, labour economics and economic history are of interest and significance, and we would welcome contributions including our own but especially those from others. These will be indicative not of the triumph of economics imperialism across the social sciences which, contra King, p. 39,[34] we do not argue, but of its uneven, varied and complex impact contingent upon the evolution and momentum of individual disciplines and topics. This is why we emphasise the prospect of alternatives drawing upon political economy in wake of the dual retreat from postmodernism and neoliberalism around which King's appeal to metaphors is unhelpful given the extent to which we demonstrate economics has colonised the subject matter of other social sciences. The reverse process to the extent that it is taking place, as for example with experimental and behavioural economics through the use of the experimental methods first used within the social sciences in psychology, is done in accordance with and not against the major pillars of orthodox economics: model building and methodological individualism (Fine and Milonakis 2011, pp. 19–22).

---

34   See also Hodgson (2011, p. 358).

This is the subject matter of our second volume where our main preoccupation has been the exploration of the processes of economics imperialism and its reception by other social sciences. As we have explained in our introduction, due to the immense terrain covered, we were highly selective in what was included and what was not. Politics, however, one of the first areas to be colonised by economics imperialists, does, contra King, pp. 47–48, get its share, F&M, pp. 36–42, but not anthropology, exactly because it has escaped almost untouched by economics imperialism. Post-Keynesianism and other heterodox schools (with one exception which could have been included in our account but was not, analytical or rational choice Marxism) have played no role in this process, which explains their non-inclusion and not any disregard for their contributions.

Coming to McNally's comments, it is significant that the new institutional economics did not take off from Polanyi (and his embeddedness) even if the interpretative focus is placed upon its origins within sociology and other than within neoclassical economics itself. Rather the origins reside with Granovetter (and his embeddedness) who confesses to have been uninfluenced by, even ignorant of, Polanyi, whilst seeking to disrupt the "functional economism" of those such as Williamson, F&M, pp. 88–9. As Hodgson (2007) has observed, the boundaries around economic sociology (and new institutional economics) are extremely fuzzy but, in contrast to him, we continue to acknowledge that there are distinct disciplinary differences between how the subject matter is treated.

On a related point, McNally is much too harsh on Zelizer. Her approach to money is not a short step to freakonomics as he suggests, although there is no doubt that Zelizer's varieties of monies could provide it with building materials.[35] So there are huge difference between those ranging across (economic) sociology and more so for being attentive to sociologically determined meanings (Zelizer). Similar differences prevail across economic geography, as in the differences with those such as Krugman whose extensive corpus of work on economic geography and trade hinges entirely on the slightest of deviations from the standard technical apparatus by allowing for increasing returns to scale.[36] What defines economics imperialism is its deep attachment to rational

---

35 See debate between Zelizer (1994 and 2000) and Fine and Lapavitsas (2000).
36 Just to forestall charges of undue prejudice, that our location of the causes and sources of economics imperialism derive exclusively from economists rather than non-economists, it is worth highlighting that Williamson and Ostrom were jointly awarded the Nobel prize for economics 2009, the later the first woman and political scientist as such, see Fine (2010b).

choice, however much this may be concealed and/or complemented by other factors. Whilst rational choice in the particular form of utility maximisation has become de rigueur across mainstream economics, it is far from confined to that discipline, with the potential for other disciplines to engage in, and not just be the victim of, economics imperialism if generally laid down by economics (formal models and statistical investigation).

These differences with McNally over our interpretation of particular contributors may simply reflect the more detailed filtering through which we have viewed them, leading him to be harder and potentially cruder. Similar considerations apply to his wish that we should have made more of an effort to offer an alternative political economy rooted in Marx's method and theory.[37] This absence reflects a strategic endeavour to engage that mixed bag of heterodox economists (who share little in common other than antipathy to orthodoxy) and equally that mixed bag of political economists located primarily within other disciplines (who share little in common other than recognition of the importance of the economic for their studies). We consider value and price theory as an indispensable reflection of the study of capitalism. Indeed, as argued elsewhere, we consider as one of the main drawbacks of (old) institutionalists and Hodgson in particular, who reduce capitalism to a portfolio of institutions, to be exactly the lack of a theory of value and price. There is a striking parallel here with Krugman for whom capitalism is a bundle of increasing returns and transportation costs whose minimal theoretical departure from the conceptually fragile, technical requirements of neoclassical orthodoxy means he is incapable of providing a theory of value.[38] Yet, in their different ways and for different audiences, these are radical scholars, whose followers must be addressed on their own terms, as well as by reference to alternatives.

McNally does point to a major if not total absence in our work of critical assessment of theories of finance, particularly salient in the current conjuncture. As already mentioned, our books have drawn limits on what is addressed and in what depth.[39] There are a couple of points that we want to raise in this connection. One is the need to understand and divide neo-liberalism into two phases, roughly separated by the early 1990s in which "shock therapy" gave way

---

37 Callinicos (2011, p. 269) makes a similar point.
38 See Arrow (2000) and Fine (2010a) for further discussion.
39 Subsequent work has addressed finance as financialisation but with greater attention to material developments themselves as opposed to the impoverished orthodoxy that has proven a dismal failure in tracking events whether through the efficient market hypothesis or, as alternative, the inefficient market hypothesis (Fine 2009b) most recent at the time. But see also Bayliss et al (2018) and Fine (2022).

to making markets work. Whilst neo-liberalism has always involved extensive state intervention on behalf of private capital in general and private finance in particular, the scholarship and ideology have shifted as has policy to some degree as the state is required both to temper the effects of the first phase in terms of dysfunction and economic and social stability, and yet to continue to promote the penetration of private capital into new areas through the active and overt intervention of the state (we have done all the privatization we can, so now let's get the state to support the private sector with public-private partnerships and the like).[40]

There is after all an extraordinary cushion now protecting mainstream theories of finance from appropriate systemic considerations (in part dependent upon money being assigned to macroeconomics and finance to microeconomics, so that, for example, bankruptcy and credit crunches never meet). It has long separated risk (the probabilistically knowable) from uncertainty (the unknowable such as what is the nature of this crisis and with what it is going to be replaced?). It has turned risk into something that is calculable and so can be priced so that uncertainty is unwittingly priced by risk as proxy. But arbitrage in financial markets effectively reduces profits from trading in risk to zero. So, to the extent that such a theory is transformed into practice, as with Black-Scholes pricing formula for derivatives, the growth of finance depends upon the growth of uncertainty (and its priced transformation as if risk). Such growing uncertainty can either be generated by external factors, by the extension of finance to new uncertain areas, or by trading more and more in uncertainty as risk through proliferation of financial assets themselves. The latter two have been extensive over the past thirty years and may be denoted by financialisation. But orthodoxy tends to see this as extending the market for risk more (efficient market hypothesis) or less (inefficient market hypothesis) efficiently, but it indicates the growing penetration of uncertainty by risk and its commodification as such.

This critique of orthodoxy can go in a number of directions. One, represented by the performativity school with lineage in actor-network theory, sees the theory or the economists as making the markets. The other is to look for the origins of uncertainty itself within the capitalist system and develop a theory of finance accordingly.

Last, on the question of the absence of discussion on critical realism raised by Fleetwood, as argued elsewhere, there is much to commend in critical realism in and of itself and in critique of the (lack of) methodology of mainstream

---

40   Again, some updating with a third phase now added, see Fine (2020a and b) for example.

economics.[41] Minor reservations apart, though, our concern both analytically and strategically has been to move beyond, or around, methodology to the substance of political economy and economics itself, something on which critical realism has been notably weak, defensive and unduly eclectic. Priority to methodology has a pleasing logical appeal but cuts limited ice within and against a discipline that is totally oblivious to it.

8 The Road Ahead

So much of the past, what of the future? Will the result be stasis, involution, fragmentation and revolution (see King)? Although it is still too early for a definite answer, we have tried in our other article in the pages of this journal to trace the possible trajectory of these developments and give some tentative answers (Fine and Milonakis 2011). Our view that the core of mainstream economics is stable reflects our understanding of what it is and how it became so, with extraordinary and intolerant commitment to model building and a familiar technical apparatus around utility and production functions, on the one hand, and methodological individualism on the other, although this is complemented by methods that are becoming less rigid around statistical use of empirical evidence, behavioural assumptions, reliance upon game theory, and so on. We do acknowledge the proliferation of such developments around the margins of the discipline and accept, at least logically, that these could have some impact on the discipline. If, however, these developments are set against the deadweight of orthodox training and mainstream publishing, and to the extent that these developments are tied to the two pillars of mainstream economic theorising, model building and methodological individualism, their impact is bound to remain marginal. There are now, and relatively recently, an awful lot of heavily technically trained, single-minded mainstream economists (only in our own lifetimes have the mathematical economists gone from being novas to black holes), and they are hassling for new directions in an overcrowded milieu. It is as well to be aware of what they share in common as opposed to the chaotic differences that mark their originalities and the discipline's fashions. Significantly, all commentators seem to overlook the extent to which freakonomics is not merely popularisation but the very image of a less than dramatically new orthodoxy in the making.

---

41 See Fine (2004b, 2006 and 2007), the last not least in debate with Fleetwood (2006). More recently, see Fine (2015).

As regards the future for political economy, our prognostications about its brighter prospects across the social sciences, other than economics itself, are not challenged. The crisis has no doubt strengthened that prospect. King in particular, though, questions what we mean by political economy, and what we would ourselves propose. What we do seek is to draw upon the rich insights and traditions of the past as a means of genuinely reincorporating the social and historical, through a renewed transdisciplinary political economy with contemporary capitalism as the main object of analysis. And although we believe that the chief source of these insights is Marx's legacy, our own work demonstrates the insights to be gained from those who do not subscribe to, or are even hostile to, Marxism.

With regard to the contribution of our books, we are not blameless for the extent to which the reviews share an almost esoteric and even marginal air in light of the current crisis that erupted only after these books were primarily completed, given the preoccupation with, but not goal of, the HET that they incorporate. But our books are much more focused on future prospects for political economy than are the reviewers, especially in relation both to needs (the study of contemporary capitalism) and to the most fertile ground for them through transdisciplinarity and interdisciplinarity in the wake of the dual retreats from the extremes of postmodernism and neo-liberalism that we identified prior to the crisis and which draw no commentary. Far from being negated by recent developments, these perspectives are strengthened. It is commonplace to observe that neither orthodoxy nor heterodoxy has gained much purchase practically in response to the crisis, one because it is unable to do so, and the other because it has neither the resources nor organised support to establish alternatives. There is, then, something of a limbo across policy, ideology and scholarship as neo-liberalism has lost legitimacy (whilst remaining as a sort of default option), and nothing has been able to emerge to replace it other than diluted forms of Keynesianism primarily pursued in mindless support of the financial system. Having said this, intellectually, the shape of things show a somewhat different picture with all sound attempts at explaining crises certainly before but also after the crisis coming from heterodox traditions in economics. And practically there are hopeful signs in the launch of the World Economics Association as the heterodox equivalent of the American Economic Association, which already numbers more than 10,000 members and the hugely successful Paris conference organised by three major heterodox Associations, the International Initiative for Promoting Political Economy (IIPPE), the Association of Heterodox Economics (AHE) and the French Association of Political Economy (AFEP) last July drawing around 700 participants, as discussed in Fine and Milonakis (2011). In a sense, both orthodoxy in economics and policymaking, and not just the financial system, have hit their Minsky moment, and the way forward is for political economy to be vigorously pursued across the social sciences.

References

Arestis, P. and M. Sawyer (eds) (2004) *The Rise of the Market*, Camberley: Edward Elgar.

Arrow, K. (2000) "Increasing Returns: Histographic Issues and Path Dependence", *European Journal of History of Economic Thought*, vol 7, no 2, pp. 171–80.

Ashman, S. (2012) "Economics and Political Economy Today: Introduction to the Symposium on Fine and Milonakis", *Historical Materialism*, vol 20, no 3, pp. 3–8.

Backhouse, R. (2012) "Political Economy: History with the Politics Left Out?", *Historical Materialism*, vol 20, no 3, pp. 24–38.

Bateman, M., S. Blankenburg and R. Kozul-Wright (2018) *The Rise and Fall of Global Microcredit: Development, Debt and Disillusion*, London: Routledge.

Bayliss, K., B. Fine and M. Robertson (eds) (2018) *Material Cultures of Financialisation*, London: Routledge, reproduced from special issue of *New Political Economy*, vol 22, no 4, 2017.

Callinicos, A. (2011) "Book Review: *From Political Economy to Economics*", *Science and Society*, vol 75, no 2, pp. 267–9.

Choonara, J. (2010) "Book Reviews: *From Political Economy to Economics* and *From Economics Imperialism to Freakonomics*", *International Socialism*, no 127, available at http://isj.org.uk/economic-development/.

Colander, D. (2010) "Book Reviews: *From Political Economy to Economics* and *From Economics Imperialism to Freakonomics*", Middlebury College Economics, Discussion Paper, no 10–03.

Damodaran, S., S. Gupta, S. Mitra and D. Sinha (eds) (2023) *Development, Transformations and the Human Condition: Volume in Honour of Professor Jayati Ghosh*, New Delhi: Routledge, forthcoming.

Fasenfest, D. (ed.) (2022) *Marx Matters*, Leiden: Brill.

Fine, B. (2001a) "Economics Imperialism as Kuhnian Revolution?", *International Papers in Political Economy*, vol 8, no 2, pp. 1–58.

Fine, B. (2001b) *Social Capital versus Social Theory: Political Economy and Social Science at the Turn of the Millennium*, London: Routledge.

Fine, B. (2003) "From the Newer Economic History to Institutions and Development?", *Institutions and Economic Development*, vol 1, no 1, pp. 105–36.

Fine, B. (2004a) "Economics Imperialism as Kuhnian Revolution", in Arestis and Sawyer (eds) (2004), pp. 107–44.

Fine, B. (2004b) "Addressing the Critical and the Real in Critical Realism", in Lewis (ed.) (2004), pp. 202–26.

Fine, B. (2006) "Debating Critical Realism in Economics", *Capital and Class*, no 89, June, pp. 121–29.

Fine, B. (2007) "Rethinking Critical Realism: Labour Markets or Capitalism?", *Capital and Class*, vol 31, no 1, pp. 125–29.

Fine, B. (2009a) "The Economics of Identity and the Identity of Economics?", *Cambridge Journal of Economics*, vol 33, no 2, pp. 175–91. See Chapter 5.

Fine, B. (2009b) "Financialisation, the Value of Labour Power, the Degree of Separation, and Exploitation by Banking", https://eprints.soas.ac.uk/7480/2/BenFine_FinancialisationLabourPower.pdf.

Fine, B. (2010a) "Flattening Economic Geography: Locating the World Development Report for 2009", *Journal of Economic Analysis*, vol 1, no 1, pp. 15–33, http://users.ntua.gr/jea/JEA%20Vol.%20I,%20No%20I,%202010/jea_volume1_issue1_pp15_33.pdf.

Fine, B. (2010b) "Beyond the Tragedy of the Commons: a Discussion of *Governing the Commons: the Evolution of Institutions for Collective Action*", *Perspectives on Politics*, vol 8, no 2, pp. 583–86.

Fine, B. (2010c) *Theories of Social Capital: Researchers Behaving Badly*, London: Pluto Press.

Fine, B. (2015) "Neoclassical Economics: an Elephant Is Not a Chimera But Is a Chimera Real?", in Morgan (ed.) (2015), pp. 180–99.

Fine, B. (2020a) "Framing Social Reproduction in the Age of Financialisation" in Santos and Teles (eds) (2020), pp. 257–72.

Fine, B. (2020b) "Situating PPPs", in Gideon and Unterhalter (eds) (2020), pp. 26–38.

Fine, B. (2022) "From Marxist Political Economy to Financialisation or Is It the Other Way About?", in Fasenfest (ed.), pp. 43–66.

Fine, B. (2023) "Social Capital: the Indian Connection", in Damodaran et al (eds) (2023), forthcoming.

Fine, B. and C. Lapavitsas (2000) "Markets and Money in Social Theory: What Role for Economics?", *Economic and Society*, vol 29, no 3, pp. 357–82.

Fine, B. and D. Milonakis (2003) "From Principle of Pricing to Pricing of Principle: Rationality and Irrationality in the Economic History of Douglass North", *Comparative Studies in Society and History*, vol 45, no 3, pp. 120–44.

Fine, B. and D. Milonakis (2009) *From Economics Imperialism to Freakonomics: the Shifting Boundaries between Economics and Other Social Sciences*, London: Routledge.

Fine, B. and D. Milonakis (2011) "'Useless but True': Economic Crisis and the Peculiarities of Economic Science", *Historical Materialism*, vol 19, no 2, pp. 3–31.

Fine, B. and D. Milonakis (2012) "From Freakonomics to Political Economy", *Historical Materialism*, vol 20, no 3, pp. 81–96.

Fleetwood, S. (2006) "Rethinking Labour Markets: a Critical Realist-Socioeconomic Perspective", *Capital and Class*, no 89, June, pp. 59–89.

Fleetwood, S. (2012) "'From Political Economy to Economics' and Beyond", *Historical Materialism*, vol 20, no 3, pp. 61–80.

Friedman, M. (1953) "The Methodology of Positive Economics", in Friedman (ed.) (1953), pp. 3–43, reprinted in Hausman (ed.) (2007), pp. 145–78.

Fullbrook, E. (ed.) (2009) *Ontology and Economics: Tony Lawson and His Critics*, London: Routledge.

Giddens, A. (1986) *Sociology: a Brief but Critical Introduction*, Basingstoke: Macmillan.

Gideon, J. and E. Unterhalter (eds) (2020) *Critical Reflections on Public Private Partnerships*, London: Routledge.

Gunn, C. (2012) "Book Review of *From Political Economy to Economics*", *Review of Radical Political Economics*, vol 44, no 2, pp. 240–1.

Hanappi, H. (2011) "Book Review: *From Political Economy to Economics*", *European Journal of the History of Economic Thought*, vol 18, no 4, pp. 619–22.

Hausman, D. (ed.) (2007) *The Philosophy of Economics: an Anthology*, Cambridge: Cambridge University Press.

Hayek, F. (1942–4) "Scientism and the Study of Society", originally published in three parts in *Economica*, vol 9, no 35, pp. 267–91, 1942; vol 10, no 37, pp. 34–63, 1943; vol 11, no 41, pp. 27–39, 1944, reprinted in F. Hayek, *The Counter Revolution in Science: Studies in the Abuse of Reason*, Glencoe, Illinois: The Free Press, 1952.

Hodgson, G. (2007) "Marshall, Schumpeter and the Shifting Boundaries of Economics and Sociology", available at https://uhra.herts.ac.uk/handle/2299/2691.

Hodgson, G. (2011) "Sickonomics: Diagnoses and Remedies", *Review of Social Economy*, vol 69, no 3, pp. 357–76.

Hodgson, G. (2012) "From Social Theory to Explaining Sickonomics: a Response to Dimitris Milonakis and Ben Fine", *Review of Social Economy*, vol 70, no 4, pp, 492–507.

Hofferberth, E. (2022) *Pathways to an Equitable Post-Growth Economy: Towards an Economics for Social-Ecological Transformation*, University of Leeds, unpublished PhD thesis.

King, J. (2012) "Sixteen Questions for Fine and Milonakis", *Historical Materialism*, vol 20, no 3, pp. 39–60.

Lawson, T. (1997) *Economics and Reality*, London: Routledge.

Lawson, T. (2003) *Reorienting Economics*, London: Routledge.

Lewis, P. (ed.) 2004, *Transforming Economics: Perspectives on the Critical Realist Project*, London: Routledge.

Mader, P., D. Mertens and N. Van der Zwan (eds) (2020) *International Handbook of Financialization*, London: Routledge.

Marx, K. (1972 [1852]) *The Eighteenth Brumaire of Louis Bonaparte*, in *Marx, Engels, Lenin on Historical Materialism*, Moscow: Progress Publishers.

Marx, K. (1973 [1957–8]) *Grundrisse*, translated with a Forward by Martin Nikolaus, London: Penguin Books.

McNally, D. (2012) "From Fetishism to 'Shocked Disbelief': Economics, Dialectics and Value Theory", *Historical Materialism*, vol 20, no 3, pp. 9–23.

Milonakis, D. and B. Fine (2007) "Douglass North's Remaking of Economic History: a Critical Appraisal", *Review of Radical Political Economics*, vol 39, no 1, pp. 27–57.

Milonakis, D. and B. Fine (2009) *From Political Economy to Economics: Method, the Social and the Historical in the Evolution of Economic Theory*, London: Routledge.

Milonakis, D. and B. Fine (2012) "Interrogating Sickonomics, from Diagnosis to Cure: a Response to Hodgson", *Review of Social Economy*, vol 70, no 4, pp. 477–491.

Milonakis, D. and G. Meramveliotakis (2012) "Homo Economicus and the Economics of Property Rights: History in Reverse Order", *Review of Radical Political Economics*, vol 45, no 1, pp. 5–23.

Morgan, J. (ed.) (2015) *What Is This 'School' Called Neoclassical Economics?: Debating the Origins, Meaning and Significance*, London: Routledge.

Pirgmaier (2018) *Value, Capital and Nature: Rethinking the Foundations of Ecological Economics*, University of Leeds, unpublished PhD thesis.

Roncaglia, A. (2009) "Book Review: *From Political Economy to Economics*", *European Journal of the History of Economic Thought*, vol 16, no 3, pp. 527–29.

Samuelson, P. (1947) *Foundations of Economic Analysis*, Cambridge: Harvard University Press.

Samuelson, P. (2016) "My Life Philosophy", *The American Economist*, vol 61, no 1, pp. 61–68.

Santos, A. and N. Teles (eds) (2020) *Financialisation in the European Periphery: Work and Social Reproduction in Portugal*, London: Routledge.

Sato, H. (2012) "Book Review: *From Economics Imperialism to Freakonomics*", *The Developing Economies*, vol 50, no 2, pp. 195–96.

Schumpeter, J. (1981[1954]) *History of Economic Analysis*, London: Routledge.

Swingewood, A. (2000) *A Short History of Sociological Thought*, Basingstoke: Macmillan.

Zelizer, V. (1994) *The Social Meaning of Money*, New York: Basic Books.

Zelizer, V. (2000) "Fine-Tuning the Zelizer View", *Economy and Society*, vol 29, no 3, pp. 383–89.

CHAPTER 8

Freakonomics as Thickening End of the Symbolic Wedge

Postscript as Personal Preamble

This chapter, unlike most of the others in this volume, has never appeared in print in any form.[1] It was intended to be a joint response from Dimitris Milonakis and myself to an article by Jack Vromen (2009) that, as is made clear in what follows, we were disappointed to find not only misrepresented our own positions in Fine and Milonakis (2009) but also misreading of the significance of both freakonomics and economics imperialism and, seemingly, failing to take them seriously.[2]

In the event, our response remained confined to my own draft alone, with pressure of other obligations preventing Dimitris from adding his own contribution. However, I was pleased to find upon revisiting it that my draft was able to stand alone subject to minimal polishing. Significantly, the retrieved electronic version dates from at least early April, 2010, but includes reference to the third phase of economics imperialism. This phase is where the core technical apparatus and architecture, TA^2, of mainstream economics is freely, if rarely consistently and coherently, complemented by whatever other factors are perceived to be relevant. In other words, TA^2 can be deployed or discarded at will, what was later to be called its suspension.[3]

In preparing this volume, I came across for the first time, the contribution of Nik-Khah and Van Horn (2012). Given overt attention to economics imperialism is entering a watershed leading to decline at this time, this contribution may be unique in drawing explicit attention to three different interpretations of economics imperialism, to which they add their own and fourth (or at least as far as freakonomics is concerned). For them, the three interpretations are: our own (taking economics imperialism as an established and ongoing

---

1 This chapter is newly drafted for this volume.
2 As suggested in Chapter 2, in his stance on freakonomics and economics imperialism, Vromen appears to belong to a school of economic methodology that takes a balanced view on it, although Vromen seems to be more balanced (i.e. extreme) than the others in misreading its own imbalance.
3 For full accounts of TA^2 and suspension, see the last chapter of this volume.

fact); Vromen's with economics imperialism a myth and freakonomics just a bit of fluffy fun; and that of John Davis, and others, in which economic imperialism has been a fact but is now in decline because of favourable influence of other social sciences (reverse economics imperialism) with correspondingly strategic opportunities for heterodoxy to accelerate and influence the mainstream's subsequent trajectory. Their own position is closest to the last but that economics imperialism, and freakonomics in particular, is a peculiar and particular consequence of the power, influence and energy of Chicago economics, something which they see as brought to light only through close archival research. In a nutshell, Nik-Khah and Van Horn (2012, p. 271):

> Whereas Fine and Milonakis understand Levitt to be part of a sweeping, century-long project in economics, Vromen portrays Levitt as part of a novel 'economics-is-fun' genre. We believe a more promising route to understanding Levitt [freakonomics] would be neither to locate him within a broad, sweeping century-long narrative about neoclassical economics [Fine and Milonakis], nor in a historically unprecedented genre [Davis], but instead within a specific part of the postwar Chicago School.

In this light, the main purpose here is to correct how our understanding of economics imperialism is being presented by Nik-Khah and Van Horn. But, before doing so, it is vital to record agreement with, and appreciation of, the archival research on this matter and more broadly as far as the Chicago school is concerned. In particular, Nik-Khah and Van Horn document how the Chicago school literally and ever "proudly" promotes economics imperialism. Whilst Gary Becker is usually taken as the leading figure, they offer an excellent account of George Stigler's role in promoting economics imperialism (especially for law and politics) as part of Chicago's neoliberal project.[4]

How, then, could Nik-Khah and Van Horn have got Chicago so right and, yet, us so wrong, see below? The answer is very simple. They only see economics imperialism (and freakonomics as its offshoot) as deriving from the Chicago school. So, it is confined to its influence and activity for which, of course, archival research is vital in bringing out its core characteristics as well as its idiosyncrasies and extremes of which freakonomics is a part. But, by our own account, this is to define economics imperialism by what we categorise as its first phase alone as if its second and third phases simply do not

---

4 This is part and parcel of the broader promotion of neoliberalism (see Mirowski and Plehwe 2015).

exist. This is perverse to the extreme not least as my own interest in economics imperialism was not prompted by, and presented as, the intellectually head-banging endeavours of the Chicago imperialists but its more nuanced and less transparent versions deriving from market information economics. If economics imperialism is only seen as what Chicago does and influences as part and parcel of a neoliberal project, then inevitably it is going to wax and wane with the prominence of Chicago in these respects and is exclusive to it. To put this another way, it is as if Arrow, Samuelson, Solow, Stiglitz, Akerlof, Krugman, Romer (all Nobels "against" Chicago), and so the list could run on, have no role to play in economics imperialism whereas, by our own account, they are vital if not central from its second phase onwards. Chicago has long been superseded in the trajectory of economics imperialism, as was already transparent and remarked as crucial fifteen years before Nik-Khah and Van Horn continue to designate it as having been what it is all about. Unsurprisingly, then, they tend to favour Davis's position, subject to contextualising the role of Chicago.

Against this general (mis)framing of economics imperialism, errors of interpretation of our own position are more understandable if still unacceptable with a closer read of our texts. First, on the reading of freakonomics itself, we do see it in the context of a century-long sweep in the development of mainstream economics but not as rigidly determined by it, see below also. Rather, despite deriving from Chicago training and milieu, freakonomics is remarkable for both drawing upon it and rejecting it at the same time, something we see as both anticipating and contributing to the emergence of the third phase of economics imperialism through "suspension".

Second, nor do we see economics imperialism as rigidly determined by an inevitable trajectory for mainstream economics. Admittedly, there is posed a historical logic to economics imperialism – how its TA^2 was established through implosion (throwing out what was inconsistent with it) but then using that very same TA^2 to analyse what had to be discarded to establish itself. This is a matter of historical fact and conceptual logic, with a path disrupted materially by the Great Depression of the thirties and intellectual sensitivities around what happens to distribution theory, quite apart from how to deal with monopolisation, technical progress, and institutions ranging from the major corporation through to trade unions. But, crucially, the historical logic of economics imperialism leaves open, as subject to contestation, whether and how TA^2 is deployed both within economics itself as well as, our main business, by economics imperialism in its relations with other disciplines where the historical logic comes up against the traditions, practices and resistances of other disciplines. Such considerations again reveal an inclination to impose a rigidity upon our account which is simply not there (with need to be corrected by close archival research which, in the event, heavily confirms our discussion of the first phase of economics imperialism albeit necessarily not engaging with its successors).

Third, along the same theme of undue determinism on our part is the view that our account of economics imperialism tends to view it as unceremoniously and homogeneously swamping the other social sciences (as was Chicago's proud mission). Nothing could be further from the truth as our position from the outset has always been that the incidence and impact of economics imperialism is both discipline and topic dependent with the implication that it needs to be studied and explained as such. Indeed, there are, or have been, more or less no go areas for economics imperialism (especially where the discursive and interpretative are involved, such as consumption and anthropology); there are areas where swamping is involved, such as development economics (with implications for development studies) spearheaded by the World Bank, the new economic history, with the result of a division with social history, and the new economic geography; and there are uneasy compromises across institutionalism and anything involving 'capital' whether human, natural or social alongside a plethora of others (Baron and Hannan 1994). Tellingly, the rise across the social sciences of "financialisation", on the face of it a topic to be owned by economics, has found its place everywhere other than (mainstream) economics (Mader et al (eds) 2020).

The two pieces by Vromen and Nik-Khah and Van Horn have, then, in common superficial readings of our account of economics imperialism, in which it is misinterpreted to such an extent that it is presented as its opposite on major issues such as how deterministic and pervasive it is. To whatever extent this will have influenced the reception and prominence of economics imperialism especially to the extent that its significance has been misinterpreted more generally. In other words, misreading of economics imperialism has dovetailed with other reasons for underestimating it – especially that it ranges over so many issues such as history of thought, interdisciplinarity, methodology, the nature of neoclassical and heterodox economics, and strategies for pluralism and political economy.[5] Unfortunately, the concluding upbeat assessment of the prospects for critique of economics imperialism appear to have been misfounded.

---

5 See Chapter 2 and preamble to Chapter 9.

1 Response to Jack Vromen[6]

In his recent contribution, Jack Vromen (2009) deploys a clear distinction between economics-made-fun,[7] of which the leading example is freaknonomics, and making fun of economics. For the latter, he renders a rare combination of entertaining and scholarly narrative, including an account of the failure of freakonomics to appreciate when fun is fun so seriously does it take itself. But, in addition, to the distinction between these two genres, Vromen is also aware of the differences between economics imperialism and freakonomics, so much so that he wishes to suggest, as the title to his piece makes explicit, that freakonomics is not or, at the very least, falls far short of economics imperialism, EI. This conclusion is hardly surprising since it tends to be conflated with a much stronger proposition that EI itself *does not* exist. If so, of course, there is no way in which freakonomics can be representative of EI. Indeed, as will be suggested below, some if not all of Vromen's commentary even implies that EI *cannot* exist.

Not surprisingly, given that Milonakis and myself are leading proponents of the hypothesis that EI is alive and well in the contemporary world of social science, Vromen is highly critical of our interpretation of it and of freakonomics, see Fine and Milonakis (2009) and Milonakis and Fine (2009) for the prehistory. He offers a number of arguments in riposte but he both misrepresents our contributions and overlooks much of its core content, possibly because of an undue focus upon freakonomics as representative of an EI of which he tends

---

6 As mentioned, a previously unpublished piece.
7 Note that Fleury (2012) locates the origins of economics made fun in the much earlier attempts to render economics relevant to students in light of charges of irrelevance, student protests in the 1960s and the need to attract students to the discipline in content and teaching methods, p. 27/8: "In many respects, the development of an "issues-oriented" approach to teaching economics was similar to the emergence of the scholarly literature on economics imperialism. Even before Becker's (1976) The Economic Approach to Human Behavior, textbooks of a new kind applied economic reasoning to various issues that belonged to the traditional domain of other social sciences. They similarly claimed that the distinctive characteristic of economics was its method and set of tools. Finally, some of the most virulent textbooks depicted the economist as the only relevant social scientists to address important policy question and economics the only useful social science. This echoed other attempts, such as Mancur Olson's, to drive out other social sciences from social policy making … But the reasons for such developments were different. From the point of view of teaching, introducing economics as a particular mode of thinking and applying it to various social issues wasn't initially meant to draw new boundaries inside social scientific knowledge, but only to make the teaching of economics more efficient. The expansion of economics' scope was the outcome of the specific response of economists to educational problems that affected most academic disciplines at the time".

to deny an existence. To start with, for freakonomics itself, as he observes, we take it to be EI *driven to the extreme*. But, equally without attribution, he identifies this with its being "depicted ... as the crowning achievement of economics imperialism to date" and "to be the apex of this trend", p. 78.

These characterisations are, however, very different from one another although possibly reflecting different interpretations of what it means to be extreme. For us, it is the opposite of crowning achievement and apex that would surely mean that freakonomics is at the core as well as in the vanguard of EI. Yet, despite the title of our volume (Fine and Milonakis 2009) opportunistically drawing upon the popularity of the term, it only devotes a few pages to freakonomics. And this is within a section entitled "Freakonomics – abnormal economics as normal". Indeed, we go out of our way to emphasise how unusual freakonomics is that, "there is apparent distance between freakonomics and economics imperialism although, not surprisingly, it does not approach absolute detachment", p. 106. In other words, freakonomics is at the extreme margins of economics (and EI) and departing from it in ways which we indicate.[8]

More specifically, as Vromen acknowledges, EI is interpreted as having gone through two phases – the first associated with as if perfect markets, the second with as if imperfect markets but with both based upon utility maximising individuals. These old and newer phases of economics imperialism are now complemented by a third, newest, phase in which the optimising individual is complemented by other behavioural motivations. This is certainly characteristic of freakonomics and, in this sense alone, it is in the vanguard of EI. As we observe, "freakonomic analysis is *not* reduced to rational economic behaviour alone", emphasis added. Otherwise, though, freakonomics is "idiosyncratic", p. 107. This renders incomprehensible Vromen's suggestion that we "argue that the economic analysis in *Freakonomics* is still committed to the view that individuals pursue their self-interest, and that they do so in an instrumentally rational optimizing way", p. 87. Vromen spends a large part of his article proving that freakonomics (and EI more generally) is not exclusively dependent upon such rationality but this is simply uncontroversial. We suspect, then, that our differences over the nature of freakonomics are minimal other than in reflecting more substantive differences concerning EI upon which we would argue it draws.

---

8 To make the point provocatively, right or wrong and as a spoof of freakonomics itself, it could be argued that Catholicism provides an incentive structure and opportunity set that drives priests to the extremes of paedophilia without this meaning that it would be the religion's crowning, or apex of, achievement.

Thus, to suggest, as Vromen does (almost certainly wrongly) that freakonomics has no interest in influencing other social sciences (as opposed to simply raising the status of economics as a discipline by displaying its analytical range to what Vromen dubs the "outlandish") bears little on the issue of EI itself as it is marginal to it. And, in passing, to suggest that freakonomics is explained merely as a consequence of providing incentives and motivations to young economics scholars (in wishing to be "more interesting and exciting", p. 85), and in informing their perceptions of editors of economics journals of the status of their discipline, is itself surely an unwitting spoof of freakonomics, an example of making fun of economics and economists. This surely does not count seriously, as is claimed, as a "sociology of economics". At the very least, as argued in our book, the overcrowding of the job market by narrowly trained and homogenised economists is a crucial factor in spilling out into outlandish topics for originality. And, equally, there is a need to explain why this incentive structure should arise when it does with some account of the broader intellectual and material environment spawned prodigiously by neoliberalism, see below, none of which enters into Vromen's account that seems entirely aloof of the contemporary scene.

This aside, the more substantive disagreements with Vromen, once properly recognised, over EI are threefold. First is a matter of language, and our use of pejorative terms such as parasitic, arrogant, ignorant, contemptuous, exploitation and appropriation. Presumably, such terms might be deemed to have a chance to be considered appropriate if the hypothesis of EI were accepted. As it is not, Vromen prefers a more neutral terminology, specifically rejecting the analogy and terminology of (economics) imperialism itself (however well understood because he seems to identify it with its much narrower aspect of plunder). Indeed, he goes much further than this, p. 79, emphasis added:

> Unlike natural resources, which are private goods, subjects are more like public goods. Their "use" by the one discipline does not diminish the opportunities for other disciplines to "use" them. Disciplines *cannot be dispossessed of their subjects* in the same way that countries can be dispossessed of their natural resources.

Now this is either a tautology (natural resources are not scholarship – and nor are they private goods by nature) or it is an explicit denial of the possibility of EI. It is also, of course, a remarkable sociology of economics (and freakonomics and economics as fun) as if the social sciences are akin to going to a public park in which anyone can have a go on the swings (and without questioning the location, access to, and content of the park). Accordingly, Vromen suggests our pejorative terms misrepresent the way in which economists use (and do not abuse) concepts drawn from the other social sciences. As is made explicit, "Economists do not steal anything from other social sciences nor abuse them in any other sense by using their concepts", p. 81.

But the omitted issue here is exactly how these concepts drawn from the other social sciences are denuded by incorporation within economics, not only transformed but reduced. And, of course, this is the rationale for the pejorative language for the use of such concepts within economics, quite apart from the justification provided by their (disputed) projection onto new areas of application within the other social sciences (even if these were previously addressed in a more rounded fashion within economics itself in the past but of no interest as such to today's orthodoxy or, indeed, freakonomics).

As we have argued in our books, this process of deconceptualisation is profoundly influenced by the technical apparatus with which economics proceeds as if by second nature. For example, as critically observed in Fine (2009a), Akerlof's work on identity seeks to fit it within a framework of utility functions and externalities. This is significant since, as Vromen observes, Akerlof is perceived as bringing the concepts of the other social sciences to economics rather than vice-versa. His treatment of identity is a telling illustration but, even if Akerlof is less extreme in other applications and is only importing to, rather than exporting from, economics, how economics as a discipline and economists as a profession have evolved are not determined by Akerlof's intentions nor even the substantive content of his own work but how these are received and used systemically and by others. For he, and others, have opened the floodgates for movements in the opposite direction.

This is already to have moved to the second issue raised by Vromen against the hypothesis of EI, much more substantive than language. This is what we have termed reverse economics imperialism, that the other social sciences are influencing and/or invading economics as much as if not more than vice-versa. We discuss and dismiss this in our book, and even provide an index entry, although our arguments are not acknowledged by Vromen (although his and more are anticipated). Essentially, we do not deny that there is a flow of concepts in both directions (just as the British Museum contains the Elgin Marbles by way of pursuing Vromen's analogy of plunder). But the use of non-economic concepts by economists is not and cannot be anything other than on their own terms. And, for fish and chips to be displaced by chicken tikka masala as the UK's favourite take-away food is evidence of, not against, British imperialism (as is the ethnic composition of the UK population, let alone how they are disadvantaged).

So, the presence of the outlandish within economics is not evidence of reverse EI. As Vromen himself only begrudgingly accepts in his final paragraph, pp. 96/7:

> One might argue, of course, that to date this reverse influence of other social sciences on economics has been very small and also that in accommodating concepts and insights from other social sciences economics has badly distorted them. These are important issues that deserve serious further discussion. But discussing them under the heading of "economics imperialism" impedes rather than helps their informed and satisfactory resolution.

Indeed, we do argue otherwise and consider that economics imperialism is essential for discussing these issues (both within and without economics). Significantly, Vromen's earlier discussion of reverse imperialism is couched in terms of the sort of public good, symmetry of opportunity, or even inequality at the expense of economics, that has already been highlighted, p. 81:

> If one insists on calling this a form of academic imperialism, 'sociology imperialism' or 'psychology imperialism' would be more apt than 'economics imperialism': sociology or psychology have been successful in getting their concepts established in economic analysis. I think it would be even better, however, to abstain from talking of imperialism altogether here. Sociologists and psychologists did not force or impose anything on economists. Economists have voluntarily accommodated concepts from sociology and psychology.

The problem here is that the concepts imported from the other social sciences tend to be in name alone and made to fit within the economists' analytical framework whereas those exported from economics carry much more uncompromising analytical baggage with them at the expense of their colony.

There is, admittedly, a tension here in how we conceive of EI. For, if economists only deploy concepts from other social sciences within their own analytical framework, then surely they are simply doing economics on a broader terrain, but within their own discipline. This can only be resolved by interrogating the shifting relations between, and content within, disciplines and is to move to the third issue raised by Vromen against the hypothesis of EI, the lack of evidence for or, more exactly, empirical investigation of, EI.⁹ He suspects there is none by virtue of empirical evidence (of journal publications by economists in non-economics journals) and motivation of most economists. Once again, though, he overlooks the arguments we provide even if it does not come in the form of metrics of journal content (although it could).

Observe initially our emphasis upon the uneven incidence and nature of EI across the social sciences by discipline and topic, in major part because of the nature of the subject matter itself and the intellectual traditions to which it is attached. Nonetheless, there are clear examples of EI. One is the new economic history that has given rise to a division of the *colonised* discipline into two separate and parallel fields of economic history and social history, from the time that it emerged in the late 1950s as cliometrics (a form of old EI) before evolving into the newer economic history based on market imperfections.¹⁰ Similar outcomes have resulted with the emergence of the new economic geography, Krugman's Nobel Prize for economics being preceded, as we observe, by the first Alonso prize for developments in economic geography, awarded by the Regional Science Association International. With Nobels in mind, the award to Elinor Ostrom is hardly indicative of reverse economics imperialism but of the incorporation of economic concepts into political science. Consider her 2010 critique of Richard Posner, Ostrom (2010) – and let us not forget the economic approach to law for which he was the leading pioneer – in response to his Damascus conversion to Keynesianism, something he confesses to have taken for granted due to his flawed trust in the environmental ethos of Chicago economics. She manages to discuss both policing and education without reference to class, race or gender, etc, and rounds them up with public goods, differentiated as follows in line with narrowest of mainstream economics, emphasis added, p. 113:¹¹

> Public goods and services differ substantially in regard to their *production functions* and *scale* of their effects.

---

9   Yet, what is sauce for the goose is sauces for the gander and without such empirical evidence, how can Vromen draw conclusions as strongly as he does?
10 Apart from cliometrics, for us, it is incomprehensible that Vromen should imply that the old EI should have been confined to a limited influence *within* economics alone. Has he not heard of human capital for example that has become a standard concept across the social sciences?
11 For further discussion, see Fine (2010a).

No doubt the same is true of the public good of (absence of) EI! But last, and by no means least by way of illustration of EI, is the new development economics, not only a recolonisation of the subject matter within economics itself, displacing the old or classic development economics but also a major assault across the broad swathe of interdisciplinary development studies (whose practitioners will surely be astonished at the suggestion that EI is at least non-existent and potentially impossible).[12]

For each of these, and more, Vromen's claim of lack of evidence for EI is surely remarkable not least because both victims (or should that be beneficiaries?) and perpetrators (colonising missionaries?) are acutely aware of the processes involved. In other areas, especially where postmodernist currents are prominent, EI has tended to make very little headway as in anthropology (despite the formal-substantive debate around the first phase of EI). The new economic sociology is much more mixed and the new institutional economics much less so.

But more disturbing for us even than the denial of EI for lack of evidence is the lack of material and intellectual worldliness in Vromen's contribution. He scarcely discusses the substantive content and dynamic of economics at all – predominantly confining himself to referencing a few works pointing to the incorporation of individual motivations other than utility maximisation into freakonomics and economic orthodoxy more generally. Even for this, he does not mention the debate raging within heterodoxy over whether such changes represent a dissolution of the mainstream from the margins from without, for which Colander (2000) is the leading representative, and an implication drawn that heterodoxy should court the mainstream to influence whatever comes next.[13]

In short, it is as if developments within economics to which we point as underpinning the evolving nature and influence of EI exist in some alternate universe other than the one we jointly occupy. Two quotations neatly represent the way in which EI has shifted its foundations. For Lucas (1987, p. 108), "the term 'macroeconomic' will simply disappear from use and the modifier 'micro' will be superfluous". And for Elmslie (2010, p. 12):

> The 1980s and 1990s saw many cases of mainstream economic theory crowding out heterodox theory by using the everexpanding standard set

---

12 For the relationship of the new development economics to EI, see Fine (2009b) and for it and the new economic geography as well, see Fine (2010b).

13 See our debate, Fine and Milonakis (2012a) with Hodgson (2011 and 2012), and forthcoming volume on mainstream economics.

of tools to better understand issues long part of heterodox theory ... Thus, Krugman can be held at least partly responsible for the identity crisis that has plagued heterodox economics for the past 30 years, as orthodox theory came to dominate many traditionally heterodox areas of research.

As Vromen acknowledges, then, EI has certainly reconquered its own traditional terrain and more (something he sees as an argument against the hypothesis of EI as such topics belonged to economics in the first place).[14] But the result has been a decimation of, and intolerance to, heterodoxy of all varieties, history of economic thought, methodology, and a grasp on economic realities other than through what are often dubious econometric practices underpinned by even more dubious analytical content. Without wishing to demonise, the source of the intellectual monopoly (not public good) involved has been heavily influenced and sustained by the Americanisation of the discipline and the agenda-setting influence of neoliberalism, globalisation and other elements within the new world order however these might be interpreted. In the absence of these key elements for a sociology of economics, is it surprising that, within economics, the only choice that Vromen sees as being on offer are freakonomics or addressing bigger more central economic issues. Different traditions within economics other than orthodoxy are taken as granted to be absent but again without comment let alone explanation. And discussion of the content and dynamic of other social sciences is notable for its almost total absence other than as reverse imperialism for providing a more rounded account of individual behaviour.

Such developments within economics have been part and parcel of the EI to which we would point and which Vromen would deny. From our perspective, his is not only a serious misreading of intellectual developments by virtue of transparent evidence but, equally, conducive to missing opportunities for engaging with the economic, economics, and interdisciplinarity in ways that are more fruitful than through EI. For, just as the global crisis has exposed the weaknesses and poverty of economics, however little admitted, so EI has done so intellectually as the discipline seeks to extend the application of its principles across disciplines and topics for which its methods are alien

---

14 Significantly, Vromen appeals to Coase and Williamson for his hypothesis of "economics regaining economic subjects that they seemed to have lost". For Williamson, but also for Coase, as discussed at length in our book, there is both the timing of his prominence to explain and the use of his work in exactly the opposite manner and interpretation than he intended. This is all closely related to the rise of market imperfection economics and its use as part of the foundations for the second phase of EI.

and unacceptable but its subject matter, the economy, inescapable. The task, then, is not simply to expose EI for what it is rather than to deny its existence, but also for this to rebound back upon economics in its own outlandish territory.

In conclusion, we welcome Vromen's account of fun-made-of-economics and do not differ enormously with him over his characterisation of freakonomics (even though he misinterprets us outrageously). But his explanation for the emergence and popularity of freakonomics is extraordinarily weak, relying upon a miniscule set of proximate factors (without evidence to back them), leaving aside all manner of intellectual and material developments within economics, the economy and more broadly across society and the social sciences. Even this would not be worthy of comment were it not for the extrapolation of the putative absence of EI from freakonomics to its absence altogether, and that its use serves only as an impediment to discussion of the relations between economics and the other social sciences, p. 97. Although Vromen claims, falsely, an absence of empirical support for the hypothesis of EI, his arguments seem to be based purely on speculative reasoning around interdisciplinarity as a public good with which all are free to play as they choose. Those at the rough end of both mainstream economics and EI know otherwise. Indeed, it is surely ironic that the fate of evolutionary economics and the philosophy of economics, to which Vromen has himself made such distinguished contributions, should not occur to him not so much as examples of EI but as symptomatic of its nature and origins.

And, if he would but look its impact. Having charted and debated EI over what is now almost two decades, we are disappointed to find it dismissed by speculative reasoning and by reference to freakonomics and making fun of economics as thin end of this wedge into the social sciences (and heterodox economics) for mainstream economics. But we are comforted by the fact that first reactions to the hypothesis of EI have often been outraged denial, followed by cautious acceptance and, ultimately, proudly declared illustration. Perhaps this explains why the hypothesis of EI has rarely been challenged as such in print given the process of gestation to its acceptance is shorter than to publication, see special issue of *Historical Materialism*, for example, Ashman (2012) and our own contribution (Fine and Milonakis 2012b). Hopefully, Vromen is the exception that proves the rule and we look forward to his substantive account of how developments within economics have influenced developments outside of economics in his own areas of expertise.

References

Ashman, S. (2012) "Economics and Political Economy Today: Introduction to the Symposium on Fine and Milonakis", *Historical Materialism*, vol 20, no 3, pp. 3–8.

Baron, J. and M. Hannan (1994) "The Impact of Economics on Contemporary Sociology", *Journal of Economic Literature*, vol XXXII, no 3, Sept, pp. 1111–46, reproduced in Swedberg (ed.) (1996), pp. 530-66.

Becker, G. (1976) *The Economic Approach to Human Behavior*, Chicago: Chicago University Press.

Colander, D. (2000) "The Death of Neoclassical Economics", *Journal of the History of Economic Thought*, vol 22, no 2, pp. 127–44, reproduced in Colander (2001), pp. 46–62.

Colander, D. (2001) *The Lost Art of Economics*, Cheltenham: Edward Elgar.

Elmslie, B. (2010) "One Small Step for Man: Paul Krugman, the 2008 Nobel Laureate in Economics", *Review of Political Economy*, vol 22, no 1, pp. 1–17.

Fine, B. (2009a) "The Economics of Identity and the Identity of Economics?", *Cambridge Journal of Economics*, vol 33, no 2, pp. 175–91. See Chapter 5.

Fine, B. (2009b) "Development as Zombieconomics in the Age of Neo-Liberalism", *Third World Quarterly*, vol 30, no 5, pp. 885–904.

Fine, B. (2010a) "Beyond the Tragedy of the Commons: a Discussion of *Governing the Commons: The Evolution of Institutions for Collective Action*", *Perspectives on Politics*, vol 8, no 2, pp. 583–86.

Fine, B. (2010b) "Flattening Economic Geography: Locating the World Development Report for 2009", *Journal of Economic Analysis*, vol 1, no 1, pp. 15–33, http://users.ntua.gr/jea/JEA%20Vol.%20I,%20No%20I,%202010/jea_volume1_issue1_pp15_33.pdf.

Fine, B. and D. Milonakis (2009) *From Economics Imperialism to Freakonomics: the Shifting Boundaries Between Economics and Other Social Sciences*, London: Routledge.

Fine, B. and D. Milonakis (2012a) "Interrogating Sickonomics, From Diagnosis to Cure: a Response to Hodgson", *Review of Social Economy*, vol 70, no 4, pp. 477–91.

Fine, B. and D. Milonakis (2012b) "From Freakonomics to Political Economy", *Historical Materialism*, vol 20, no 3, pp. 81–96. See also Chapter 7.

Fleury, J.-B. (2012) "The Evolving Notion of Relevance: an Historical Perspective to the 'Economics Made Fun' Movement", *Journal of Economic Methodology*, vol 19, no 3, pp. 303–16.

Hodgson, G. (2011) "Sickonomics: Diagnoses and Remedies", *Review of Social Economy*, vol 69, no 3, pp. 357–76.

Hodgson, G. (2012) "From Social Theory to Explaining Sickonomics: a Response to Dimitris Milonakis and Ben Fine", *Review of Social Economy*, vol 70, no 4, pp, 492–507.

Lucas, R. (1987) *Models of Business Cycles*, Oxford: Blackwell.

Mader, P., D. Mertens and N. Van der Zwan (eds) (2020) *International Handbook of Financialization*, London: Routledge.

Milonakis, D. and B. Fine (2009) *From Political Economy to Economics: Method, the Social and the Historical in the Evolution of Economic Theory*, London: Routledge.

Mirowski, P. and D. Plehwe (2015) *The Road from Mont Pèlerin: the Making of the Neoliberal Thought Collective*, with a new preface, Cambridge: Harvard University Press.

Nik-Khah, E. and R. Van Horn (2012) "Inland Empire: Economics Imperialism as an Imperative of Chicago Neoliberalism", *Journal of Economic Methodology*, 19, no 3, pp. 259–82.

Ostrom, E. (2010) "Organizational Economics", *Journal of Institutional Economics*, vol 6, no 1, pp. 109–15.

Posner, R. (2010) "From the New Institutional Economics to Organization Economics: With Applications to Corporate Governance, Government Agencies and Legal Institutions", *Journal of Institutional Economics*, vol 6, no 1, pp. 1–37.

Swedberg, R. (ed.) (1996) *Economic Sociology*, Cheltenham: Edward Elgar.

Vromen, J. (2009) "The Booming Economics-Made-Fun Genre: More than Having Fun, but Less than Economics Imperialism" *Erasmus Journal for Philosophy and Economics*, vol 2, no 1, pp. 70–99.

CHAPTER 9

Vicissitudes of Economics Imperialism

Postscript as Personal Preamble

This short piece (Fine 2008) was commissioned to appear in the first contribution to a Speaker's Corner in the *Review of Social Economy*, the longstanding journal of the Association of Social Economics. I took the opportunity to press the case for acknowledging and critically engaging with economics imperialism. The piece originally appears as a polemic, without references and footnotes, much like my very first explicit piece on economics imperialism, published as a Polemic in a new section of *Capital and Class* (Fine 1997).

The Association has been good to me, putting me on editorial boards, and subsequently inviting me as a keynote conference speaker (Fine 2013). But this piece remained in a Corner. It is reported as only having attracted four citations, and economics imperialism is notable for its limited presence in continuing articles in the journal. This is disappointing for two reasons. First, it has contributed to the watershed leading to the neglect of economics imperialism as its Chicago/Becker version was eclipsed by its market imperfections progeny. Second, it neglected a way of promoting political economy within economics, not least with the eruption of the demand for pluralism in the wake of the Global Financial Crisis. And, third, it neglected opportunities for influence, publications and career development through engagement within other social sciences.

1 Speaker's Corner

I know of few neoclassical economists who have suffered for their intellectual commitments. For economics, the passage from school to Nobel Prize is paved in orthodoxy, with Chicago well ahead amongst the few who make it, followed by idiosyncrasy as a poor second, and heterodoxy scarcely making it on to the winner's podium. By contrast, I know of few heterodox economists who have not struggled to find appropriate employment, recognition and publication both in absolute terms and relative to their much less talented orthodox counterparts. We have to be at least as good as they are in what they do; they need know nothing about what we do. And this situation has worsened over the past few decades to such an extent that the very survival of heterodoxy is threatened, other than at the diminishing margins of the discipline.

Not surprisingly, then, social economics would appear to have fallen on hard times. Although, under the banner of economics imperialism, neoclassical economics has long laid claim to the social (as non-market and/or as non-individual), it does so only on its own terms of the optimising individual whether in a world as if perfect market or, more recently, a world as if responding to market imperfections. From Becker to Akerlof,[1] the technical apparatus of the orthodoxy reigns supreme, as evidenced by their recent sorties into social capital and identity, respectively, which reveals how close these two Nobel Laureates are to one another. This all places genuine social economics and interdisciplinarity in the pigeon hole of heterodoxy, where it is simply dismissed by orthodoxy for lacking what are ignorantly and dogmatically claimed to be scientific and rigorous standards (even though the orthodoxy always sets aside inconvenient mathematical and empirical results to suit – from the Cambridge Critique of Capital Theory through to empirical patterns of international trade).[2]

In short, economics as a discipline is marked by lack of attention to heterodoxy, history of economic thought, interdisciplinarity and methodology. Its deductive methods and corresponding technical apparatus of utility and production functions are extraordinarily intellectually fragile by reference to method, theory, conceptualisation and even simple appeal to evidence. Yet, the orthodoxy commands a stranglehold over the discipline that has strengthened to the point of a monopoly that it would itself abhor if found in the market place (although there are those who see orthodoxy's dominance as some sort of Microsoft survival of the efficient fittest).

Some are arguing that the introduction of new techniques and considerations at the borders of the discipline, from game theory to behavioural economics, are forging a future pluralist orthodoxy out of current heterodoxy. I consider this is the opposite of what is happening in the sense that the core principles of mainstream economics are as strong as ever within the discipline and alternatives are correspondingly weaker. Whilst the intellectual fragility of the orthodoxy is further exposed by scrutiny of any addition to, or revision of, its underlying assumptions, it has long learnt to live with such tensions in relying upon continuing techniques and methods even when complemented with the incompatible. We question rationality, for example, only by building

---

1 See previous volume on economics imperialism, especially Chapter 5, for Becker, and Chapter 5 of this volume for Akerlof.
2 See forthcoming volume on mainstream economics.

upon it. Paradoxically, then, the same technical apparatus is being extended across a wider plane of economic and social analysis without regard to the intensified limitations that result from piling heavier explanatory burdens on sorely inadequate and inappropriate principles. It is appropriate, and a token victory for social economics, that economics should recognise that it is unable to explain the economy by virtue of its economic analysis alone, that interdisciplinarity is essential. But it would have been better for the mainstream to have interrogated the weakness of its own principles as opposed to extending them to the non-economic (although New Classicals continue their introverted explanations within the discipline). Freakonomics appropriately captures self-deprecation as self-promotion.

To some extent, such economics imperialism is a consequence of the universal applicability of the marginalist principles – perfected and consolidated through the formalist (and Americanising) revolution of the 1950s – even though this universality could only be established through setting aside all but the narrowest of methods, concepts, techniques, variables and assumptions. Initially confined to a part of economic behaviour and a part of the economy, they could be extended to cover all economic and social life as if utility and production functions sufficed in presence of a perfect, or imperfect, market and possibly complemented by other motives or influences.

How this bizarre situation came about is of interest and importance but it is not my concern here – although I would observe that the extremities of today have been realised within my own life-time as an economist, and the interwar period was entirely different, especially as the newly borne and evolving marginalist microeconomics was confined in scope if not in ambition. When I began economics in the late 1960s, heterodoxy was taken seriously and was debated across all of the leading journals. Although I was myself recruited to do economics because I had a degree in mathematics, there were ample opportunities both to learn to command that orthodoxy, and to dissent from it. This is no longer the case, and it means that the current generation of heterodoxy is not liable to be reproduced, at least within the discipline, for heterodox economics is stronger in other disciplines – paradoxically, possibly at its strongest in Business and Management Schools in the UK for example. In short, the demands of the orthodoxy in economics are now so great, in content and compliance, that there is little room for presence let alone voice of alternatives. Those interested in economics have to jump the hoops. Those interested in the economy might justifiably avoid doing so by running in or to other fields.

This places a heavy burden of responsibility on the current generation of those committed to social economics as they are uniquely placed to guard its own traditions as well as to advise of the continuing weaknesses of orthodoxy, especially as the latter seeks to colonise the other social sciences through its variety of "new" fields. I am not convinced that social economists are making best use of their collective resources to this end although I am wary of blaming the victims, doomed to decline if not extinction within the discipline. Like heterodoxy, social economics is, in some respects commendably, diverse in approach and scope. This can be so much so that the only thing that its practitioners at most seem to share in common is an antipathy to orthodoxy. I also suspect there is an understandable professional and psychological disposition to wish to be taken seriously by orthodoxy, especially amongst those less on the social and more on the economics side of things. But the chances of achieving respectability in the eyes of the mainstream are remote, and the associated costs liable to defeat the purpose of the exercise, legitimising, consolidating and advancing the orthodoxy rather than undermining it.

Whilst keeping the beacon of social economics alive within the discipline is imperative, opportunities are not only brighter but positively radiant across the other social sciences despite, or even because of, the designs of economics imperialism. Across the intellectual scene, the last two decades have witnessed what I term a "dual retreat" from the extremes of the agendas set by postmodernism and neo-liberalism. There has been an upsurge of interest in the nature of contemporary capitalism in place of interpretative deconstruction and debating the relative merits of market versus state and whether the latter is withering away. The rise of "globalisation" as the leading concept across the social sciences since the early 1990s, before which it had never been mentioned, is striking evidence for the reorientation of social sciences towards more materially grounded approaches, concerned with how the world is and systemically so.

Inevitably, what might be termed the return to the real across the social sciences is accompanied by an enhanced interest in the economic but, for the vast majority of social science, the methods and techniques of mainstream economics are alien. This places the continuing if marginalised traditions of social economics, and political economy more generally, in an advantageous position. On the other hand, knowledge of, and commitment to, heterodox economic analysis across social science has eroded during the dominance of postmodernism just as it has, for entirely different reasons, within the discipline of economics itself. Often non-economists are now simply looking for an economic "fix" to provide their contributions with an apparent roundedness, which is why notions such as globalisation and neoliberalism are so popular, just as social capital, institutions, path dependence, and so on, provide a non-economic fix for the economists. Or the economic is seen as contingent, one factor to be taken into account alongside others, an add-on as opposed to an irreducible element of any social analysis.

These perspectives lead to a number of conclusions about the future path of the social sciences and the place that social economics might play within them. First, developments within and across disciplines and topics are liable to be diverse, with different outcomes depending upon prevailing traditions and dynamics of subject matter, how postmodernism and neo-liberalism were previously negotiated, and how economic considerations are being introduced or re-introduced. Economics imperialism, for example, has tended to be at its weakest where contextual content and meaning are unavoidable as in ethnographic anthropology or study of the material culture of consumption. It has been at its strongest where simple notions of rationality have or can establish themselves (as with rational choice politics), and especially where statistical methods can be heavily deployed, as with new growth theory for example, where social analysis is reduced to the inclusion of one or more variables in a multiple regression.

Second, such diversity of responses to economics imperialism suggests that intellectual outcomes are more open than they have been for some time. There is no fixed formula within or across disciplines and topics for how the dual retreat and economics imperialism will be incorporated, or rejected. Where rational choice has previously been present, for example, economics imperialism has greater chances of prospering. But the abiding weaknesses of rational choice from stances rooted in social theory are legion: the absence of key categories such as class, power, conflict; undue reliance upon methodological individualism and deductivism; failure to examine the meaning of categories of analysis and their historical and social specificity and scope of application.

These considerations, though, do not preclude the presence of economics imperialism. In case of the new economic geography, for example, it has prospered simply by neglecting the weight of scholarship concerned with the social construction of space and ploughing ahead in parallel with its deductive models. The new institutional economics has been more mixed but with a trend towards reductionist reliance upon the optimising individual in a path-dependent world. The new economic sociology has begun to move in the opposite direction, with increasing emphasis on the cultural content and meaning of economic relations.

Third, then, this means that individual and collective effort has the potential to have disproportionate if uncertain influence on the future direction of the social sciences and the nature of the economic analysis that they incorporate. As previously indicated, social economics has a particular role to play in light of its critical command of orthodoxy. But it also has something much more to contribute because of its capacity to engage the universal concepts of social science, such as class, power and conflict, and imbue them with an economic content that is specific to the object of study, and especially capitalism in its material and cultural forms. It is also better placed, as far as social science is concerned, to address issues of contemporary concern that are systemically derived, such as globalisation, neo-liberalism, environmental sustainability, as well as the moral economy of poverty, justice and equity.

In short, the task of social economics – and it is both exciting and guaranteed success – is not primarily to nibble futilely at the margins of orthodoxy but to exert a major influence upon the place of economic analysis across the social sciences (and to draw, as always, on the insights that are given in return). This leads directly, as an alternative to economics imperialism in developing an economics for the social sciences, to the following questions, traditional within political economy.

First, capitalism is a system based on profitable expansion in which class, power and conflict have structured as well as socially and historically contingent features. What is the appropriate value theory through which the processes of capital accumulation can be addressed? Orthodoxy is notably weak in this respect as it hops between a value theory (general equilibrium) without dynamics, and a dynamics (new growth theory, for example) without value. The traditions of classical political economy are crucial in this context, especially Smith and Marx, as they sought to assess how value is formed as accumulation proceeds. But, equally, value theory needs to be able to explain how and why sustained periods of economic growth are punctuated by slowdowns and crises. And what is historically and conceptually distinctive about capital and capitalism, and the money and commodity forms that they inhabit.

Second, what is the relationship between the financial and industrial systems in the process of accumulation? Arguably, financialisation is the defining feature of the current phase of capitalism, with a proliferation of financial markets and intermediation to such an extent that their dominance has been especially if unevenly dysfunctional for both economic and social provision, as well as lessening the pace of "real" accumulation. In this light, what is the relationship between (fractions of) classes and the state and how do they resolve and sustain differences in national systems of accumulation?

Third, how do the new world order, US hegemony, and the factors associated with "globalisation" impact upon the prospects for growth and development? This inescapably places political and cultural factors on the economics agenda, and the issue of how to incorporate them in a genuinely interdisciplinary approach. There is also the problem of addressing the economics of non-capitalist societies or those in transition, and the continuing relationships between capitalist and non-capitalist economic systems. China looms large in this respect, across all of the issues associated with social economics, from the violence of transition to re-incorporation into the world economy.

In short, whatever the prospects for social economics within economics, and whatever the prospects of economics itself, the comparative advantage that social economics has in these and related questions should be exploited to the full.

References

Fine, B. (2008) "Vicissitudes of Economics Imperialism", *Review of Social Economy*, vol 66, no 2, pp. 235–40.

Fine, B. (2013) "Economics: Unfit for Purpose", *Review of Social Economy*, vol LXXI, no 3, pp. 373–89, shortened version of "Economics – Unfit for Purpose: the Director's Cut", SOAS Department of Economics Working Paper Series, No. 176, 2013.

CHAPTER 10

Economics and Interdisciplinarity: One Step Forward, N Steps Back?

Postscript as Personal Preamble

The last piece in this second volume on economics imperialism was published a number of years after all of the others, and over twenty years after the first. Unsurprisingly, it takes the opportunity to bring together and summarise the evolving analytical content of my approach to economics imperialism. All of the key elements are present:

- The historical logic of economics imperialism – historically economics was confined to the study of markets but logically established a technical apparatus, TA1, that was of universal application.
- The implosion of conceptualisation to establish both TA1 and its corresponding technical architecture, TA2, of general equilibrium and efficiency considerations.
- The subsequent explosion of economics imperialism, both internally within economics itself and unevenly across other disciplines and topics, by bringing back in (BBI) those very considerations that had to be excluded to establish TA².
- And the passage of economics imperialism through three phases – the old based on as if perfectly working markets, the new as non-market response to imperfectly working markets, and the newer through 'suspension' of TA², with corresponding flexibility to draw at will from across the social sciences.

But the contribution is not just a retrospective. It also seeks to identify how heterodox economics, pluralism and political economy can best respond to the challenges posed by an unremittingly hostile and institutionally powerful mainstream economics that is increasingly veiling its inadequacies through claims of being more rounded in its assumptions and methods, not least through learning from other social sciences. Collective and tolerant endeavour needs to be wedded to openness in critical debate. Whilst the key task is the reconstruction of economics as political economy – how economics deals with the economy – the weaknesses of the mainstream will be exposed by its incursions across other disciplines and topics, offering strategic opportunities to highlight alternatives not only for interdisciplinarity but also for and against the mainstream's intradisciplinarity.

1 Economics Is as Economics Does[1]

The purpose of this piece is to assess the prospects for political economy, especially in the context of interdisciplinarity. A necessary starting point for making such an assessment is the current state of mainstream economics. I approach this obliquely in the first instance, and anecdotally. I was recently invited to give a lecture at the Institute of German Historical Research in London as part of a series to mark the 200th anniversary of Karl Marx's birth, May 5th, 1818, and I sought to address the series' theme of Marx's continuing influence on contemporary social science. Other talks in the series included politics, sociology, anthropology and history. I explained that the one on economics would necessarily be extremely short as Marx had predominantly been excluded from mainstream economics today, since the mainstream totally dominates the discipline with little room for, let alone tolerance of, alternatives.[2] This is so whether deriving from Marx, other classical authors, or political economy or otherwise more widely. As a result, I offered to give a lecture explaining why this was so, whether this was or was not a sign of health of the dismal science, and what sets economics apart as a social science in being so negligent of Marx (and others), themes to which I will return below.

First, though, let me recall an earlier lecture I gave a few years ago for the Association of Social Economies, in which I suggested that the mainstream is unfit for purpose, focusing on just one of the many dimensions for which this is so, that is its own heavy ethical content which it seeks to deny as being present in view of its putative scientific/positive as opposed to normative content (Fine 2013). In preparing the lecture, I undertook a simple test of the self-confidence of the discipline, comparing it with sociology. In the wake of the Global Financial Crisis of 2007/8, GFC, I searched the scholarly literature employing the terms 'crisis of sociology' and 'crisis of economics'. Sociology

---

[1] Revised from Fine (2019). Based on a plenary address to the founding conference of the Portuguese Association of Political Economy, held at Lisbon, ISCTE-IUL, 25–27 January 2018. Thanks to journal editors and referees for most helpful comments and for Scott M. Culp for editing.

[2] For evidence on this of their own, and reference to others, see Javdani and Chang (2019) and Aigner (2021).

had a steady stream (if not a torrent) of contributions, numbering in the thousands, persisting over time and suggesting a commendable degree of self-critical examination. Economics, by contrast, barely totalled one hundred, most of these dating to a debate from the 1930s on Schumpeter. Especially in the wake of the GFC, one has to wonder whether this lack of critical self-examination is a mark of the mainstream's success or of its failure![3]

This is indicative of one of a number of other features of the mainstream: 1) its absolute self-confidence; 2) its lack or misuse (if not abuse) of the history of economic thought; 3) its lack of engagement with alternatives; 4) its poverty of methodology; 5) its lack of realism; and 6) denial of, and so lack of attention to, normative content and issues.[4] As a result, the absence of Marx from the mainstream is not an isolated exception, as much as the same is true of all major figures in the history of economic thought, and, other than opportunistically, most major figures in social science as well. Does this mean that there is no interdisciplinarity with respect to and within mainstream economics? I would suggest not at all, hardly surprising as I have been critically peddling the notion of economics imperialism, the colonisation of the subject matter of other social sciences by economics, for twenty years or more now. Let me explore this in detail in order both to specify the nature of contemporary mainstream economics, its approach to interdisciplinarity, and the potential for alternatives.[5]

2   Economics Imperialism

The term economic(s) imperialism dates from the 1930s, but it only really gathers momentum after the Second World War, WWII. From there, it has gone through three phases, ones which I have called the "old", the "new" and the "newer". The first phase reflects the immediate post-WWII period, the second corresponds in part to a reaction to the monetarist counter-revolution built upon the first phase (although this second phase had a dynamic and logic of its own), with the current phase just about preceding but intensified by the GFC.

---

3   For an account of the "superiority" (if not the arrogance) of economists, see Fourcade et al (2015).
4   Discussed at length in Fine (2013).
5   The main thrust of what follows is to be found in Milonakis and Fine (2009) and Fine and Milonakis (2009) but for some more recent material and reflections around other themes, see my other later contributions (Fine 2010, 2011, 2016a-c, 2017a and b and 2018, Fine and Dimakou 2016, and Fine and Milonakis 2011), where extensive references to, and discussions of, the broader literature can be found.

Analytically speaking, the origins of economics imperialism lie in what I have termed its historical logic, which will require a bit of a narrative in the history of economic thought to specify. With the marginalist revolution of the 1870s, especially through Marshall rather than Jevons, Menger and Walras,[6] we receive the key concepts of what I call the Technical Apparatus, TA1, which has remained persistent within mainstream economics to the present day. It is the apparatus attached to utility and production functions and their application to supply and demand through the market. In what was to be termed microeconomics from the 1930s, and as the junior partner to macroeconomics that distinguished itself and became the senior branch given the pressing problems of unemployment, TA1 set itself two major problems. The first refers to the properties of supply and demand functions, given that they derive from optimising individuals, and the second addresses what I call the technical architecture, denoted by TA2, which gave rise to the problem of forming the aggregate economy out of those individuals coordinated through the market, otherwise known as general equilibrium, and whether it exists and is unique, stable and Pareto efficient. Forge these two problems and TA1 and TA2 together and we get what might be designated as TA^2.[7]

The first of these problems was solved in the late 1930s and the second in the 1950s, via what are known, respectively, as the Hicks-Slutsky-Samuelson conditions and by Arrow and Debreu for general equilibrium. I am less concerned with these solutions than with the *process* and *context* by and within which they occurred. I call the process an *implosion* – for it involved making whatever assumptions are necessary to be able to derive meaningful results, assumptions such as fixed individuals, preferences, endowments, technologies, single motivation, fixed goods, etc., even technical assumptions within its own frame such as no externalities, increasing returns, concavities and imperfect competition.

These are the origins of the mainstream's deviation from whatever we mean by realism since, whatever the extent of use of empirical information in econometrics or otherwise, it is theoretically embedded in assumptions that suit the theory rather than to conform with the evidence.[8] Theoretically, we do whatever is necessary to get what we want. Indeed, this actually sets a standard

---

6 Marshall's *Principles* was the main microeconomic textbook until the end of the 1930s, laying out and applying the discipline's core technical apparatus. General equilibrium, despite preoccupying Walras, only drew concerted attention from the mid-1930s (Marshall 1959 [1890]).
7 The idea of technical apparatus/architecture derives from Al-Jazaeri (2009).
8 Made explicit by Friedman (1953) in dismissing the need for realism in assumptions, although the so-called F-twist was rejected as such by Samuelson (1963).

method within the discipline; make whatever assumptions (and exclusions) we need for our purposes and reality will have to fit, giving rise to all sorts of problems, even on its own terms, as a result of what are known as aggregation problems, the theory of the second best, the Cambridge critique of capital theory, and so on. This is indicative of a myth that the mainstream purveys of itself, that it is first and foremost committed to mathematical rigour. This may be so in obtaining mathematical results themselves if by virtue of mathematical reasoning alone. But such rigour derived from the mathematics is far from being carried over when observing the implications of mathematical reasoning, which asserts that most standard assumptions and results are implausible (as with existence, uniqueness, efficiency and stability of general equilibrium, for example).

So much for the process by which these results were derived with corresponding implications for the content of economic theory that was to become standardised, natural to economists if totally unnatural in relation to realism. The context in the interwar period within which such TA^2 microeconomics emerged and began to flourish was one in which it did so alongside the increasingly prominent and more significant macroeconomics and what we now call the old or, more recently, the original institutional economics, both to distinguish it from the new and to indicate that it remains relevant, respectively. The latter had, and increasingly, covered a wide range of what became more generally dubbed as applied economics, reflecting inductive, practical fields with mixed methods suitable to the subject matter at hand (public economics, labour economics, business cycles, technical change, and so on). This was very strong at the time in the United States and, alongside economic history, comprised core components of teaching and research, concerning itself with unavoidably contemporary developments for those who cared to see them, not least with the rise of large corporations, labour movements, technical change, consumerism and short- and long-term business cycles. These traditions survived into the post-WWII period but were subject to erosion and even marginalisation as such, if not immediately and only gradually.

When I began studying economics in the late 1960s, such subjects were still a core part of the curriculum but had already begun to be subject to accelerating capture in light of, and as raw material for, the internal colonisation of the discipline by microeconomics and its more limited methods, see below. Further, the so-called formalist revolution of the 1950s, which began the heavy mathematisation of the discipline,[9] adopting the methods of the newly-established

---

9 For discussion of the mathematization of economics, see Milonakis (2017).

microeconomics, heavily consolidated the division between economics and the other social sciences (with its wider range of methods and conceptualisations including that of the economy).

So, with the two basic microeconomic problems set and solved on their own terms, microeconomics and its core TA² were established at the heart of at least one major field within the discipline. I can now specify the historical logic of economics imperialism, for, *historically*, TA² was derived out of addressing the problem of the consequences for supply and demand in the context of an entirely idealised and isolated market system. What are the (formally-derived) implications for supply and demand curves arising out of one part of individual economic behaviour in the context of a disembedded market? But, remarkably, and logically, the core concepts that were deployed (self-interest, inputs and outputs, efficiency, equilibrium and optimisation) depended purely upon universal, general, asocial, ahistorical (use whatever terms you wish) concepts with no relation to the market as such – specifically utility and production functions and the mathematical formulations (with optimisation) associated with them. Hence, this gave rise to a tension of *historical* confinement to the market at one extreme, reflecting the origins of TA² and a *logic* of universal, not market-confined conceptualisations and potential application, at the other.[10] As a result, there was potential to move in the direction of greater scope of application of TA², to apply supply and demand as it were beyond the market, according to whatever took the economists' fancy and to whatever extent it would be accepted by fellow economists or even those from other disciplines. Against the historical origins of TA², the logic pushed towards using its methods and tools to expand its application. The implosion to establish the TA², and its subsequent implications, was to be thrown into reverse, slowly and surely at first but, as will be seen, in an increasingly explosive manner, as it gathered momentum.

This, then, gave rise to the first phase of economics imperialism, a reflection of this historical logic, with the most notable exponent being Gary Becker. What characterises this first phase, the old economics imperialism, is that it seeks to apply TA² not only to its initiating problem of the implications of individual optimising behaviour in a market context (supply and demand) but across other economic and social problems, in principle without limit. It comes to treat the non-market, the social, as if a market were present, as if family members trade with one another, for example, or criminal activity is

---

10   This is how Robbins (1935 [1932]) came to be interpreted in defining economics ahistorically and asocially as the allocation of scarce resources to competing ends.

simply a matter of trading potential rewards against potential punishment at the margin. Initially, the most prominent applications were to be found with human capital theory (treat skills and learning and their application as if a fixed asset), the new economic history (or cliometrics, which treats the past as if models of supply and demand) and public choice theory (politics as if like markets). But in the context of the post-war boom and the intellectual triumph of Keynesianism, microeconomics remained subservient to macroeconomics (in the form of IS/LM), and there remained some continuing strength of applied economics, as well as respect for, possibly intellectual intimidation by, disciplinary boundaries.

But the stagflation of the 1970s gave rise to the monetarist counterrevolution most closely associated with Milton Friedman. Yet, ultimately, and equally and intellectually much more important or wide-ranging, something else was gathering momentum, possibly less likely to be recognised because of the dramatic demise of the previously hegemonic Keynesianism both as a field of macroeconomic scholarship and as a rationale for much more wide-ranging interventionism. For, generally, the monetarist counter-revolution also signalled a watershed for the reversal of the macroeconomic/microeconomic hierarchy within the discipline. In turn, it was associated with two effects of importance for our narrative. First, the applied fields became subject to "theory", i.e. microeconomics, and became squeezed out as alternatives, most notably in the appropriately dubbed new development economics and the Washington Consensus, examples of the first phase of economics imperialism (treat everything as if, and to be made into, perfectly working markets) par excellence. This signified the extent to which economics imperialism was *internally* colonising the discipline of economics, not least macroeconomics itself, with its reduction to microeconomics. With the New Classical Economics (NCE), and the emergence of rational expectations, representative individuals, and so on, macroeconomics was increasingly driven to the extremes of microeconomics, and assumptions to suit the theory rather than the subject matter.

Second, and subsequently, there came the restoration of (hydraulic) Keynesianism[11] through asymmetric information, market imperfection economics, consolidating (rather than breaking with) the reliance upon microeconomics, and many of the extreme assumptions attached to the New Classical Economics, such as rational expectations, representative individuals, and reduction of finance to the supply of and demand for money. In time, the

---

11 By which we mean, here and elsewhere, the hegemonic IS/LM framework of the Keynesian period, as opposed to the many varieties of Keynesianism that have both co-existed with and succeeded it (see Fine and Dimakou 2016).

New Consensus Macroeconomics emerged, and rose to hegemony until it was rudely shattered by the GFC, exposing even for its exponents how impoverished macroeconomics had become in content and scope.[12] With real business cycles, and technical change treated as random shocks, the NCE was macro treated as micro, and not only taken to extremes but also in extreme ways. Lucas (2003) famously declares that micro has the prospect of making macro superfluous, possibly by defining as economics only what can be done by microeconomics.[13]

Inevitably, there were (orthodox) Keynesian reactions against such extremes, although they are striking for incorporating rather than rejecting much of the initiatives attached to NCE (especially in terms of continuing reliance upon microeconomics and rational expectations if not perfectly working markets and completely ineffective state intervention).[14] Such were the market *imperfection* foundations for what was to give rise to the second phase, the new, economics imperialism. Unlike the old economics imperialism, which treated the non-market as if market (the choice between apples and pears is exactly the same as between war and peace, for public choice Nobel prize-winner James Buchanan), the new economics imperialism treats non-market as if it were a response to market imperfections. So, for example, the family, the state, institutions, customs and culture are all to be explained as the response

---

[12] For Blanchard (2008, p. 1), erstwhile Chief Economist at the IMF, italics added: "For a long while after the explosion of macroeconomics in the 1970s, the field looked like a battlefield. Over time however, largely because facts do not go away, a largely shared vision both of fluctuations and of methodology has emerged. Not everything is fine. Like all revolutions, this one has come with the destruction of some knowledge, and suffers from extremism and herding. None of this deadly however (sic). *The state of macro is good*". Subsequently, five *mea culpas* were confessed in explaining how the state of macro was no longer good, that: low inflation should be a primary target of policy; this could be achieved through the single instrument of the interest rate; fiscal policy was of limited significance; financial regulation was not a macroeconomic matter; and, with the Great Moderation, continued stability was more or less guaranteed (Blanchard et al 2010).

[13] Thus, as opposed to stochastic risk, "in cases of uncertainty economic reasoning will be of no value" (Lucas 1981, 224).

[14] Thus, for the neoclassical Keynesian, Solow, extreme distaste for the NCE is expressed and widely cited as follows (Klamer 1984, p. 146): "Suppose someone sits down where you are sitting right now and announces to me that he is Napoleon Bonaparte. The last thing I want to do with him is to get involved in a technical discussion on cavalry tactics at the Battle of Austerlitz. If I do that, I'm getting tacitly drawn into the game that he is Napoleon Bonaparte". But Solow's own promotion of the economy as a single production function, and treatment of technical change as a residual in the 1950s is no less extreme and, indeed, facilitated further the macro as micro extremes of what was to follow, however much unpalatable to him as a Keynesian.

to the failure of the markets to work perfectly. As a result, non-market relations emerge, if still on the basis of optimising behaviour. These have the potential either to improve equilibrium outcomes or even to worsen them (as would be argued by those who believe in market perfections where interventions to improve upon the market merely make it work worse).

This held out the prospect of a more widespread and palatable economics imperialism from the perspective of other social sciences, in light of not reducing everything to be market-like, thereby giving rise to a whole range of "new" or renewed fields for the mainstream – such as the new economic sociology, the new welfare economics, the new institutional economics, the revitalisation of the new economic history (led by Douglas North with the startling claim that institutions matter), the new growth theory, and the shift from new to "newer" development economics (and from Washington to post Washington Consensus).[15] This is all reflected in what can be termed a "bringing back in", or the BBI syndrome. This is paradoxical, even perverse, since given that the TA^2 could only be established by omitting legions of considerations in order to be able to establish core results, that apparatus was now to be more broadly applied, precisely in order to address those considerations upon which its legitimacy depended on them being absented.

As is well-known, the emblematic example of the new market imperfections economics is Akerlof's market for second-hand cars considered to be "lemons". Asymmetric information between buyers and sellers means the market is inefficient. Those wishing to get together to exchange a superior (inferior) car at higher (lower) price cannot do so since such cars are indistinguishable from one another for the buyer and so must sell at the same price. Higher quality cars may be excluded from the market at too low a price, and lower quality cars crowd in at price higher than value. This is inefficient as such but it is also possible that there will be excess supply (demand) if prices settle high (low) or absence of markets altogether if no one trusts quality sufficiently. But this has nothing to do with second-hand cars in particular. The same could happen in any market. Concerned dealers might group together and offer a warranty scheme, a non-market, collective solution. By the same token, this is the embryonic form of the state, culture, habit, institutions, etc. Microeconomic market imperfections are enabled to explain the non-market as responses to those imperfections.

---

15 Also space was found for game theory and its application to behavioural economics (strategising to optimise rather than allowing for other behavioural motivations in the first instance).

So, microeconomics and market imperfections allow more or less any economic and social variable to be incorporated on the basis of optimising individuals. This potential inclusion of variables as a response to market imperfection holds the key to the current, third and newer phase of economics imperialism, emerging prior to but accelerated by the GFC. This phase is characterised, relative to the market imperfections phase, by what I call 'suspension'. The BBI could only become increasingly significant once TA² was so strongly and unquestioningly deployed that it could be done so without being threatened by confrontation, combination even, with inconsistent assumptions or conceptualisations around what has been left out. Most notable, for example, is bounded rationality, and behavioural economics more generally, and game theory (treated with suspicion as TA² was being consolidated because of its behavioural interdependencies). But the BBI associated with the new phase of economics imperialism is akin to an original sin, motivating the inclusion of any variable as subject to optimisation. But, by the same token, once these variables have been introduced on this basis, it is a simple step to continue to use them on whatever basis is chosen without necessarily relying completely and exclusively on optimising behaviour alone.

As a result, the exclusive preoccupation with optimisation can be suspended, but it is not discarded. It might be combined with other motivations and constraints other than the market. Even where optimisation (especially as utility maximisation) is abandoned altogether, there is a tendency for it to remain present in the form of what individuals would do if they or the world in which they live were perfect. Such suspension enriches the scale and scope of BBI, allowing for mixed theories in the formulation of the loosest of models – throw in variables and estimate, dovetailing with increasing presence of econometrics which allows a corresponding shift in meaning of model from theory to an equation or six. The world becomes a Cobb-Douglas function, or CES (constant elasticity of substitution) if you can manage it, most notably in empirical applications of the new, endogenous growth theory. And, with suspension, the mainstream economist can claim no longer to be neoclassical, to have become more realistic, and even to be interdisciplinary and heterodox in departing from what has gone before – although the reality is that the methods, theories and conceptualisations of the latest phase of economics imperialism remain negligent of, and hostile to, those of other disciplines and heterodoxy especially regarding the analysis of the systemic, power, conflict, class and so on that take suspension too far from core dependence upon TA².[16]

---

[16] There are also claims not only of understanding the world as deriving from markets, working perfectly or otherwise, but also of capacity to create better-performing markets

3 Acknowledging the Strengths, Exposing and Exploiting the Weaknesses

In short, economics and economics imperialism in its latest phase of suspension is so powerful and confident in its core, TA^2, that it is able to breach it at will in extending itself to ever more areas of application. In a sense, it is fake news within the realm of academia. It also projects itself from an extraordinarily powerful position of institutional, Americanised strength, over training of PhDs, control of journals, command of Nobel Prizes, and so on.

But, equally, matching the overwhelming and even increasing institutional hold of the mainstream over the discipline, there are striking and increasingly overt intellectual weaknesses. The first and most stunningly obvious one is incapacity relative to the GFC – the inability to explain, even after the event, how it could have happened. Second is the lack of a coherent world vision – whether Ricardian, Keynesian or even monetarist – which commands general support despite the unanimity on unquestioned methods, centred on, even if suspended from, TA^2. Third is the inability of economics to explain the economy, the need to draw upon other social sciences and non-economic variables to do so, an implicit acceptance that economics as such is unfit for the economy without supplementation from the non-economic and the other social sciences. Fourth, once the mainstream trespasses onto other disciplines, outside its extreme methods, conceptualisations and assumptions, it exposes itself to critical alternatives drawn from the other social sciences. Fifth, the systemic and interpretative aspects of the other social sciences and the humanities are the least amenable to economics imperialism although weak assaults are and can be made; mainstream economics is extremely uncomfortable with the non-individualistic or what can be derived from it, not least with respect to issues of power and conflict, and equally ill at ease with the critical examination of the meaning and reconstruction of concepts and their normative content.

The most recent and obvious example of most of these weaknesses is provided by the concept of financialisation. This has exploded across the social sciences over the last decade but it has as yet had no presence at all within the mainstream,[17] with the presumption that all that has happened in the

---

through appropriate design and regulation of markets and behaviour. Here, there are affinities with the performativity thesis (for example, the role of Black-Scholes in creating financial markets) but see Fine (2016b) for a critique.

17 See Dymski (2015) although, unsurprisingly, diluted understandings of financialisation have begun to appear within mainstream literature. See also Mader et al (eds) (2020).

intervening period can be sufficiently addressed through the suspensions previously suggested, broader behavioural assumptions in particular to the fore. But, whilst understandably prominent as a deficiency of the mainstream, brought to light by the GFC, this is merely the tip of the iceberg of a legion of deficiencies driven even by a suspended methodological individualism: how we deal with innovation, distribution, monopolisation, globalisation, neoliberalisation, the exercise of power, conflicts, their meanings, contextualisation and corresponding determinants.

This allows for a more positive turn in our account, especially where interdisciplinarity is concerned and through which mainstream economics is exposed by the mainstream let alone radical social science. For it is precisely with its narrow and reduced conceptualisation of the economy that mainstream economics' weaknesses have their other worldly mirror images in other social sciences. Nor is this merely a matter of logic and differences in interdisciplinary boundaries and inner content. Following a period of postmodernism, without ever fully discarding its fecund successors (varieties of post- this and that -isms) over the past twenty years, the social sciences have taken a more material or realist turn, as reflected in the treatments of neoliberalism and globalisation and, as already mentioned, financialisation. Attention has turned to how these developments with respect to neoliberalism, globalisation and, increasingly, financialisation, have affected everything from systemic functioning to the daily lives of situated individuals as opposed to those defined by exogenously given utility functions.

The result has been a blossoming of political economy across the social sciences and a sort of Cold War between it and mainstream economics, in which limited serious engagements take place other than in the unfulfilled demands of students for the Rethinking of Economics and its more pluralistic teaching. This is why the formation of Political Economy associations are so important in bringing together critiques of the mainstream, its putative interdisciplinarity, and its intolerance of alternatives. This has underpinned my own intellectual motivation in part for a number of decades, not least in how to sustain and to reproduce traditions and knowledges of alternatives, with critical knowledge of (and to be turned against) the increasingly intolerant monopoly of the mainstream.

Rhetorically speaking, where does this leave political economy and interdisciplinarity strategically, given the huge scope for analytical criticism? It is not, then, especially through 'suspension', to be underestimated how much the mainstream is capable of striking back by making minimal concessions through economics imperialism itself, as if such developments were capable of negating all criticisms from pluralist perspectives. There is thus the need for continuing to expose and critique the mainstream, even if doing so is arduous and unrewarding in certain respects. Also, as reflected in the movement for a pluralist economics, one must be mindful that there is considerable potential for both unity and division despite what might otherwise appear to be a common purpose. Across almost all criteria, mainstream economics is methodologically, conceptually, theoretically, by its standard assumptions even, positioned at far extremes from the various perspectives of other social sciences let alone political economy. Accordingly, there is so much to criticise from so many different standpoints that often the only thing critiques need to have in common is the multiplicity of (and not necessarily shared) ways of disagreeing with the mainstream, whether minimally or as outright rejection. With the latest phase of economics imperialism as suspension, we are all pluralists now – although it is commonplace to find that mainstream economists accept pluralism in principle (or as a strategic response to what is perceived to be uninformed grumbles) whilst the practice is to reject alternatives as unscientific by some unspecified or ill-formed criteria (generally lack of mathematical modelling around TA^2, suspended or otherwise).

In short, with suspension, we are all pluralists now although some are far more pluralist than others. To some degree, this situation plays into the hands of the latest phase of economics imperialism in a number of ways. First, it can selectively plunder heterodox economics in a marginal way, just as previously it has plundered social sciences, for variables to include in its (suspended) deployment of TA^2. Second, this allows for what might be termed mainstream heterodoxy as a defence of the discipline – consider that we are responding to criticism, we are becoming more realistic, we are interacting with other social sciences. Third, this gives rise to claims that, far from perpetrating economics imperialism, economics is becoming more rounded, and even subject to, a reverse imperialism (as if the adoption of Indian cuisine in the United Kingdom, takeaways in particular, at the expense of fish and chips, is evidence of historical reversal of British cultural imperialism).

In this light, vigorous debate on whether the current nature of the mainstream and its relationship with other social sciences is vital to situating and promoting alternatives. And there is such debate, on which considerable disagreements have arisen. An example of this is how Tony Lawson, the leading exponent of Critical Realism in Economics (CRE) has argued that neoclassical economics does not exist or, at the very least, is a misleading term insofar as it does not have a common theoretical and conceptual core and certainly does not continue the traditions nor renew classical (political) economy. However, I would suggest that a trip to any number of lecture rooms, textbooks or journals, let alone economics departments, would indicate otherwise at least as far as core analytical content is concerned.[18] For Lawson, mainstream economics is defined by its deterministic, deductive methodology as opposed to substantive theory, and this is reflected in its increasing reliance upon mathematical modelling. A different if, to some degree, consistent interpretation is offered by Colander (2010) in which he sees neoclassical economics as disintegrating from outside, as new methods and factors are brought to bear, drawn for example from other social sciences (i.e. reverse imperialism and more).

As is apparent, I disagree with both of these interpretations and can explain why they might be termed a real illusion. In the case of mathematics (and econometrics) the discipline relies upon the false presumption that it is emulating some invented notion of the methods of the natural and physical sciences. But, as I have sought to emphasise, alongside increasing mathematisation, there remains a core analytical content around TA^2 even if suspended in the latest phase of economics imperialism. And the idea that this represents the disintegration of the mainstream from without is contradicted by the simple observation that, as the mainstream has expanded its scope and methods, it has become even more (and not less) tolerant of alternatives beyond what are very narrow, if slightly expanded, boundaries. Indeed, put the issue of the disintegration of the mainstream before any heterodox economist seeking a job, or student seeking a course of political economy or history of economic thought, economic methodology, etc. Instead, as I have argued, at the heart of mainstream economics lies TA^2 even though it is now embedded in suspension, giving the appearance of no such thing as neoclassical economics (Lawson) and its disintegration from outside (Colander).

Such different takes on the nature of the mainstream, and its interdisciplinarity, have significant implications on how to situate opposition and alternatives. For Lawson, the main line of attack is through social ontology where the mainstream is admittedly weak but not debilitatingly so. Tellingly, the mainstream has primarily and studiously ignored, even dismissed, methodological issues for decades. Whatever the intellectual merits of Lawson's approach – and they are considerable – there must be doubts over its impact in persuading those within the mainstream to abandon it, and whether they might be better drawn to do so by questioning many of its extreme characteristics apart from those derived from its impoverished and ill-considered methodology. In short, CRE is just one amongst any number of avenues for critical assessment of the

---

18   For my own critique and more general debate over Lawson's stance, see Fine (2015) and Morgan (ed.) (2015), respectively.

mainstream and for posing alternatives.[19] And contra Colander, the idea that the mainstream will disintegrate from the outside through concerted but compliant contribution from heterodoxy is far-fetched.[20]

Nonetheless, my own inclination is unambiguously to lean towards being tolerant of all of the forms of heterodoxy, whilst engaging in vigorous and critical debate over alternatives, mindful of the extent to which the monopoly of the discipline of economics by the mainstream renders any opposition extremely difficult, fragile and to be welcomed and nourished. In this light, there is much to be said both for intellectual integrity – saying how it is as opposed to what is acceptable to the mainstream – and never forgetting that pluralism is a stance of equal voice in very unequal circumstances, given the mainstream's dominance.[21] But in the realm of scholarship, at least in principle, it is the power of ideas and arguments that should prevail, and we have superior weapons across methodology, realism and interdisciplinarity, however interpreted, especially as the mainstream exposes its weaknesses through economics imperialism. So, whilst we must be aware of the dangers of intellectual opportunism parading itself as strategic compromise, in the realm of ideas, intellectual integrity should take pride of place, alongside tolerance of its blooming wherever and however it can.

As a result, those engaged in heterodox, pluralist and/or interdisciplinary political economy should not underestimate the challenges they face from a hostile and dominant mainstream. But opportunities will open and close, possibly within economics itself (in response to student demands for example) as well as within other disciplines. In the UK for example, political economy is strong within business and management schools for peculiar reasons; that it is interdisciplinary and successful (students think it gets them a job), that it corresponds to financial and hence intellectual independence and has some

---

19 Interestingly, Hodgson (2018) strongly supports the idea that TA² remains paramount, at least through dependence upon utility maximisation if, ironically, he ignores the role of production functions. He puts this down to the inability to falsify the U max hypothesis empirically. He argues that reference to ethics and broader individual motivation may be the most effective strategy in displacing the mainstream. However, this overlooks the extent to which the mainstream remains committed to its core even where it can be falsified, not least the Cambridge Critique of Capital Theory in which he has himself somewhat previously made a telling contribution in pointing to neglect of its implications (Hodgson 1997).

20 For a spirited critique of Colander, and especially that heterodoxy does not have anything to offer other than critique, see Lee (2013).

21 Consider, for example, how many departments of economics would join an association of pluralist economics.

attachment to the real world (of business or otherwise), or that it represents an institutional strength of heterodoxy (Critical Management Studies), and a history of restructuring many disciplines under a single umbrella, at times under the leadership of radical academics from the 1960s as they attain institutional seniority. More generally, and more important, the turn against postmodernism (where it is not being reinvented) and towards the real in light of the privations of neoliberalism, and the stark realities of the GFC and its consequences, have meant that political economy has been centrally located in many disciplines and topics across the social sciences.

Different countries will have different disciplinary trajectories and contexts although the overall trend everywhere has been for the reduction and marginalisation of political economy even where it might previously have been both strong and vibrant. At an individual level, as opportunities equally open and close, compromises are needed with respect to publications and teaching, and these should be tolerated whilst advocating for progress towards alternatives to the mainstream. Such developments are that much stronger and secure the more they are linked to, and supported by, associations of political economy, these in turn committed not only to the critique of the mainstream but also to interdisciplinarity. Having played a role in founding the International Initiative for Promoting Political Economy, iippe.org, a decade ago, and now serving as its Chair, I have been delighted that it has been able to engage with similar organisations, not least the Association française d'économie politique, AFEP (http://assoeconomiepolitique.org/), the Turkish Social Sciences Association, TSSA (tsbd.org.tr/), and the Brazilian association Sociedade Brasileira de Economia Política, SEP (sep.org.br). IIPPE has held joint conferences with AFEP (another in 2019), and TSSA, and has longstanding relations with SEP. The same will apply to the newly-formed Rethinking Economics for Africa, REFA (http://www.rethinkeconomics.org/re-group/rethinking-economics-africa-wits/) which has just held its founding conference. IIPPE held its 2016 Conference in Lisbon and a future joint conference surely represents a promising step for promoting political economy both within and across national and disciplinary borders.

References

Aigner, E. (2021) "Global Dynamics and Country-Level Development in Academic Economics: an Explorative Cognitive-Bibliometric Study", Department of Socio-Economics, Institute for Multi-Level Governance & Development, Vienna University of Economics and Business, Social-Ecological Discussion Paper in Economics, no 7, https://www-sre.wu.ac.at/sre-disc/sre-disc-2021_07.pdf.

Al-Jazaeri, H. (2009) *Interrogating Technical Change through the History of Economic Thought in the Context of Latecomers' Industrial Development: the Case of the South Korean Microelectronics, Auto and Steel Industries*, SOAS, University of London, PhD thesis, unpublished.

Arestis, P., G. Palma and M. Sawyer (eds) *Capital Controversy, Post-Keynesian Economics and the History of Economics: Essays in Honour of Geoff Harcourt*, Volume 1, London: Routledge.

Blanchard, O. (2008) "The State of Macro", NBER Working Paper, no 14259. Accessed on 22.09.2018, at http://www.nber.org/papers/w14259.pdf.

Blanchard, O., G. Dell'Ariccia and P. Mauro (2010) "Rethinking Macroeconomic Policy", IMF Staff Position Note. Accessed on 22.09.2018, at http://www.imf.org/external/pubs/ft/spn/2010/spn1003.pdf.

Colander, D. (2010) "Moving Beyond the Rhetoric of Pluralism: Suggestions for an 'Inside-the-Mainstream' Heterodoxy", in Garnett et al (eds) (2010), pp. 36–47.

Decker, S., W. Elsner and S. Flechtner (eds) (2018) *Advancing Pluralism in Teaching Economics: International Perspectives on a Textbook Science*. London: Routledge.

Dymski, G. (2015) "How to Engage with the Global Crisis: the Shape of Jazz to Come", *International Initiative for Promoting Political Economy*, 10 September. Accessed on 22.09.2018, at http://iippe.org/wp/wp-content/uploads/2015/10/Dymski-IIPPE-keynote-as-presented.pdf.

Fine, B. (2010) "Flattening Economic Geography: Locating the World Development Report for 2009", *Journal of Economic Analysis*, vol 1, no 1, pp. 15–33, http://users.ntua.gr/jea/JEA%20Vol.%20I,%20No%20I,%202010/jea_volume1_issue1_pp15_33.pdf.

Fine, B. (2011) "The General Impossibility of Neoclassical Economics", *Ensayos Revista de Economía*, vol 30, no 1, pp. 1–22.

Fine, B. (2013) "Economics – Unfit for Purpose: the Director's Cut", SOAS Department of Economics Working Paper Series, no 176, Accessed on 22.09.2018, at http://www.soas.ac.uk/economics/research/workingpapers/file81476.pdf. Revised and shortened to appear as "Economics: Unfit for Purpose", *Review of Social Economy*, vol LXXI, no 3, 2013, pp. 373–89.

Fine, B. (2015) "Neoclassical Economics: an Elephant Is Not a Chimera but Is a Chimera Real?", in Morgan (ed.) (2015), pp. 180–99.

Fine, B. (2016a) *Microeconomics: a Critical Companion*, London: Pluto.

Fine, B. (2016b) "From Performativity to the Material Culture of Legal Expertise?", *London Review of International Law*, vol 4, no 3, pp. 477–94.

Fine, B. (2016c) "The Endemic and Systemic Malaise of Mainstream Economics", FESSUD Working Paper Series, no 190. Accessed on 22.09.2018, at http://fessud.eu/wp-content/uploads/2015/03/FESSUD_WP190_The-EndemicSystemic-Malaise-of-Mainstream-Economics.pdf.

Fine, B. (2017a) "Die Untote Welt der Mainstream-Ökonomik", *Zeitschrift für Kulturwissenschafe*, vol 11, no 2, pp. 85–102, in English as "The Undead World of Mainstream Economics", SOAS Department of Economics Working Paper, no 206, 2017.

Fine, B. (2017b) "From One-Dimensional Man to One-Dimensions Economy and Economics", *Radical Philosophy Review*, vol 20, no 1, pp. 49–74.

Fine, B. (2018) "In and Against Orthodoxy: Teaching Economics in the Neoliberal Era", in Decker et al (eds) (2018), pp. 78–94.

Fine, B. (2019) "Economics and Interdisciplinarity: One Step Forward, N Steps Back?" *Revista Crítica de Ciências Sociais*, no 119, pp. 131–48.

Fine, B. and O. Dimakou (2016) *Macroeconomics: a Critical Companion*, London: Pluto.

Fine, B. and D. Milonakis (2009) *From Economics Imperialism to Freakonomics: the Shifting Boundaries between Economics and Other Social Sciences*, London: Routledge.

Fine, B. and D. Milonakis (2011) "'Useless but True': Economic Crisis and the Peculiarities of Economic Science", The Isaac and Tamara Deutscher Memorial Prize Lecture, *Historical Materialism*, vol 19, no 2, pp. 3–31.

Fourcade, M., E. Ollion and Y. Algan (2015) "The Superiority of Economists", *Journal of Economic Perspectives*, vol 29, no 1, pp. 89–114.

Friedman, M. (1953) *Essays in Positive Economics*, Chicago: Chicago University Press.

Garnett, R., E. Olsen and M. Starr (eds) (2010) *Economic Pluralism*, London and New York: Routledge.

Hodgson, G. (1997) "The Fate of the Cambridge Capital Controversy", in Arestis et al (eds) (1997), pp. 95–110.

Hodgson, G. (2018) "Are Rumours of the Death of Max U Exaggerated?", paper circulated for the Cambridge Realist Workshop, November 12th..

Javdani, M. and H.-J. Chang (2019) "Who Said or What Said?: Estimating Ideological Bias in Views among Economists", Institute of Labor Economics, IZA, Bonn, Discussion Paper, no 12738, https://www.iza.org/publications/dp/12738/who-said-or-what-said-estimating-ideological-bias-in-views-among-economists, published in *Cambridge Journal of Economics*, Javdani, M. and H.-J. Chang (2019) "Who Said or What Said?: Estimating Ideological Bias in Views among Economists", Institute of Labor Economics, IZA, Bonn, Discussion Paper, no 12738, https://www.iza.org/publications/dp/12738/who-said-or-what-said-estimating-ideological-bias-in-views-among-economists, published in *Cambridge Journal of Economics*, 2023, beaco71, https://doi.org/10.1093/cje/beaco71.

Klamer, A. (1984) *Conversations with Economists: New Classical Economists and Opponents Speak Out on the Current Controversy in Macroeconomics*, Totowa, NJ: Rowman & Allanheld.

Lee, F. (2013) "Heterodox Economics and Its Critics", in Lee and Lavoie (eds) (2013), pp. 104–132.

Lee, F. and M. Lavoie (eds) *In Defense of Post-Keynesian and Heterodox Economics: Response to the Critics*, London: Routledge.

Lucas, R. (1981) *Studies in Business Cycle Theory*, Cambridge, MA: MIT Press.

Lucas, R. (2003) "Macroeconomic Priorities", *American Economic Review*, vol 93, no 1, pp. 1–14.

Mader, P., D. Mertens and N. Van der Zwan (eds) (2020) *International Handbook of Financialization*, London: Routledge.

Marshall, A. (1959[1890]) *Principles of Economics: an Introductory Volume*, London: MacMillan, eighth edition.

Milonakis, D. (2017) "Formalising Economics: Social Change, Values, Mechanics and Mathematics in Economic Discourse", *Cambridge Journal of Economics*, vol 41, no 5, pp. 1367–1390.

Milonakis, D. and B. Fine (2009) *From Political Economy to Economics: Method, the Social and the Historical in the Evolution of Economic Theory*, London: Routledge.

Morgan, J. (ed.) (2015) *What Is This 'School' Called Neoclassical Economics?: Debating the Origins, Meaning and Significance*, London: Routledge.

Robbins, L. (1935[1932]) *An Essay on the Nature and Significance of Economic Science*, London: MacMillan.

Samuelson, P. (1963) "Problems of Methodology: Discussion", *American Economic Review*, vol 53, no 2, pp. 231–36.

Index

Where terms appear continually throughout a chapter, they may not be (fully) indexed.

10Cs. *See also* Chaotic, Closed, Collective, Commodified, Conforming, Constructed, Construed, Contested, Contextual, Contradictory 89, 106n32

abstractions 105, 143, 149
accumulation 52, 63, 79, 84, 184
actor-network theory, ANT 157
addiction 78, 79, 79n17
advantage, comparative 7, 43, 185
advertising 78, 83, 106
AFEP, French Association of Political Economy 159, 201
agent 24, 38, 74, 110, 131, 138, 146
aggregation problems 54, 63, 82, 87, 94, 95, 102, 124, 124n7, 127, 189
ahistorical 4, 8, 63, 70, 71n6, 73, 74, 76, 82, 84, 191, 191n10
Aigner, E. 32n18, 32n19, 42, 43, 187n2, 201
Akerlof, G. 5, 34, 43, 55, 87–93, 93n13, 96n17, 111, 113, 115, 116, 143, 143n18, 166, 171, 180, 180n1, 194
Algan, Y. 45, 203
Al-Jazaeri, H. 189n7, 202
Allais, S. 15, 43
allocation 37n23, 70, 112, 131, 191n10
Amariglio, J. 116
Ambrosino, A. 37, 43
American 25, 90, 93n13, 159
American Economic Association, AEA 159
Americanisation 62, 175, 181
Andersson, D. 19, 43
anthropology 22, 24, 25, 33n20, 58, 93, 143, 155, 167, 174, 183, 187
appearance 58n22, 84n23, 152, 199
appliances. *See also* durables 70, 71, 73–78, 80–82
applied economics 190, 192
arbitrage 157
Arestis, P. 160, 202, 203
arrogance 30, 31, 170, 188n3
Arrow, K. 102, 102n27, 123–126, 127n12, 128–132, 156n38, 160, 166, 189
Ashman, S. 138, 160, 176, 177

asocial 4, 8, 70, 71n6, 84, 137, 191
assault
  against mainstream 32
  by mainstream 17, 56n15, 174, 196
  sexual as economics of crime 127n12
assets 49, 146n23, 157, 192
Association of Heterodox Economics, AHE 159
Association of Social Economics, ASE 179
Atkinson, A. 78, 78n6, 84
atomistic 109, 113
Auslander, L. 84, 84n22
austerity 13, 120, 121
Austrian 140, 152
authoritarian 71
axiomatic 91n9, 92, 126, 130

Backhouse, R. 139, 139n10, 142, 143, 145, 147, 148, 151–153, 160
Bailly F. 17n5, 44, 51n5, 65
banana 113
bananarama 113n40
Bank of England 92
Bank, Grameen 137n4
Barberà S. 92, 116
Baron, J. 167, 177
barter 34n20
Basu, K. 84, 85
Bateman, M. 137n4, 160
Bayliss, K. 25n13, 44, 70n3, 71n6, 73, 85, 106n32, 114n43, 116, 121n1, 132, 156n39, 160
Becker, G. 2–5, 17, 28–30, 33, 34, 39, 49, 51, 51n6, 54–56, 55n14, 60, 65, 70, 72n7, 73, 74, 74n10, 76, 78, 79, 85, 90, 91, 93, 93n14, 104, 108–110, 113, 113n41, 116, 136, 150n32, 165, 168n7, 177, 179, 180, 180n1, 191
Bédécarrats, F. 91n8, 116
behaviour 95, 196n16
  non-rational 5, 23, 26, 31, 35, 36, 51, 54, 79, 90, 91, 110, 158, 169, 175, 194n15, 195, 197
  rational/optimising 22, 24, 31, 35, 91, 124, 158, 191, 194, 195

behavioural economics. *See also*
    neuroeconomics 18, 24–26, 35–37, 91,
    114, 143, 154, 180, 194n15, 195
Bénabou, R. 108n33, 116
Bernstein, M. 62n25, 65
bicycles 75
biological 79, 143
Birch, K. 9, 10
Birkbeck College, University of
    London 92, 123
Black-Scholes 157, 196n16
Blanchard, O. 193n12, 202
Blankenburg, S. 160
Blaug, M. 59n23, 62n28, 65
Bögenhold, D. 21, 22, 44
Bossert, W. 92, 116
boundaries, between disciplines. *See also*
    division, between disciplines VII, 17,
    23, 29, 29n16, 30, 31, 33n20, 34, 53, 129,
    144, 155, 168n7, 192, 197, 199
Bowden, S. 4, 50n4, 65, 70, 85
Boylan, T. 57n19, 65
Brewer, R. 83, 85
British 71, 135, 140, 152, 171, 198
bulimia 107
business and management studies 17, 50,
    135, 154, 181, 200
business cycles 141, 190, 193
business history 56n15

Callinicos, A. 138n8, 143n16, 149n30,
    156n37, 160
Cambridge capital theory 46, 68, 85, 88,
    91n10, 94, 122, 178, 180, 190, 200n19
Campbell, C. 58n22, 65
capabilities 31, 120, 128
capital VII, 53, 60, 63, 72, 74, 74n10, 80, 84,
    94, 110, 110n36, 124, 137, 157, 167, 184, 190
  consumer 79
  fixed 80, 81
  human 15, 16, 40, 54, 60, 74, 74n10,
    110n36, 173n10, 192
  motivational 110, 110n36
  natural 137
  personal 74, 79
  social VII, 8, 14, 41, 55n14, 74, 79, 104n31,
    110, 113, 137, 137n4, 180, 182
Capital and Class 179

capitalism 19, 34n20, 62–64, 72, 75, 81, 137,
    138, 156, 157, 159, 182, 184
Carrier, J. 54n12, 65, 66, 71n6, 85, 86
causation 19n8, 73, 82, 128, 131, 137, 143, 147–
    149, 155n36
Cedrini, M. 19, 33n20, 36n21, 37, 43,
    44, 47, 65
Chang, H.-J. 32n18, 32n19, 40, 42n26, 44, 46,
    187n2, 203
Chaotic. *See also* 10Cs 106
Cherrier, B. 130, 132
Chester, L. 44, 45
Chicago 37n23, 50, 104, 109, 118, 165–167, 173,
    177, 179
chicken tikka masala 171
childcare 27n14, 79
children 72, 77, 109
China 185
choice. *See also* preferences 17, 23, 34, 50n4,
    57, 70, 77, 82, 83, 87, 94–96, 98–101, 104,
    105, 108n34, 109, 113, 120, 121, 123–130,
    126n11, 127n13, 142, 156, 175, 183, 193
  binary 125, 126n11
  consumer 82
  individual 18, 95, 104, 105, 111, 113
  logic of 94, 96, 97, 100
  of identity 95, 96, 98–101
  public 8, 23, 131, 192, 193
  rational 16–18, 24, 31, 34, 36, 39, 54, 59, 61,
    64, 89, 91, 104, 105, 155, 156, 183
  social 9, 92, 94, 100–102, 120–131, 122n4,
    125n8, 126n11, 128n13
Choonara, J. 138n8, 160
Chuah, S. 23, 44
classes 52, 53, 60, 63, 82, 99, 105, 107, 128,
    146, 173, 183, 184, 195
classical political economy 7, 52, 53, 124,
    134, 152, 184, 198
climate change VII, 2, 13, 21, 28
cliometrics. *See also* economic history 8, 56,
    74, 173, 173n10, 192
Closed. *See also* 10Cs 106n32
Coats, A. 62n25, 65
Coffin, J. 83, 83n21, 85
Colander, D. 38, 44, 114, 116, 138n8, 160, 174,
    177, 199, 200, 200n20, 202
Cold War 126, 126n10, 130, 197
Coleman, J. 104, 104n31, 110, 116

INDEX 207

collective 84, 131, 131n16, 137, 146, 182, 183, 194
Collective. *See also* 10Cs 106n32, 120, 186
colonisation by economics. *See also* phases of economics imperialism VII, 29, 50, 51, 54n11, 55, 58, 59, 61, 74, 87, 93, 108, 126, 134, 136, 154, 155, 173, 174, 182, 188, 190, 192
combined and uneven development 19
commercial 17, 34n20, 72, 75, 81, 84
commodification 84, 157
Commodified. *See also* 10Cs 106n32
commodities 34n20, 97, 184
community 30, 57, 120, 137
competition 8, 20, 37n23, 112, 189, 191n10
complexity economics 26, 37, 40
conflict 63, 77, 91, 105, 107, 109, 110, 122, 127n13, 128, 137, 138, 183, 184, 195–197
Conforming. *See also* 10Cs 106n32
Connell, R. 53n9, 65
conservative 87
Constructed. *See also* 10Cs 106
constructed. *See also* deconstruction and 10Cs 35, 54, 59, 80, 83, 106, 108n34, 110, 112, 114, 127
construction. *See also* deconstruction and 10Cs 56, 57, 61, 83, 92, 97, 106, 111, 183
construed. *See also* 10Cs 35, 80
Construed. *See also* 10Cs 106
consumer 4, 35, 58, 70, 73, 74, 77, 78n16, 79, 81, 82, 83, 84n23, 97, 105–107, 114n43, 128n13
consumerism 190
consumption 25n13, 58, 58n22, 70, 70n3, 73, 74n10, 75, 78, 78n16, 79, 81–84, 84n23, 90, 106, 128n13, 167, 183
  conspicuous 90
contamination 105n32
contemporary, the VII, 18n6, 19, 52, 57, 62, 115, 159, 168, 170, 182, 184, 187, 188, 190
Contested. *See also* 10Cs 107
Contextual. *See also* 10Cs 106
Contradictory. *See also* 10Cs 107
Convert, B. 16n3, 44
Cornwall, R. 56n16, 65
corporations. *See also* firms 80, 105n32, 190
cosmetics 84n23
covid 7n6
credit 27n14, 78, 79, 81–83, 157

crime 5, 54, 127n12
crisis 49, 50, 136, 140, 141, 151, 157, 159, 175, 187
  in economics 136, 140, 159, 175
Crisis, Global Financial, GFC 15, 41, 49, 50, 87, 130, 136, 147, 179, 187
critical realism 8n7, 57n19, 143, 157
Critical Realism in Economics, CRE 8n7, 122n2, 198
Cullenberg, S. 112n39, 116, 118
cultural 24, 40, 58, 61, 63, 82, 84, 106, 106n32, 112, 113, 183, 184, 198
culture 4, 23, 56, 61, 102, 112, 193
cultures 71
cumulative 19n8
curriculum 190
custom 22, 35, 51, 55, 56, 60, 64, 193

Dagnes, J. 33n20, 44
Daly, H. 108, 116
Damodaran, S. VIII, 160, 161
Davern, M. 16, 44
Davis, J. 37, 38, 43, 44, 90, 91n7, 113, 113n41, 114, 114n42, 115, 116, 165, 166
de Grazia, V. 58n22, 65, 83–86, 84n22
Decker, S. 9, 10, 202, 203
deconstruction 182
deductive 112, 124, 126, 148n27, 149, 150, 153, 180, 183, 199
dehistoricisation. *See also* ahistorical 33n20, 34n20, 152
demand 3, 7, 8n7, 32, 41n26, 52, 58n21, 59, 76, 77–80, 82, 96, 179, 189, 191, 192, 194
demands 75, 147, 181, 197, 200
democracy 128, 130
demography 4, 58
desocialisation 152, 153
determinants 13, 81, 83, 94, 96, 108n34, 197
determination 94, 101
determine 40, 42, 53, 63, 72, 73, 73n8, 77, 81, 83, 90, 92, 94, 95, 99, 105, 106, 114, 129, 146, 149, 155, 166, 171
determinism 7, 121, 167, 199
development 7, 55
development economics. *See also* Washington Consensus and post Washington Consensus 14, 20, 41n26, 91n8, 120, 122, 167, 174

development studies. *See also* Washington Consensus and post Washington Consensus   14, 19, 41n26, 55, 129, 167, 174
dialectics   129
diet   107
diffusion, of durables   59, 70, 73–75, 78, 81
diminishing returns   23, 71n6
disabled   127
discourse   17, 23, 27, 84n23, 130, 167
diseases, of affluence   71n6
dismal science   34, 43, 62, 144, 145, 154, 187
distribution   53, 58n22, 77, 83, 94, 130, 166, 197
division, between disciplines. *See also* boundaries, between disciplines   26, 28, 29, 29n16, 53, 54n11, 56, 61, 112, 167, 168n7, 173, 191
dominance   16, 21, 32n19, 38, 42, 64, 99, 152, 180, 182, 184, 200
drug dealers   5
du Gay, P.   65, 68
dualism   16, 34n20, 36, 75, 99, 103, 125, 154, 159, 182, 183
Dubner, S.   5, 6, 11, 14, 46
Dugger, W.   105n32, 109, 117
durables. *See also* appliances   4, 70, 73, 74, 76, 80, 81, 82, 84, 84n23, 128n13
Dymski, G.   196n17, 202
dynamics   7, 13, 59, 60, 90, 108, 174, 175, 183, 184, 188
dysfunction   35, 41, 42, 137, 157, 184

Earp, F.   105n32, 117
eclecticism   74, 158
ecological economics   19, 138, 138n5
econometrics   42, 62n28, 175, 189, 195, 199
economic geography   19, 19n8, 30, 155, 167, 173, 174n12, 183
economic history   VII, 4, 8, 8n8, 56, 56n15, 73, 74, 135, 137, 137n3, 142n15, 145, 152, 154, 173, 190
  new   4, 56, 70, 73, 167, 173, 192, 194
  newer   142n15, 173
Economic History Review   71
economics imperialism, reverse   25, 26, 30n17, 34n20, 38, 39, 136, 143, 154, 165, 171–173, 175, 191, 198, 199

economics of identity   5, 34, 90, 91, 94, 95, 96n17, 107–109, 111–113, 115
economics of organisations   89
economies of scale. *See also* increasing returns   7
economism   155
education. *See also* capital, human   15, 16, 41, 54, 104, 168n7, 173
efficiency   8, 22, 52, 59, 63, 77, 92, 93, 156n39, 157, 168n7, 180, 186, 189–191
efficiency-wage   92
elasticities   76, 76n12, 195
electricity   78, 80
elite   32n19, 62n28, 78, 78n16
Elizabethan   80
Elmslie, B.   174, 177
Elsner, W.   9, 202
embedded   16, 22, 23, 34, 52, 155, 189, 191, 199
empirical   16, 36, 52, 62, 64, 70, 71, 73, 76n12, 80, 82, 83, 115, 128n13, 148, 149, 158, 173, 173n9, 176, 180, 189, 195, 200n19
empiricism   148
employers   104
employment   28, 72, 75, 77, 79, 80, 103, 110, 110n36, 179
emulation   90, 105n32, 199
endogenous   60, 63, 93, 95, 104, 195
endowments   53, 95, 189
engineering   25, 25n13, 61
enterprise. *See also* corporations   81, 90
entitlements   25, 120, 121, 128, 128n14
environment
  intellectual   VII, 21, 41, 60, 104, 126, 137, 138, 173, 184
environmental economics   138, 138n5
envy, physics   24n12
epistemological   19, 25, 26, 29, 29n16, 145
equilibria   101, 102
equilibrium   8, 21, 52, 53, 59, 79n19, 93, 101, 123, 184, 186, 189, 189n6, 190, 191, 194
essence   146n23, 149
ethics   24, 108n34, 121, 124n6, 126n9, 200n19
Ethics and Social Welfare   120
ethnic   107, 122, 171
ethnography   58, 183
European Association for Evolutionary Political Economy, EAEPE   134n1

INDEX

evolution 3, 5, 21, 28, 33, 34, 37, 84, 90, 121, 126, 130, 135, 139, 143, 144, 150–152, 154, 176
evolutionary economics 37, 176
evolutionary game theory 37
evolutionary psychology 28
exchange 34n20, 72, 84, 139n10, 140, 194
exemplar, Kuhnian 143n18
exogenous 60, 63, 82, 94, 95, 101, 104, 105, 110, 131, 197
expectations, rational 147, 151, 192, 193
explosion, of economics imperialism 8, 58, 126, 186, 193n12
externalities 5, 30, 61, 95, 101, 124, 171, 189

Falgueras-Sorauren, I. 37n23, 45
Falk, P. 58n22, 65
falsifiability 57, 57n19, 59
family VII, 28, 29, 58, 58n22, 74, 83, 84, 109, 111, 120, 191, 193
famine 120, 122, 128, 128n14
Fasenfest, D. VII, 45, 160, 161
fashion 82, 102, 106, 109, 140, 158, 171
female 70, 75, 77, 83, 95, 107
femininity 83, 95
fields, disciplinary 15, 16, 17, 18, 23, 27, 29, 40, 51, 84n23, 120, 123, 125, 126, 129, 131, 137, 140, 153, 173, 181, 182, 190–192, 193n12, 194
film 5
finance 20, 25, 41, 49, 50, 55, 136, 143, 156, 156n39, 157, 192
financial 49, 50, 55n13, 136, 140, 141, 157, 159, 184, 193n12, 196n16, 200
financial economics 55n13, 136
Fine, Anne 92
Fine, K. 92, 99, 102, 118, 127, 133
financialisation 13, 15, 41, 121, 136, 137, 156n39, 157, 167, 184, 196, 196n17, 197
firms. *See also* corporations 50, 58n21, 104, 109, 110, 110n36, 148
Flechtner, S. 9, 202
Fleetwood, S. 139, 139n10, 140, 143, 147, 149, 150n32, 157, 158n41, 162
Fleury, J.-B. 20n10, 45, 130, 132, 168n7, 177
fluctuations 193n12
Fontana, M. 36n21, 44
food 76n12, 77, 80, 107, 171

form 18, 19n8, 27n14, 31, 51, 64, 74, 81, 83, 88, 91n9, 100, 110, 123, 124, 144, 146, 148–150, 150n32, 152, 156, 164, 172, 173, 192, 194, 195
formal 77, 83n21, 89, 93, 95, 100, 102, 113, 123, 126, 129, 156, 174
formalism 34, 57, 61, 124, 129, 139, 152, 181, 190
forms 13, 20n10, 24, 33, 34, 36, 39, 59, 72, 73, 129, 130, 141, 148, 159, 184, 200
Foster, N. 86
foundations 23, 29, 102, 103, 122n2, 153, 174, 175n14, 193
Fourcade, M. 25, 26, 45, 188n3, 203
Frader, L. 85, 86
fragmented 9, 13, 36, 37, 39, 64
freakonomics 5, 6, 9, 14, 134, 155, 158, 164–166, 164n2, 168–171, 169n8, 174–176, 181
freedoms 130
French 103, 151, 153, 159
Frey, B. 23, 46
Friedman, M. 113, 147, 147n26, 148, 148n27, 162, 189n8, 192, 203
F-twist 189n8
Fullbrook, E. 139n11, 162
fun 9, 165, 168, 168n7, 170, 176
functions
    production 3, 6, 21, 94, 110, 113n41, 115, 124, 124n7, 158, 173, 180, 181, 189, 191, 193n14, 200n19
    utility 3, 21, 87, 94, 96, 97, 100, 102, 103, 103n30, 110, 113, 114, 124–126, 171, 197
Furlough, E. 58n22, 65, 83, 84–86

Gabriel, Y. 58n22, 67
game 101
game theory 26, 38, 114, 126n10, 158, 180, 194n15, 195
Garnett, R. 65, 67, 202, 203
gas 78
gender 58n22, 77, 82, 105, 107, 173
geography 58n22
German 103n28, 140, 151, 152
Giddens, A. 153, 162
Gideon, J. 45, 46, 161, 162
gift 19, 34n20, 58n20, 137
Gilead, T. 15, 46
Gintis, H. 62n27, 65

globalisation. *See also* Crisis, Global Financial, GFC   VII, 3, 15, 28, 32n19, 41, 61, 63, 138, 147, 175, 182, 184, 197
goods   8, 75–79, 80–84, 95, 124, 189
   private   170
   public   131, 170, 173
Grameen Bank   137n4
Grayot, D.   36, 46
groups   37, 95, 111, 120, 140, 194, 201
growth   184
growth theory, new   15n2, 183, 184, 194, 195
Guérin, I.   116
Gunn, C.   138n8, 162
Gupta, S.   VIII, 160
Gutting, G.   59n23, 67

Hadjimichalis, C.   19, 19n8, 46
Hanappi, H.   138n8, 162
Hannan, M.   167, 177
Harley, S.   62n25, 68
Hausman, D.   162
Hayek, F.   141, 147, 162
Heasman, M.   67, 86
hegemony   21, 184, 192, 192n11, 193
Heilbron, J.   16n3, 44
Hennessey, K.   49, 67
heterodox economics   VII, 1, 13, 14, 30, 32n18, 33, 41, 43, 61, 90, 91, 135, 139, 141, 167, 175, 176, 181, 186, 198
heterodoxy   3, 8n7, 9n10, 9n9, 20, 20n9, 38–40, 115, 121, 122, 122n2, 136, 137n2, 159, 165, 174, 175, 179–182, 195, 198, 200, 200n20, 201
Hicks-Slutsky-Samuelson conditions   189
hierarchy   18, 192
Hill, C.   97, 118
historians   71
historical   3, 7, 8n8, 27, 39, 40n24, 42, 53, 58n22, 60, 71–74, 80, 82, 84, 124, 134, 140, 142–145, 142n15, 151–153, 159, 166, 183, 186, 189, 191, 198
   logic, of economics imperialism   3, 7, 166, 186, 189, 191
historically   72, 74, 80, 82, 84, 90, 105, 165, 184, 186, 191
history   VII, 1–4, 7, 8, 8n8, 20, 21, 25, 27, 27n14, 29, 39, 40, 42, 49, 52, 53, 56, 56n15, 58n22, 64, 71–73, 87, 93, 113, 115, 122, 126, 130, 135, 139, 141, 142, 142n15, 144, 146, 151–153, 167, 175, 180, 187–189, 199, 201
history of economic thought   3, 7, 8, 21, 27, 39, 42, 52, 53, 115, 135, 139, 141, 142, 144, 175, 180, 188, 189, 199
Hodgson, G.   9n9, 10, 40, 40n25, 62n25, 67, 135, 139n10, 140, 142n14, 143, 144n19, 146n24, 150n32, 152, 154n34, 155, 156, 162, 174n13, 177, 200n19, 203
Hofferberth, E.   138n5, 162
Holbrook, M.   58n22, 67
Holt, R.   38, 44
homo economicus   31, 90
homo sociologicus   31
Hoover Institute   49
household economics, new   74n10
households   54, 58n22, 72, 73n8, 74–82, 83n21
human nature   24, 71, 73

Ianovski, E.   118
iBUILD   25n13
identities   87, 90, 94–97, 98n23, 99, 99n24, 100, 101, 104–107, 108n34, 109, 111, 113, 114, 114n43
identity   5, 24, 58n22, 87, 89–91, 93–96, 96n18, 97–115, 99n24, 103n30, 108n34, 114n42, 143n18, 171, 175, 180
ideological   21, 60
ideology   17, 21, 24, 34, 64, 71n6, 146, 157, 159
IIPPE, International Initiative for Promoting Political Economy, iippe.org   41n26, 137n2, 159, 201, 202
illusion, real   199
impact   1, 5, 36, 55, 60, 78, 90–92, 109, 115, 121, 122n2, 154, 158, 167, 176, 184, 199
imperfect   58, 61n24, 136, 169, 181, 189
implosion, of economics   7, 8n7, 63, 124, 166, 186, 189, 191
impossibility theorems, social choice   100–102, 124, 125, 128
incentives   50, 56, 61n24, 62n26, 70, 169n8, 170
income   70, 76, 78, 81, 83, 114
incommensurable   127
increasing returns. *See also* economies of scale   155, 156, 189
Indian   VIII, 122, 198

indifference   98, 99, 123, 127*n*11, 127*n*13
individualism   51, 54, 64, 71, 89, 103, 105, 109, 112, 121, 131, 143, 154, 158, 183, 196, 197
  methodological   54, 64, 89, 105, 121, 131, 143, 154, 158, 183, 197
induction   103, 148, 149*n*30, 153, 190
industrial   7, 17, 49, 62*n*26, 90, 107, 135, 153, 154, 184
  relations   17, 62*n*26, 135, 154
inefficiency   76, 156*n*39, 157, 194
inequality   122, 125*n*8, 172
inflation   193*n*12
information, asymmetric   194
infrastructure   7, 25*n*13
innovation   23, 111, 197
Institute of German Historical Research   187
institutional   4, 9*n*10, 23, 38, 88, 89, 144*n*19, 155, 190, 196, 201
institutional economics
  new   8, 70, 89, 89*n*5, 155, 174, 183, 194
  old   20*n*10, 90
institutionalised   17, 21, 31, 32
institutionalism   17, 90, 91, 167
institutions   21, 22, 35, 40, 53, 55, 56, 60, 64, 84, 89, 93, 110, 143, 146, 150*n*32, 152, 156, 166, 182, 193, 194
instrumentalism   127, 146, 147*n*26, 148, 148*n*27, 169, 193*n*12
insurance   49
interdisciplinarity. *See also* individual disciplines   3, 7, 9, 12, 20*n*10, 24, 25, 25*n*13, 30*n*17, 32, 40, 115, 137*n*2, 159, 167, 175, 176, 180, 181, 187, 188, 197, 199, 200, 201
interdisciplinary. *See also* individual disciplines   7, 18*n*6, 20*n*10, 25, 26, 28, 31, 36, 39, 42, 81, 90, 138, 142, 174, 184, 195, 197, 200
interests   21, 40, 131, 144, 150
international   19*n*8, 63, 120, 180
interpersonal   125, 127, 128
interventionism   20*n*10, 35, 61, 120, 157, 192, 193, 197
intrapersonal   125
invaluable   13, 127

Jabbar, H.   46, 31
Javdani, M.   32*n*18, 32*n*19, 46, 187*n*2, 203

Jo, T.-H.   44, 45
Johnson, D.   10, 118
justice   131*n*16, 140, 184

Kellecioglu, D.   20, 29, 46
Keynesianism   20, 37*n*23, 61, 64, 96*n*17, 124, 141, 151, 153, 159, 173, 192, 192*n*11, 193, 193*n*14, 196
King, J.   62*n*25, 67, 139, 139*n*10, 140, 142*n*14, 143, 144*n*20, 148, 148*n*27, 150, 151, 152, 153, 154, 155, 158, 159, 162
Klamer, A.   193*n*14, 203
knowable   111, 157
Kondratev, A.   92, 118
Kotz, D.   70*n*2, 86
Kozul-Wright, R.   160
Kranton, R.   5, 34, 43, 87, 88, 91, 93, 115, 116, 143*n*18
Krijnen, C.   23, 46
Kuhn, T.   57, 59, 59*n*23, 67
Kuhnian   57*n*18, 143*n*18
Kuorikoski, J.   16*n*3, 23, 46

labour   17, 20, 29, 34*n*20, 53, 62, 62*n*26, 70, 72, 73*n*8, 75, 76, 83*n*21, 124, 135, 154, 190
  domestic   70–72, 75, 77
  markets   20, 29, 62, 62*n*26, 70, 75
labour economics   17, 135, 154, 190
Lamoreaux, N.   56*n*15, 67
Lang, T.   58*n*22, 67
language   56, 57, 60, 73, 112, 130, 131*n*16, 170, 171
Lapavitsas, C.   50*n*4, 55*n*13, 67, 155*n*35, 161
Lavoie, M.   203, 204
law   17, 18, 19*n*6, 97, 130*n*16, 165
law and economics   17, 18, 18*n*6, 30, 173
Lawson, T.   7, 7*n*5, 8*n*7, 10, 40, 40*n*25, 57*n*19, 59*n*23, 67, 114*n*44, 118, 138*n*8, 139*n*11, 149, 149*n*29, 149*n*31, 162, 198, 199, 199*n*18
Lazear, E.   2–4, 11, 17, 34, 46, 49–52, 50*n*3, 51*n*5, 51*n*7, 54–61, 55*n*13, 56*n*17, 61*n*24, 62*n*26, 63, 67, 68, 88*n*2, 93*n*14, 118
Lecouteux, G.   35, 46
Lee, F.   62*n*25, 68, 200*n*20, 203, 204
Lehtinen, A.   16*n*3, 23, 46
leisure   70, 71, 73*n*8, 75, 79, 90
Leopold, E.   58*n*22, 67, 70*n*3, 78*n*16, 81*n*20, 86
Levitt, S.   5, 6, 11, 14, 46, 165

Lewis, P.   66, 68, 132, 133, 161, 162
lexicographic   97
life   2, 4, 30n17, 41, 82, 103, 106, 122, 181
    social   120, 181
    -style   82, 106
linguistic   57, 102
lipstick   84n23
London School of Economics   123
Lucas, R.   174, 177, 193, 193n13, 204
luxury   82

macroeconomics   17, 19, 20, 45, 61, 95, 96n17, 124, 143, 152, 157, 174, 189, 190, 192, 193, 193n12, 193n14
Mader, P.   137, 162, 167, 177, 196n17, 204
mainstream economics   VII, 2–4, 7, 8n7, 12, 13, 20, 21, 29, 30, 32, 32n18, 37, 37n23, 38, 41, 42, 52, 53, 53n9, 56, 62, 63, 64, 87, 91, 94, 96, 105, 115, 120, 124, 124n7, 126, 128, 128n15, 136, 138, 139, 139n10, 143, 147, 148n27, 150, 151, 153, 156, 158, 164, 166, 173, 174n13, 176, 180, 180n2, 182, 186–189, 196–199
Mäki, U.   26, 27, 27n14, 27n15, 28–30, 37, 46, 47
male   77, 95
Marchionatti, R.   19, 33n20, 37, 44, 47, 65
marginalism   53, 90n6, 139, 153, 181
marginalist revolution   7, 33n20, 34, 52, 53, 105, 110, 112, 124, 144n19, 152, 153, 189
Mariotti, S.   25, 26, 47
market imperfections   2, 6, 13, 14, 17, 29, 34–36, 53n9, 55, 60, 61, 64, 73, 93, 136, 137, 173, 179, 180, 186, 193–195
Marshall, A.   8n7, 90n6, 92, 112, 139, 143, 152, 153, 189, 189n6, 204
Marx, K.   53n9, 124, 140, 141, 143, 149, 153, 156, 159, 162, 163, 184, 187, 188
Marxism   VII, 32, 70, 135n1, 137n2, 143, 155, 159
masculinity   95
material culture   83, 89, 183
material realities   3, 13, 41, 60, 73, 106, 149, 156n39, 170, 174, 176, 182, 184, 197
mathematical   7, 22, 24, 43, 57, 59, 62, 62n28, 91, 91n9, 99, 102, 103, 111, 121, 122n3, 123, 124, 126, 127, 129, 131, 158, 180, 190, 191, 198, 199

mathematical economics   43, 62n28
mathematics   43, 92, 102, 103, 112, 122n4, 123, 126, 181, 190, 199
Mauro, P.   202
maximisation   16, 35, 54n11, 83, 88, 91, 93, 103n30, 105, 106, 108, 109, 110, 156, 169, 174, 195, 200n19
McCloskey, D.   57n19, 59n23, 68, 87, 112, 118
McNally, D.   139, 139n10, 143, 152, 155, 156, 163
McRorie, C.   24, 47
meanings, social construction of   18, 56, 58, 59, 61, 63, 71, 75, 75n11, 106, 107, 108n34, 111, 112, 114, 114n43, 127, 129, 142n14, 143, 147, 148, 155, 169n8, 183, 195–197
Medema, S.   17, 18, 30, 47
media   5, 16, 32
men   70, 77, 146
Menashy, F.   46, 31
Mendelson, E.   123, 133
Mendes Loureiro, P.   102n27, 118, 125n8, 133
Meramveliotakis, G.   9n10, 11, 146n23, 163
Mertens, D.   162, 177, 204
metaphysical   145, 148
Methodenstreit   151, 153
methodological. See also individualism   54, 64, 73, 89, 105, 121, 131, 140, 142–145, 142n14, 147, 150, 151, 154, 158, 183, 197, 199
methodology   4, 27, 29, 30, 34n20, 39, 40, 40n25, 42, 53, 57, 57n19, 59, 62–64, 74, 89, 91, 110, 112, 115, 121, 124, 135, 136, 142n14, 147, 148n27, 157, 164n2, 167, 175, 180, 188, 193n12, 199, 200
Michie, J.   19, 31, 47
microeconomic   17, 51, 55, 56, 61, 95, 129, 174, 189n6, 191, 192, 193, 193n14, 194
micro-foundations   51, 55, 56, 61, 96
Microsoft   180
Miller, D.   54n12, 58n22, 65, 66, 68, 71n6, 85, 86
Milonakis, D.   5–8, 6n4, 9n10, 9n9, 10, 11, 14, 33n20, 34n20, 40n24, 40n25, 45, 47, 50n4, 52n8, 56n15, 67, 68, 87n1, 93, 102, 112, 118, 124, 126n9, 132–135, 138, 138n6, 138n7, 139n10, 141n13, 142n15, 144n19, 146, 146n23, 151n33, 154, 158, 159, 161, 163–165, 168, 169, 174n13, 176–178, 188n5, 190n9, 203, 204
Mirowski, P.   125, 126, 133, 165n4, 178

Mitra, S.   VIII, 160
model building   110, 149, 154, 158
modernism   61, 92, 107, 112, 113, 142, 145, 154
Molho, A.   67, 68
monetarism   20, 113, 152, 188, 192, 196
monetary   114
money   114, 155, 157, 184, 192
Mont Pèlerin   49
Monty Python   121
moral   24, 29n16, 184
Moreno-Ternero, J.   92, 116
Morgan, J.   10, 11, 45, 47, 132, 133, 161, 163, 199n18, 202, 204
Moscati, I.   102, 118
mother   72
motor cars   75
movements   VII, 16, 18, 54n11, 62, 171, 190, 198
Murakami, Y.   123, 133
Murphy, K.   90, 91, 116
Mykhnenko, V.   9, 10
Myrdal, G.   19n8, 47, 134, 134n1

narrative   13, 36, 123, 142n14, 145, 150, 151, 153, 165, 168, 189, 192
nations   37, 80, 103, 106n32, 107, 124, 184, 201
natural resource economics   137
natural resources   170
natural sciences   147, 148, 199
neoclassical economics   7, 8n7, 31, 51, 58, 73, 77, 81, 83, 89, 90, 92, 94, 101, 104, 110, 114, 122, 122n2, 155, 165, 180, 198, 199
neoliberalism   VII, 3, 13, 15, 19, 20, 34, 41, 49, 71n6, 120, 121, 130, 154, 165, 165n4, 166, 170, 175, 182, 197, 201
Nesterov, A.   118
networks   105n32
neurobiology   24
neuroeconomics   6, 26, 36, 37
New Classical Economics, NCE   20, 151, 181, 192
new development economics   55, 174, 174n12, 192
new economic sociology   174, 183, 194
new family economics   4
new welfare economics   194
newer development economics   194
Nik-Khah, E.   40n24, 47, 164, 165, 167, 178
Nobel   15n2, 56, 92, 120, 123, 155n36, 166, 173, 179, 180, 193, 196

normative   29n16, 128, 129, 131, 187, 188, 196
norms   35, 55, 60, 82, 83, 93, 105, 121, 128j211n13
nudging   7, 35

obesity   71n6, 107
objectivity   60
Offer, A.   4, 50n4, 58n20, 65, 68, 70, 85
oligopoly   101, 111
Ollion, E.   45, 203
Olsen, E.   203
Olson, M.   68, 168n7
ontology, social   8n7, 27n15, 29, 40, 114n44, 121, 122, 122n2, 199
opportunism   128n15, 169, 188, 200
optimising   5, 52, 53, 55, 59, 63, 64, 74, 79, 81, 83, 93, 102, 107, 127, 169, 180, 183, 189, 191, 194, 194n15, 195
orthodox economics   154
Ostrom, E.   155n36, 173, 178
Oughton, C.   47
ownership   78, 79
Oxford Economic Papers   92

Palma, G.   202
paradigm   9n10
paradox   60, 103
paradox, Russell   96n18, 102, 103
paradox, voting   126, 127n11
Paretian liberal   101
Paris   159
Parker, W.   47
Parsons, T.   17, 53, 53n9, 112, 112n38, 119, 154
pathologised   35, 137
patriarchy   77
Pattanaik, P.   85
Peiss, K.   84n23, 86
Perelman, M.   53n9, 68
performativity   157, 196n16
personnel economics   17, 50, 51n5, 62n26
phases of economics imperialism   3, 8, 13, 14, 20, 26, 29, 34, 156, 169, 186, 188
  new (second)   2, 4, 5, 49, 70, 73, 93, 165, 195
  newer(third)   1, 4, 5, 6, 8n7, 9, 26, 34–37, 134, 137, 157n40, 164, 166, 169, 195, 196, 198, 199
  old (first)   3, 33, 73, 136
  pre-history   134, 168

Pincus, J.   55n13, 67
Pinto, F.   19n7, 47
Pirgmaier, E.   138n5, 163
plastic   80
Plehwe, D.   165n4, 178
pluralism   2, 19, 24, 29–32, 37, 38, 40, 42, 139, 167, 179, 186, 198, 200
pluralist economics   198, 200n21
pluralistic   12, 33, 38, 114, 139n12, 180, 197, 198, 200, 200n21
policies   VII, 7, 15–17, 20, 20n10, 21, 35, 36, 37n23, 40, 71n6, 78, 120, 121, 130n16, 131, 136, 137n2, 157, 159, 168n7, 193n12
policing   70, 70n3, 173
policymaking   20n10, 21, 32, 136, 160
political   54, 84, 98, 104, 131, 143, 146, 150, 151, 184
political science   25, 33n20, 64, 93, 124, 129, 130n16, 143, 155n36, 173
politics   155, 165, 183, 198
poor   114, 179
Porter, R.   83, 85
Portuguese Association of Political Economy   7n6, 187n1
positivism   57n19, 91n9, 143, 147, 148n27, 153, 187
Posner, R.   173, 178
post Washington Consensus   55, 55n13, 60, 194
post-Keynesianism   143, 155
postmodernism   3, 4, 41, 56, 56n16, 58, 60, 63, 71, 87, 103, 105, 106, 112, 113, 154, 159, 174, 182, 183, 197, 201
poverty   137, 175, 184, 188
power   15, 18, 18n6, 19, 31, 32, 53, 59, 63, 78, 84, 93, 105n32, 107, 109, 110, 122, 123, 128, 137, 149, 150, 165, 183, 184, 186, 195–197, 200
practice, in   3, 14, 19, 21, 24, 27, 30, 33, 37n23, 40, 53n9, 57, 59n23, 80, 84, 95, 99, 105
practices   3, 94, 106, 107, 120, 121, 146, 166, 175
pragmatism   27n15, 29, 43, 49, 88, 122n4
Pratten, S.   8n7, 11
preferences   6, 8, 16, 22, 23, 53, 59, 60, 70, 72n7, 78, 79, 82, 88, 92, 94, 96–102, 105, 107, 110, 121, 123–125, 127n11, 128n13, 131, 189
prices   53, 71, 77, 78, 81, 83, 101, 156, 157, 194
primitive societies   19, 33n20, 34n20

Primrose, D.   48
private   146n23, 157, 170
privatisation   121, 157
profit   63, 81, 90, 110n36, 157, 184
property rights   9n10, 19n6, 30, 145n23
provision, systems of   25n13, 70n3, 82, 84, 106n32
Pryke, M.   65, 68
psychology   21, 23–25, 51, 58n22, 93, 106n32, 111, 154, 172, 182
  social   130n16, 143
public choice   8, 23, 131, 192, 193
public-private partnerships   157

Quarterly Journal of Economics   49, 50, 88, 112
quasi-transitivity   98, 98n22, 99

race   105, 107, 173
racism   28
Radin, M.   127n12, 133
Ragkousis, A.   121, 133
random shocks   193
randomised control trials, RCT   91
real   31, 35, 62, 62n28, 106, 109, 149, 182, 184, 193, 199, 201
  world   31, 62, 62n28, 109, 201
realism   21, 23, 31, 36, 91, 91n9, 139n11, 149, 152, 157, 188, 189, 189n8, 190, 195, 198, 200
reciprocity   19, 24
reconstruction   20, 33n20, 42, 63, 96n17, 147, 186, 196
reductionism   19n8, 24, 34n20, 35, 54, 62n26, 64, 93, 109, 113, 128, 131, 169, 171, 183, 197
REFA, Rethinking Economics for Africa   201
reflexive   23, 103, 114
regional   19
Regional Science Association International   173
regression   183
regulation   193n12, 196n16
relational. See components of relations, relationships, etc   18, 103
religion   56, 169n8
representative   108, 131, 139, 151, 168, 174, 192
  individual   151, 192
reproduction   VII, 8, 41, 47, 51n5, 106n32, 108, 121, 147, 177, 181, 197

residual   77, 193n14
resources   17, 22, 62n26, 110, 124, 159, 170, 182
Rethinking Economics for Africa, REFA   201
retroduction   149
rhetoric   57n19
Ricardian   64, 196
rich   114, 128, 139n12, 144, 159
Richter, R.   89, 90, 119
rigour   2, 4, 39, 51, 51n5, 51n7, 57, 59, 91, 91n9, 102, 109, 147, 180, 190
risk   38, 102, 111, 157, 193n13
Robbins, L.   20n10, 37n23, 112, 152, 204
Robertson, M.   160
Rolin, K.   29n16, 47
Romer, P.   15, 47, 166
Roncaglia, A.   138n8, 163
Rose, S.   85, 86
Rosser, B.   38, 44
Rothman, H.   62n25, 67
Rothschild, K.   24, 24n12, 47
Roubaud, F.   116
Ruccio, D.   116
rules
   finite ranking   99
   voting   126

Samuelson, P.   113, 147, 148, 163, 166, 189, 189n8, 204
Santos, A.   10, 118, 132, 133, 161, 163
sati   107
Sato, H.   138n8, 163
Sawyer, M.   160, 202
Scandinavia   21
scarce resources, allocation of   37n23, 112, 191n10
schools of thought   72, 96, 138, 140, 141, 143, 145, 150–152, 153, 155, 157, 164n2, 165, 179, 200
Schumpeter, J.   30n17, 140, 141, 150, 152, 163, 188
Seiter, E.   79n18, 86
self-interest. See also interests   23, 34n20, 121, 124, 169, 191
Sen, A.   9, 99n24, 101, 108, 108n34, 114, 119–130, 128n15, 133
set-theoretic   97, 102
sewing   83, 83n21
sexual   108, 127n12, 135n1

sexuality   58n22, 107
shopping   58n22
signification   84
Simister, J.   86, 128n13, 133
Sinha, D.   VIII, 160
Slater, D.   61, 68
SOAS, School of Oriental and African Studies   41n26
social economics   180–185
social history   173
socialism   55n13, 60
Sociedade Brasileira de Economia Política, SEP   201
societies   19, 20, 52, 58, 72, 81, 84, 109, 113, 114, 124, 126, 131, 146, 154, 176, 184
socioeconomic   82, 83
sociological   16, 26, 29, 111, 145, 155
sociologist   16, 17, 172
sociology   16, 17, 21–23, 25, 33n20, 51–53, 53n9, 58n22, 64, 93, 104, 112, 140, 145, 152, 153, 155, 170, 172, 175, 187
   of economics   170, 175
Solow, R.   47, 124, 166, 193n14, 42
South Africa   VII, 106n32
specialisation   36, 37, 39, 40, 42, 58n22
speculation   111
Spencer, D.   17, 48, 62n26, 68
sports economics   92
stages of development   28, 34n20
stagflation   151, 192
Stålhammar, S.   19, 48
Star Trek   35
Starr, M.   203
state, the   19, 20n10, 21, 35, 63, 84, 106n32, 146, 151, 157, 182, 184, 193, 194
statistical   5, 7, 59, 62, 91n9, 156, 158, 183
Stigler, G.   54n11, 68, 165
Stiglitz, J.   49, 55, 55n13, 68, 70, 73, 92, 166
Stillman, C.   22, 48
Stilwell, F.   44, 48
stratification   63
strikes   92
structures   18, 20, 26, 38, 55, 60–62, 82, 95, 100, 106, 107, 114, 138, 146, 149, 169n8, 170, 184
students   9n10, 41n26, 62, 62n28, 92, 96, 104, 123, 129, 142, 168n7, 197, 199, 200
studies   14–17, 30n17, 41, 50n4, 83, 107, 131, 156

study 29, 32, 50n3, 53, 55n13, 56, 58n22, 59, 82, 83, 90, 104, 123, 131, 142n15, 156, 159, 183, 184, 186
subjectivity 56, 60, 76, 105
substitution 70, 195
Suomi 5
superiority 24, 25, 51, 51n7, 52, 54, 91, 188n3
supply 3, 7, 8n7, 52, 54, 58n21, 59, 60, 124, 189, 191, 192, 194
supply-side 58n21, 59, 60
suspension, of economics imperialism 6, 6n4, 7, 9, 13, 36, 37, 91, 91n9, 164, 164n3, 166, 186, 195–199
sustainability 25n13, 184
Suzumura, K. 85
Swedberg, R. 54, 54n11, 65, 68, 69, 115, 119, 177, 178
Swingewood, A. 153, 163
symbolic 9n9, 57, 93, 105, 111, 121, 135, 153
symposium 8, 40n24, 49, 120, 134–136, 138, 138n9, 139, 139n10, 139n11
synthesis 9, 131n16, 149, 149n30
systemic 14, 62, 64, 94, 105, 112, 131, 157, 171, 182, 184, 195–197
systems 7, 25n13, 38, 63, 70n3, 82, 84, 106n32, 107, 123, 157, 159, 184, 185, 191

tastes 58, 59
teaching 7, 14, 17, 32, 39, 42, 122n4, 168n7, 190, 197, 201
technical apparatus, TA1 3, 6, 21, 88, 104, 110, 113, 115, 124, 126, 153, 155, 158, 164, 171, 180, 181, 186, 189n6, 189n7
technical architecture, TA2 6, 21, 186
technical progress 124, 166
techniques 7, 57, 59, 62, 64, 102, 103, 105, 108, 110–112, 115, 180–182
technologies 6, 8, 53, 78, 79, 83, 95, 189
telephone 75, 75n11, 81
Teles, N. 132, 133, 161, 163
television 75, 78, 79, 82
tendencies 63, 78, 138, 195
terminology 170
textbooks 168n7, 198
Thompson, G. 50n4, 69
Thorén, H. 48
Thornton, T. 48
Tirole, J. 108n33, 116
Tomes, N. 108, 109, 116

trade unions 104, 105, 166
traditions VII, 4, 12, 13, 16, 17, 21, 23, 51, 53, 55, 57, 58, 60, 62, 63, 90, 94, 108n34, 113, 115, 130, 135n1, 144, 148, 159, 166, 168n7, 173, 175, 181–184, 190, 197, 198
transaction costs 9n10, 89
transition 5, 38, 127, 152, 184
transitivity. See also quasi-transitivity 97–100
transportation costs 156
trends 139, 141n13, 169, 183, 201
Trentmann, F. 117, 119
trust 19, 20n10, 24, 35, 64, 110, 173, 194
Tsakalotos, E. 124n6, 133
Turkish Social Sciences Association, TSSA 201
turnover 73n8
Tzotzes, S. 9n10, 11

UK 25n13, 50n3, 77, 171, 181, 200
UK Economic and Social Research Council, ESRC 50n3
uncertainty 94, 98–100, 103, 111, 157, 193n13
underdevelopment 19
unemployment 96, 189
unfit 187, 196
universal 7, 8, 58, 72, 73, 75, 80, 105, 111, 112, 181, 184, 186, 191
Unterhalter, E. 45, 46, 161, 162
USA 20n10, 32n19, 62n28, 184

vacuum cleaner 75
value 34n20, 72, 77, 79, 123, 124, 124n6, 131, 148, 156, 184, 193n13, 194
  normative 19, 29, 124n6, 148
  theory 34n20, 70, 72, 156, 184
Van der Zwan, N. 162, 177, 204
Van Horn, R. 40n24, 47, 164–167, 178
Van Waeyenberge, E. 10, 118, 19
variegation 2, 13, 15, 29, 33, 34, 36, 39, 40, 136
Veblenesque 121
Velthuis, O. 17, 48, 53n9, 69
voting 123, 126, 127n11, 128–130, 128n13
Vromen, J. 9, 11, 37, 40n24, 48, 164, 164n2, 165, 167–172, 173n10, 173n9, 174–176, 175n14, 178

wages 71, 73, 77, 79, 81, 92
Waller, W. 109, 119

wants   22, 96, 99, 101, 101*n*26, 126, 156, 189, 193*n*14
washing machine   76, 78, 81
Washington Consensus   192
water   121
watershed, in economics imperialism   1, 8, 12, 14, 73, 87, 135, 164, 179, 192
wealth   82
welfare   21, 84, 120, 121, 126*n*10, 129, 131
Wilkinson, F.   47
women   70, 77, 79, 107

workers   49, 77, 96, 104, 105, 109
workplace   73
World Bank   7, 15*n*2, 41*n*26, 88*n*3, 167
World Economics Association, WEA   159
Wright, J.   67, 86

Yay, T.   30*n*17, 48

Zafirovski, M.   48
Zelizer, V.   50*n*4, 69, 155, 155*n*35, 163

www.ingramcontent.com/pod-product-compliance
Lightning Source LLC
Chambersburg PA
CBHW070620030426
42337CB00020B/3863